ARTHUR LYDIARD

Also by Garth Gilmour

Run for Your Life, Minerva, Auckland, 1965
Jogging with Lydiard, Hodder & Stoughton, Auckland, 1983

with Arthur Lydiard:
Run to the Top, Reed, Wellington, 1962, and Tokyo Baseball Publishing, 1964
Running the Lydiard Way, World Publishing, USA, 1978, and Hodder &
    Stoughton, Auckland, 1978
Running with Lydiard, Moscow Publishing, 1987
Run with Lydiard, Taishukan Publishing, Tokyo, 1993
Jogging with Lydiard, Meyer & Meyer, Germany, 1994
Running to the Top, Meyer & Meyer, Germany, 1995,1997
Distance Training for Young Athletes, Meyer & Meyer, Germany, 1999
Distance Training for Women, Meyer & Meyer, Germany, 1999
Distance Training for Masters, Meyer & Meyer, Germany, 2000

with Murray Halberg:
A Clean Pair of Heels, Reed, Wellington, 1963

with Peter Snell:
No Bugles No Drums, Minerva, Auckland, 1965

with Dardir El Bakary:
Dardir on Squash, Gilmour Associates, Auckland, 1971

with Eve Rimmer:
No Grass Between My Toes, Reed, Wellington, 1978

with Sandra Barwick:
Unstoppable, HarperCollins, Auckland, 1993

with David Wright:
Swim to the Top, Meyer & Meyer, Germany, 2002

ARTHUR LYDIARD
MASTER COACH

GARTH GILMOUR

SPORTSBOOKS

First published 2004

SportsBooks Limited
1 Evelyn Court
Malvern Road
Cheltenham
GL50 2JR
www.sportsbooks.ltd.uk

British Cataloguing in Publication Data
A catalogue record for this book is available from the British Library.

ISBN 1-899807-22-5

Text design and production by *BookNZ* (www.booknz.co.nz)
Cover design by Dexter Fry
Printed in China through Colorcraft, HK
Distributed by Turnaround

Cover photographs: (*front*) Arthur Lydiard on a training run in Auckland in the
1950s; (*back, top*) Arthur Lydiard as he is today; (*back, bottom*) Alan McKnight,
Murray Halberg, Peter Snell and Barry Magee training the Lydiard way in Auckland's
Waitakere ranges.

contents

Part Two: The Nomad

To all those fortunate enough, by whatever means,
to fall beneath the Lydiard spell.

acknowledgements

The author gratefully acknowledges the willing cooperation and contributions of everyone who is mentioned in this book.

foreword

ARTHUR LYDIARD HAS been and is still one of the most influential personalities in world athletics. From his native land, New Zealand, his influence spread through the world – to Asia and Australia, to the Americas North, South and Central, and to Europe, especially Russia, Germany, Finland and Denmark.

Arthur coached and lectured extensively across all areas of athletics – the young and the old, the joggers and the élite, the fun runners and the thousands involved in the marathon boom, but the specialty that made him world-famous was developing Olympic and world champions from 800 metres to the marathon. The New Zealand genius was an innovator and a pathfinder, departing from traditional training methods to devise the 'Lydiard system', which produced athletes with superior stamina through long running and testing hills and enhanced their speed with surges and hillwork. His tapering strategy before races was masterly and a critical factor in his success.

Another crucial factor was his ability to instill confidence in his athletes. The combination allowed them to dream of achieving the impossible. That power was demonstrated by the dominance of Lydiard's first champions, from 1958 through two Olympics to 1964 and beyond. In 1961, Murray Halberg, Peter Snell and Barry Magee were unbeaten over a range of distances from 800 to 10,000 metres. Magee's only loss was by mere strides to Halberg over 3 miles.

More Lydiard-influenced stars followed: John Davies, Dick Tayler, Dick Quax, Rod Dixon and the unforgettable John Walker (coached by Arch Jelley). The tradition lived on. Across the Tasman, the great Australian distance runner, Ron Clarke, revitalised his career with a similar emphasis on long running in the Dandenong Ranges on the outskirts of Melbourne and sustained surging running on Caulfield racecourse. He broke 19 world records from 2 to 10 miles. The Lydiard-Clarke influence was the impetus for the emergence of world marathon leaders Rob de Castella and Steve Monaghetti, whom I coached with Chris Laidlaw.

Magee was the surprise package to me – a marathon runner with modest apparent speed who ran the third-fastest 3-mile and fifth all-time fastest 5000 metres. Does long work really slow you down?

Arthur made the challenging claim that the main requirement of a half-miler was endurance. Snell proved it. In December 1961, he ran a marathon in 2:41. On 27 January 1962, he ran a world mile record and on 3 February the world 800-metre and 880-yard world records. In 1964, he ran and won six races to take the very rare 800 and 1500 metres Olympic Games double in Tokyo.

Lydiard the master coach was also a master psychologist and an optimist whose runners had faith and confidence in his patient, thorough build-up methods. He believed they could achieve wonders and they did.

I thank Arthur and his athletes for their generosity and inspiration. I was fortunate to share their experiences on tour and in New Zealand. Their influence and example endured in my own running and, later, my even more rewarding coaching career. I owe much to Arthur Lydiard. Australasian athletes would do well to revisit the Lydiard system and the impossible dream of personal excellence may emerge again. As he and his runners demonstrated, there are no shortcuts.

Pat Clohessy
Brisbane 2003

introduction

THE WORLD-STARTLING TRACK and road performances of Lydiard athletes at the Rome Olympics in 1960, followed by their even more spectacular record-breaking sweep through the world in 1961, changed Arthur Lydiard's life for ever. The small, spring-steel man who masterminded those successes moved from being a misunderstood magician who really wanted to be an architect to an internationally recognised and acclaimed authority on coaching. Fame was not something he sought, but he brought it upon himself and turned a job he did not want into a success which has touched millions of people in the last half-century.

After Rome, the world – well, most of it – wanted to know more and sought to exploit this newly discovered talent. It is a mark of Lydiard's humility and humanity that, for decades, he gave advice freely to everyone who asked.

The Rome explosion and the subsequent trail that Lydiard's runners burned through the world established one dominant truth: Arthur Lydiard was an architect – not in the way of his private but aborted ambition to design buildings but as a creator of superb running machines out of the most basic raw materials.

He had learnt how to lay the foundations, painstakingly build the framework and finally add the cladding of the complete runner. Many of his athletes were masterpieces of planning and design because Lydiard didn't just shape runners, he placed them exactly at the distances for which they were physically, mentally and psychologically best suited; and he prepared them so their peak performances came at precisely the time required.

How he did it became the question asked all around the globe, except in his home country. In New Zealand, where conservatism in sporting development frequently manifests in a heads-in-the-sand mentality rather than an appreciation of new concepts and ideas, Lydiard attracted as much doubt and mockery as compliments. Many foolishly attributed his successes to a freakish streak of luck in stumbling across a collection of exceptional athletes. That dismissive stance was maintained for years, even in the face of the inarguable fact that his athletes were merely a motley collection of local lads who he amalgamated into a force that would control New Zealand's middle- and distance-running spotlight. The way in which these men met to determine which of the national titles each would like to win in the coming season smacked of arrogance. The way in which they then went forth and took those titles, season after season, from 800 metres upwards, demonstrated that it was not arrogance. It was confidence born of their faith in their own capabilities and faith in their coach's ability to hone them exactly for the critical races.

Jack Lovelock's sensational appearance at the Berlin Olympics lit a lonely flame for New Zealand athletics; Arthur Lydiard and his lads fanned it into a forest fire. And international awareness of how it was done came with the simultaneous development of the fitness cult of jogging for people of all ages, sizes, shapes and sexes. Suddenly, every man, woman and child had the opportunity to jog or run the Lydiard way and millions grabbed the chance with both feet.

Lydiard made it quite clear from the outset that what he knew about training athletes could be anyone's merely by asking. He offered to New Zealand the seeds of a plan that could have made the country a mecca for the world's élite runners. The seeds fell on stony ground. His idea was to acquire some land – Waimauku, just north of Auckland and close to coastal forests, sandhills and beaches, was a favoured possibility – where a complete training camp could be established. There he would teach all comers how to turn themselves into the Halbergs, Snells and Magees – and the coaches – of the future.

It never happened. One of the reasons might have been that the Arthur Lydiard of old – like the man today – didn't go out of his way to ingratiate himself with those who might, if their backs were rubbed the right way, supply the resources he needed. While he was completely sure of the success of his own training methods, he made no attempt to hide his disdain and even contempt for those who weren't prepared to come aboard. If you weren't with him, you were against him and you were the losers.

The critics said the Lydiard method would burn runners out; his response was that his system wouldn't and theirs would. They said his system took too long to produce worthwhile results; his answer was that theirs didn't take long enough and couldn't produce any worthwhile results anyway. His did. When it was said that his system had too many limitations, he retorted that any athlete in any sport that called for a degree of stamina – and few sports do not – would benefit from it. Even sprinters, as he and other coaches were later to prove. Even racehorses, as some trainers proved. Even canoeists and kayakers, footballers and cyclists, pistol shooters, swimmers and cricketers, tennis players and archers, yachtsmen and windsurfers. Any sportsman or woman who began to include a good measure of distance running in his or her training schedule was following the Lydiard concept: get stamina first and better results will follow. It's the foundation stone for everything else.

The 1960s were an astonishing period for track and field politics in New Zealand. The hierarchy had the means within their grasp to guarantee New Zealand a permanent and prominent place on the international athletic map and a continuing stream of medal winners on the Olympic dais. They let the opportunity slip.

Lydiard would have preferred to stay in New Zealand, but he had four teenage mouths and a wife to feed and, when job offers flowed in from around the world, he was faced with a choice: stay and struggle or leave and achieve a measure of financial security. Given the indifference and hostility towards him by many athletics officials in New Zealand, it was a classic Hobson's choice.

Lydiard left. New Zealand lost.

The world's best middle- and distance-running coach and conditioner of athletes headed off to more success, more controversy and more frustration. He discovered that, while New

Zealand was notably prodigal in kicking its own talent into homeland oblivion or exile, petty jealousies and envy existed everywhere.

He ran into unhelpful and hostile officialdom; he had to woo over, skirt around or simply ignore those coaches who weren't prepared to accept that his wisdom was superior to theirs. But, against the odds, the Lydiard lore spread through the coaching and competing world until, these days, it can be confidently said that almost no middle-distance or distance running titles or records are achieved by Western world athletes without the vital ingredient of Lydiard-style training. And the same recipe has invaded many other sports with equal success. It may be artfully disguised or subtly tampered with, but it's there. And it has never been improved upon by anyone, except for minor tweaks from Lydiard himself.

Arthur Lydiard has been described by many as arrogant. But this is a tag frequently applied to people who state that not only are they good, they are probably better than most. It is not arrogance for a leading sportsperson or business tycoon to acknowledge that he or she is number one in their field. It is silly not to recognise it when it is obvious to all, even if some won't admit it.

And that's what Arthur Lydiard has been: the self-taught number one in the art of athletics coaching.

He has been called grumpy – he is with those who treat him badly, as are many people. Before the Sydney Olympics, he said, 'Give me forty thousand dollars, give me time and I'll give you medal winners.' He was cold-shouldered. That definitely made him grumpy. He'd asked for no more than the chance to do in New Zealand what he had already achieved in Finland – to coach the coaches to produce the medallists. He could have done it for less than was spent on any one athlete who didn't perform.

He has been called intolerant. He is, with those who are not prepared to listen and learn. People who walk away are not welcomed back. Lydiard will give you loyalty till he drops, but you have to earn it. Far from being vain or arrogant, Lydiard is a modest man, almost self-effacing. He habitually omits his own contribution when he praises the successes of his athletes. He has also committed almost nothing of his life to paper. There are rare diary records, but reading them reveals little.

He has an uncanny feel for athletic potential. Even today, there is a brilliant gleam in his eyes and a flash of zest in his face when he speaks about youngsters among the local neighbourhood group who have fallen beneath his spell and begun running the Lydiard way. Many of them have been winners already but two in particular, he said, could be the next Snell and Halberg. He knows it, they know it, the rest of us can wait and see. He has been so right before. The achievement of that lustre, however, rests with them.

Arthur Lydiard is also a man of kindness and generosity, often unexpected, and of genuine, life-loving, often bawdy humour.

In July 2003 he turned 86. He has gone through periods of personal tragedy and illness, has suffered from heart trouble and lost his ability to run after some serious knee problems, which have made even walking uncomfortable. But, get him talking and the voice firms with its old aggressive confidence and authority, the keen blue eyes spark and you're listening to a man as mesmerising now as he was more than half a century ago when a handful of local lads were drawn to follow him from nowhere to stardom on the world's running stage.

I am proud and privileged to have known him for more than half my life, to have had that life changed by him and now to put his story down in print. I've been trying to uncork this very private bottle of memories and recollections for about 20 years and it is evident that time has mellowed the man. But it is still vintage Lydiard.

When I was talking to Murray Halberg during the final stages of writing this biography of the man he (at age 70) still calls 'Coach', he reminded me of the dedication in our 1963 book, *A Clean Pair of Heels*. 'It says just about everything,' he noted.

Murray Halberg dedicates this book to: The man I have cursed most on cold, wet winter days and thanked most on the victory dais – the man who has been my inspiration, guide, mentor and friend – Arthur Lydiard.

These days, those sentiments can be iterated around the world. And the world has honoured him. He has received numerous awards in recognition of his contribution to athletics and general fitness. He is genuinely touched by most of them but he never mentions them unless pressed. They are not displayed in his home as most people's trophies are flaunted. Once, in the course of making a film documentary, we found a collection of medals and other memorabilia jammed in a drawer in his games room. What were these? we asked. Arthur neither knew nor cared. Later, he revealed that his second wife, Eira, had kept his collection of cups and other awards brightly polished in a trophy cabinet but, after her death, he decided he wasn't going to clean them. Eventually, most of the collection went into a sack that was deposited in the nearest rubbish dump. No one, he said, was interested in 'bloody cups'. What he kept was consigned to the drawer where we found them.

He was proud of his White Star from Finland, that country's highest honour, and was delighted when a home for a fine statue of him was finally found at Auckland's Ericsson Stadium. He had been awarded the OBE in 1962. Many years later, in 1990, he was elevated to the exclusive Order of New Zealand, and in the same year was inducted into the New Zealand Sports Hall of Fame. In 1994 he was honoured with the Halberg Award for Services to Sport and, when the New Zealand Awards were inaugurated that year, received the first Recreation and Sport Trophy.

And in October 2003, one glaring omission from this list of tributes was finally remedied. Arthur was elected to life membership of Athletics New Zealand, the organisation that, for so many decades, had wasted the remarkable talent that could have kept New Zealand on top of the running world for decades after the glories of 1960.

As the writing of this book neared an end, I asked Arthur if he had any final thoughts. He said he would think about it and a few days later gave me a typed synopsis of his life. The man's humility and modesty is reflected in the fact that he did it all in about 500 words and most of them were devoted to thanking other people for the help and encouragement they had given him: his late first wife, Jean; Ken Jarvis, the general manager of Winstone Ltd, who created a job in order to keep him in New Zealand; Graham Davy, the Auckland athletics administrator who negotiated the Winstone deal; and the late Frank Sharp, who, as president of the Auckland Centre in 1960, organised the public appeal that financed Lydiard to the Rome Olympics and ensured that he – and New Zealand – had three remarkable middle- and distance-running medals.

Arthur wrote little about himself. His private life and feelings have been his business and nobody else's. The deeper emotions rarely surface for anyone else to see, although I did glimpse them occasionally as we worked together. But I had known him for 42 years before I learnt that his ambition had always been to be an architect. For a man who can talk fast and endlessly on the human condition and how to shape and improve it, he is the embodiment of taciturnity when it comes to talking about himself.

There is so much more to the Arthur Lydiard story than can be told in 500 words. Or perhaps, even in 80,000.

Part One: The Quest

1

growing up

On 6 July 1535, Sir Thomas More was executed in England for treason. On the same day in 1885, Louis Pasteur successfully tested his anti-rabies vaccine on an infected boy. In 1923, 6 July saw the formation of the USSR and on that day in 1957, Althea Gibson became the first black tennis player to win a Wimbledon singles title.

There were two events on 6 July 1917. One of them, T. E. Lawrence leading his Arab forces to capture the port of Aqaba from the Turks, was immediately significant. The other, which would not gain significance for many years, occurred in Auckland, when Arthur Leslie Lydiard was born into a house builder's family in Mt Eden. He grew into a small boy, tough, resourceful, but of no great stature, and there was nothing about him to suggest that, in time, he would revolutionise the conditioning of athletes, initiate a jogging movement that would sweep the world and, from a physical fitness viewpoint, make what may be seen as one of the greatest contributions of the last century to the wellbeing of men, women and children.

Mind you, when he was only five, he gave perhaps the first demonstration of his athleticism. As he remembers it, 'Escaping from my father eighty years ago may have been my unknowing introduction to running training. We lived in Auckland's Reimers Avenue, opposite Eden Park, the football stadium that hosts most of the rugby and cricket tests now played in Auckland. In those days, it was small, as I was, and it was not walled off as it is now, so I was over there all the time. I remember watching New South Wales playing rugby there against Auckland in the early 1920s and I didn't pay to get in.

'The area around the park was largely swampy and I still remember that, when I was about five, my father chased me out there. I have no idea now why he was after me, but there was no way I was going to be caught. I was moving fast and I got over the fence into this area and escaped when my father became entangled in the barbed wire. For him to be after me like that was a rare event, because we were a fairly normal family and we all got along until my father moved out when I was in my middle teens. Apart from one occasion in a city street, I did not see him again.'

Yet Arthur's parents had already seen tragedy before he was born. Their first child, Davie, born in 1915, had died of meningitis when he was only 18 months old. After Arthur, they had another son, Wally, in 1920. Oddly, just before Wally died in 2002, his wife heard him talking to himself. When she asked who he was talking to, Wally said, 'I'm talking to my brother.'

'Arthur?' she asked.

'No, I'm talking to Davie,' Wally replied. He was talking to someone he had never known.

Arthur's mother was the eldest of eight girls, so he had seven aunts. His maternal grandfather, who was a butcher, died of a heart attack when his mother was 15, leaving the family with no income. There was no social security in those days and Arthur's grandmother earned money to keep her large family by cleaning houses and doing other menial chores. It was a hard life – as well as the physical nature of the work she had to walk to all her jobs from their home just off Valley Road in Mt Eden.

The young Arthur and one of his aunts were the only members of the family who were not stricken when the influenza epidemic swept around the world after World War One and killed some 6600 people in New Zealand between October and December 1918. All the aunts were confined to beds in the Lydiards' huge Reimers Avenue house, except for one who lived with her husband in a house just behind them. He guesses they were all there because they were short of money and the house had plenty of room for them.

The married aunt's husband was working, but he never told his wife exactly what he did. He was employed on a death truck, travelling up and down the streets collecting dead bodies and taking them to Victoria Park, where they had dug huge trenches for the corpses.

The death toll all round the world was huge, but all of the Lydiard family survived.

Only a year or so earlier, when Arthur was about three, there had been a polio scare in New Zealand and he was sent out to New Lynn to stay with an aunt for a year. Today New Lynn is just another suburb, but 80 years ago it was a remote part of Auckland.

'We got there by train from Morningside and it was like living in the country. I was fascinated to see the big cattle drives down Portage Road on their way to the works at Westfield. I used to hang on my aunt's front gate and watch as hundreds and hundreds went past with their drovers and dogs around them.'

Those were the days when milkmen on horse-drawn floats used to drive around and fill householders' billycans from bigger cans of milk. No billy, no milk was the rule. There were no refrigerators, either, just a meat safe covered in muslin, which hung outside the back door, out of the sun but in the draught. Arthur recalls, 'I'm not sure we weren't healthier then than we are now.'

And the night-cart men came clattering round in the darkest hours to replace filled toilet cans with empty ones. 'Like everyone else, we had an outside toilet. If you wanted to go at night, you had to go out in the dark and follow the trail – and your nose – down the back yard. Great on a winter's night. We used to awake to the sound of the cans rattling when the night-cart men arrived.' Even in 1939, when Arthur married his first wife, Jean, and they moved into a state house in Mt Roskill, the suburb still relied on a night-cart service.

'We had no electricity, just candles and kerosene lamps for lighting, we cooked on cast-iron, coal-fed ranges. Women were marvellous cooks with the big black stoves – they seemed to know just when to open the door.'

Arthur's primary school was Edendale, 3 kilometres away in Sandringham Avenue, and he walked – or occasionally ran – there five days a week, along a loose-gravel road which wound through areas of swamp, where he could hear hordes of frogs croaking and where kids played in makeshift canoes – and occasionally drowned.

Mt Eden then was considered a long way from the centre of Auckland, but access gradually improved as roads were straightened and sealed and the tram service was extended from central city Queen Street into the burgeoning suburbs.

'But as I began schooling, the only traffic was a few Model-T Fords with their accelerators on their steering wheels, horse-drawn vehicles and people like me who used our feet or rode bicycles.'

Arthur had many photos of those days but, when his grandmother died, one of his aunts collected them and burned them all. As a result, there are no pictures of young Arthur Lydiard.

Arthur's indestructibility was demonstrated when he was still a child. The Mt Eden family house, like so many built in those days, had a long hallway running straight through the middle of it.

'I raced down that hall one day on my three-wheeled bike, the front door was open and I shot straight off the front steps. I've often wondered how I didn't kill myself, but there were no injuries at all – not on that occasion, anyway. But little kids can fall hard and don't seem to get hurt.'

The incident may seem trivial but, knowing Arthur, it's easy to picture him pedalling down that hallway flat out and determined, a trait he grew up to display in virtually everything he later did in his picturesque life.

As he grew older, Arthur spent several Christmas fortnights at the YMCA camp in the Hunua Ranges, a large forested region to the south of Auckland. He remembers them as good holidays. 'A nice old guy called Mr Adair ran the camp – it's named after him now. The first thing every morning, all the boys would run naked down to the river and dive into the cold water. There were no girls in the camp. These were the days before co-ed colleges, although I think Takapuna Grammar might have been a mixed school.

'These were days of innocence. I didn't have a sister and I was shy of girls for many years. Me and my friends just didn't associate with them; we did everything with our mates, tearing around playing rugby and other games. We had to walk everywhere we went and we didn't have any money to take girls out anyway, even if we'd had the time.'

Arthur thought nothing of walking two kilometres to Balmoral to join his football team at Potter's Park, where he played his first game of rugby for Eden, the club he remained with for many years.

Simplicity was the way of life for young Lydiard. 'I think I got to know my first girl-friend at Avondale when I was about 15. We were living at Owairaka at the time. She was nice, a little blonde, and one of a bunch of us who went picnicking all over the place; places like Tui Glen and Titirangi or up to a park in the Henderson Valley. I'd bike over to Avondale and we would travel around in a truck that someone used to hire.

'None of us had any money, but we made our own fun without it. We played a lot of cards. I remember the excitement when we got our first radio. I was about 19 then. I hadn't even heard a radio until I was about 14 when I used to go to an aunt's place for visits. A guy in a neighbouring house close to the street had a radio and we'd stand outside in the street and listen to it.'

As a youngster, Arthur moved around a lot. His father built spec houses and, as one was finished, the family occupied it while the next was built. They then moved to that one and sold the other so that another house could be started. The houses were all in the neighbouring suburbs of Mt Eden, Mt Roskill and Mt Albert, which meant there was only minimal disruption to Arthur's schooling.

'I must have gone to every Sunday school there was, except the Catholic one,' Arthur says. 'I enjoyed Sunday school and would go every Sunday morning to the one nearest to wherever we were living at the time. I was christened in the Church of England but I went to all the others, although I didn't think much of the Church of England. I found them too bloody political.'

So, as a family in those early, financially difficult times, the life of the Lydiards revolved pretty much around where they lived. Holidays were a rarity; Arthur remembers his mother and father going to Rotorua once for a whole week. That was a big deal in those days and it was probably the first and the only real holiday they ever had before they broke up.

Not unexpectedly, Arthur never went far from home in those days either, apart from to the Hunua camp. He was 10 before he ventured further south. He travelled through Hamilton to Raglan, about 170 kilometres away down the wild west coast, to spend the holidays with some relatives.

'Today, we can climb in our cars and be there in little more than an hour or so. Then, we got up early to catch a tram about 6 o'clock to the railway station, took the train to Frankton, just north of Hamilton, where we transferred to a service car, which took us to Raglan, where our relatives waited with a horse and cart to take us to their farm.'

For an outdoor lad, the trip was worth every dragging mile. He and his cousin spent their days roaming in the bush on the slopes of Mount Koriori. 'We never got ourselves lost because we knew if we followed any stream downwards we would eventually come to the road that circled the forest. I was taught to swim in Whale Bay by a Maori boy, who was one of my cousin's companions. They were wonderful holidays. I was small for my age but I could look after myself – not that it was often necessary.'

After primary school, Arthur went to Kowhai Intermediate School for two years, travelling there by tram – a wonderful service which was eventually scrapped in favour of buses.

At Kowhai, he had his first experience of the popular New Zealand school event, the 'everyone starts' steeplechase. 'In my case,' he remembers, 'it was a remote encounter which could have had no influence on my future activities. The practice was to ring the school bell to call the entire school out of their classrooms and then ring it again to start the race. But the only bell my teacher heard was the second one. By the time we got outside, everyone else was out of sight. So we didn't start.'

Arthur moved on to Mt Albert Grammar School on a day he can never forget – 3 February 1931.

'I went home from school at midday and one of the few people in our street who had a radio had passed the news from neighbour to neighbour that the east coast city of Napier had been devastated by an earthquake. The news was passed along in case anyone had friends or relatives in Napier. Hundreds of people were killed and thousands lost everything in what remains as one of New Zealand's greatest natural disasters.'

Arthur enjoyed his intermediate and grammar school years – 'I probably enjoyed primary as well, but I don't remember much about it. One of the brighter memories from Kowhai is of learning Maori songs. I was a good scholar at intermediate level. I got 100 per cent in mathematics and science and I did well in Latin and science when I moved on to Mt Albert. My career goal then was to be an architect. I was good at and relished mechanical and architectural drawing and was working well towards my ambition when my father lost all his money in the Depression and I had to leave school and go to work.

'I have always regretted that I could not keep on with architecture, although how we would have managed university I don't know. Those were the days when it was impossible to study at the tertiary level because we didn't have the money.

'Even when I got married, I had only a hundred pounds. So we had to make a little go a long way to feed and clothe the kids when they came along and look after them properly. I used to give Jean my pay envelope as soon as I got it. I never even opened it – she could spend the money better than I could. I always had a good garden and that helped a lot, but we had no money to enjoy the luxuries of life, even the little ones.

'But my childhood was virtually untroubled. Family life was good, without any problems until I was about 14. That's when my father buggered off. There was no responsibility on him in those days to look after us after that, but my mother, who was a wonderful woman, managed somehow and was very helpful to Wally and me.'

Arthur's enjoyment of Mt Albert Grammar School lasted only two years before the Great Depression fell on the country and he was forced to find a job to help the family finances. This was a bad time for builders, as it was for many other people, so his father was no longer earning much and the family needed every penny they could get. When his father left, of course, the situation became even more critical.

'The situation in the Depression was so desperate that the grounds of Mt Albert Grammar were being worked on by gangs of relief workers, men from all walks of life who had been thrown out of work. Many of them were professional people – doctors, lawyers, teachers and so on – forced to labour for a pittance to save their families from starvation and their homes from repossession.'

Because of the slump, interest in sporting activities was minimal, but Arthur ran the grammar school's steeplechase, for which no one trained, and won, with no great distinction, the junior championship and handicap sections. He was also involved in school boxing, for which there was no training either. 'I apparently had some natural aptitude because I fought about six times without being beaten. I cannot recall how I won, I just did.'

One recollection of those early days is that in his school final, Arthur was matched against a lad who was taller, had a longer reach and was rated one of Auckland's better amateurs. Arthur's solution to all that was to fill the air with leather as soon as the bell went and so defeat his opponent by sheer aggression and determination. It was another example of his approach to life, his tendency to overcome overwhelming odds by pure resolve.

His parents weren't very sports-minded at all. At the time he won those events, they didn't attend the prize presentation ceremonies. His mother wasn't particularly well at the time and his father wasn't interested. 'They didn't discourage me; they just didn't provide much support.'

With the need to make money to keep the family afloat, Arthur's father wangled him a job in Warren Farmer's foundry, a manufacturer of milking machines based in Hobson Street, in the heart of Auckland city. He worked in the store for a time and then, despite his comparative lack of size, he was told to swing a 26-pound sledgehammer to smash up pig iron. That he carried on cheerfully with this muscle-straining slavery might indicate why he was successful as a boxer and why, in time, he was able to push his body to extremes that most would shy away from.

'Because I was under 16, I did not have to pay any tax, but the company took it anyway. They were paying me 15 shillings a week but I received only 12 shillings and sixpence. I guess the two and sixpence went into the boss's pocket rather than to the tax department. It was a lot of money not to get in those days.'

Arthur pedalled his bicycle between home and work every day, recalling that there wasn't much traffic about and the only thing he had to be wary of were people getting on and off the trams in the middle of the roadway. Quite possibly, they also had to be wary of him. He rode his bicycle, head down and backside up, as if he was facing a personal challenge. He always raced the trams and, once, took on a racing cyclist and beat him on a hill, unaware that the man he was challenging was the junior Auckland champion.

Arthur worked for a year at the foundry, until it went bankrupt. One of his aunts then got him a job in Bridgens shoe factory, where she was the secretary. It was a good job and it meant he escaped having to go off in the labour force to work in the Waitakere Ranges to the west of Auckland, or to any other remote region.

'I stayed with the company for 24 years. I did consider setting up my own company, but the shoe-making business isn't like being a butcher or an electrician, where you can work on your own. A shoe factory needs a lot of specialised staff – cutters, machinists, finishers and so on.'

One day in the life of Arthur the shoemaker is recorded. Apparently, he hit his thumb with his hammer and, as usual when this happened, everyone around laughed. Arthur's response was, 'At least I'm not taking half an hour off like you lot would', and he immediately used his forefinger in place of his thumb to steady the nail. As luck would have it, his first swing of the hammer hit that finger too, but he immediately pushed forward the next finger and, on his third attempt, hit the nail and went on with his work. If he was hurt, and he must have been, he didn't let it show.

In 1958 Arthur moved to the Zenith shoe factory, in Penrose, where his brother Wally was working. He became manager there, and just two years later he was making an impact at the Rome Olympics. His day job and his sporting passion were closely linked. 'My boys were wearing shoes I had made for them, because I had developed my own last for running shoes.'

The running shoe design skills that Arthur was to demonstrate around the world were typical of his resourceful nature. By the standards of the 1960s his level of marathon training was extraordinary and the shoes that were commercially available weren't good enough for the high mileages he was running. The shoes he designed were made with very thick microcellular rubber soles, which gave good traction on the roads. The band of runners he had gathered around him wore the same Lydiard-style shoe. The soles wore down very quickly and he was constantly resoling them for both himself and his runners; but it was typical of his attention to detail that he watched for the first signs of wear on the heels and immediately took them off to Zenith and rebuilt them. His awareness of the importance of looking after their shoes was one of the reasons his runners never suffered from injuries, even when they were grinding out up to 320 kilometres a week in scheduled and supplementary training.

Just how Arthur Lydiard got himself into this demanding regime and induced others to join him is perhaps the most extraordinary phase of an extraordinary life.

2

running for his life

ASK A DOZEN athletes why they took up a particular sport and you'll probably get a dozen differing answers. Many factors – physiological and psychological – influence whether a person pursues football, softball, cricket, swimming, running or any other pastime. But if those reasons were analysed, you would almost certainly find one common element: the influence of someone whose attitude to their sport inspires the young to follow them. In New Zealand, for decades, the inspiration was usually a star of the national game of rugby. For Arthur Lydiard, it was two otherwise ordinary men distinguished by an intense interest in running and fitness. He says now that, without them, he would probably never have become a runner and, if he had not become a runner, he would not have become a coach. As he says, it is impossible to become any kind of a coach 'except perhaps a bad one' without immersing yourself in practical experience first.

Perhaps, therefore, those two men deserve to be placed alongside him in the annals of athletics. One was Jack Cargill, in his day one of the best sprinters in New Zealand, who set an unstoppable ball rolling by introducing Arthur to the Lynndale Club. At his first meet, Arthur started in a half-mile and a mile on generous handicaps and managed to win both. It was an early sign of a trait that has marked Arthur's entire career – he has never liked being beaten. The second man to influence Arthur was Jack Dolan, also of Lynndale, who came on the scene later and helped sort out a confused young man and show him what running was really all about.

Having joined Lynndale, Arthur continued running, without

training, because his main interest at this stage was rugby football. He played for the Eden Club as a side-row forward and for six years in a row was in the team which won its Auckland grade championship.

'Then I was promoted to the senior side and found myself a small man among the giants of senior forward packs, so I became a back, playing anywhere from halfback to wing. In my three years as a senior, I was never in a team which won a championship.

'I remember when I was still a kid, my Eden team was drawn against a tougher team one weekend. I'm not sure which year this was. Our coach said to our hooker, "Have a look at the other side and see if they've got their sleeves rolled up or down." The kid had a look and reported they had their sleeves rolled up. "Right," the coach said, "roll your sleeves up and when the ball comes into the scrum, put your hand down and roll the ball their way." He did and we got a free kick.'

Arthur chuckles over this story as evidence that, all those years ago, even the youngsters were into football trickery. 'There's not much new in beating the rules,' he says.

Arthur is remembered as a tireless and extremely dynamic loosie. He stood less than five and a half feet (1.7 metres) tall but, when he got the ball and dropped his shoulders, he went forward so hard and low to the ground that he was a problem to stop. He once went over the tryline with four opponents hanging on to him, one of them on his back. Being beaten was not in his nature. Being intimidated wasn't either.

In early 1939, Arthur married Jean Young. War broke out the same year, while Arthur was playing rugby at Victoria Park. The team were given the news at half-time and it did not occur to anyone that, by the end of the war, half of them would be dead.

A few weeks later, in another rugby match, Arthur injured his left shoulder, which has ever since limited his ability to lift his arm high and straight. The defect meant he was not considered suitable for the army, and he was assigned to the Home Guard for the duration of the war. 'You did what you were told in those days,' he remarks.

So while the war rolled inexorably on overseas, life in New

Zealand continued only somewhat changed for the Lydiard family. Jean and Arthur's first son, Roy, was born in February, 1943. They had three more children, Fay, Gary and Bruce.

Arthur still ran in the summer and occasionally won races, but only at club level. 'I wasn't interested in climbing to championship levels because the sport gave me little real pleasure. It hurts to run when you're not fit, even when you kid yourself you are. So in some years I might have started in only one or two races and I rarely ran more than a dozen.'

Among his rivals were Norm Cooper, who was a former national 3-mile champion, and Bill Savidan, the national mile champion from 1927 to 1929, 6-mile champion seven times between 1927 and 1937 and 1930 Empire Games 6-mile gold medallist. 'He was the first of our great distance runners and I don't imagine they were as aware of me as I was of them, although we were much the same in at least one respect – not at all serious about running as we judge seriousness by today's standards. Running was still something most of us did to fill in time between rugby seasons.'

And then Jack Dolan entered Arthur's life and changed it irrevocably. Jack, who went on to become Lynndale president for 25 years, was a number of years older than Arthur but by no means an old man. His great pleasure was to see others running or at least involved in a healthy recreation and he inveigled Arthur into joining him on a 5-mile training jog. 'It nearly killed me. I thought I was fit from football and Jack showed me how pathetically wrong I was.

'But his enthusiasm was the most whole-hearted I have experienced and, while he physically exhausted me, he also mentally stimulated me. For the first time, I thought about fitness in its true sense and that led to the further thought: if this is what I am like at 27, what state of fitness will I be in when I am 47?'

It was, in some ways, laughable – and laughable, says Arthur as he looks back, is what the sport of athletics was in New Zealand in those days.

'For instance, I didn't run with the harriers; I trained only on the track and that was negligible. We mainly raced ourselves fit, combining club competition and training with, perhaps, a little extra effort before a major event. If we had done the

Auckland harriers began the season with the Great Eastern road race from Pakuranga to Ellerslie. This is the 1945 start with Arthur, aged 27, tucked back in the middle of the front runners. Wearing C14 is Auckland mile champion Norm Ambler. *B.Snowden*

Arthur lies second as the leaders pass through Newmarket in the 1946 Onehunga to Auckland race.

Arthur, running for Lynndale, wins a mile at Newmarket's Sarawia Park.

Arthur returned to competitive running to help his marathon pupil Ray Puckett and emphasised his power by running second to him in the national marathon in 1958.

The indomitable Murray Halberg in his prime.

Bill Baillie demonstrates the art of cross-country fencing.

Barry Magee, who chased Murray Halberg hard but beat him only once, is now a coach rated by Arthur as ready for national appointment.

Arthur meets former New Zealand Prime Minister Sir Keith Holyoake after the 1960 Olympic Games in Rome. *The Dominion*

Ray Puckett demonstrates one of Arthur's stretching and limbering exercises.

Arthur with his team at the 1960 Olympic Games in Rome. From left, Murray Halberg, Ray Puckett, Barry Magee, Arthur, Peter Snell and Jeff Julian. *NZ Herald*

opposite of everything we were being told or thought, we would have been working along much better lines.

'We might wander down to the track a couple of times a week; we might jog for a half-mile or mile and sprint a couple of times. If we were really charged with enthusiasm and vigour, we might even *run* a full half-mile. But we would normally be on the track for no more than fifteen minutes before we showered, drank a bottle of stout and went home, glowing with pride at our dedication and our levels of speed and fitness.

'Today's athletes train faster than races were won in in those casual pre-Second World War days, when Harold Nelson took more than thirty minutes to win the New Zealand 6-mile title and a runner was considered terrific if he could run between 14:14 and 14:18 for 3 miles. The average athlete then could not hope to run twenty 440s at speed because he didn't have the strength. Today, properly conditioned runners handle that workload with ease. The then-impossible has become a now-doddle.'

Arthur agrees that there are still runners gifted with natural speed who can get away with doing little more in the way of training than in those pre-war days. A stand-out example for him was the Jamaican George Kerr, who chased Peter Snell and Roger Moens home in the 1960 Olympic 800 metres final. 'I have often wondered what he could have achieved had he supplemented his wonderful natural speed with stamina training to enable him to sustain his speed over greater distances.'

So Arthur, while he was, he supposed, a reasonable sort of runner, was also a confused one. 'At one meeting, an athletic "expert" approached me after I had run a race and said sagely, "Lydiard, young man, your stride is too short." Obligingly, I lengthened it in the next event, after which another "expert" came up and said, "Lydiard, you should shorten your stride. It's too long."

'But that kind of confusion did nothing to kill my new outlook on running. I decided that, from now on, I was going to enjoy it and that led to my first discovery or, if you like, my first inspiration.'

It was Arthur's first step along a road he never dreamed existed on the map of his life.

3

conquering confusion

IN RETROSPECT, THE inspiration that triggered Arthur Lydiard seems simple enough, but it was revolutionary then: that the initial step to enjoying running is to achieve proper fitness; not just the ability to run half a mile once a week without collapsing, but the ability to run great distances with ease at a steady speed.

'I began running seven times a week and wading through all the literature in the Lynndale club library, finally settling on a book by English coach F. A. M. Webster, who impressed me most for his common sense. I now consider he knew more about athletics than anyone else I have read and his only fault was that he did not train his athletes hard enough.

'I also broke sharply from the accepted tenets of athletic training about food and drink. I refused to go through the agonies of "drying out" before a race and I rejected the tradition of building up on steaks. I used Webster's theory of more regular training and the alternation of fast work with steady work and walking sessions and I soon found that, contrary to all established practice, I could drink anything I wanted to – it didn't stop me from running just as fast – and it wasn't necessary to eat rich red meat before a competition.

'I found later that a cup of tea immediately before starting a marathon was a stimulus – something that Emil Zatopek discovered much later on.'

Arthur soon decided Webster's schedule was not tough enough for him, since his concern was getting fit for life, not just for racing, and he was starting at an age when athletes were considered to be finished, too old, a belief which he, too, then accepted.

'So I stepped my training up to seven days a week and I cut out the walking Webster had put in his schedules. I reasoned that, unless the exercise was strenuous, it could not add anything to my condition. I increased my runs up to twelve miles, which, in those days, was considered a hell of a long way.'

And, late in 1945, Arthur was back into active racing. He was 28, he sensed he had begun to discover something about good running and he wanted to put it to the test in competitive racing. He made such an impression that he was chosen to captain the Auckland cross-country team in the national championships. Auckland won and, although he had run well earlier, Arthur was the only man in the team to run poorly. The races were held in Dunedin and he discovered that he didn't travel well.

'So I didn't represent Auckland again until 1947, by which time I was a scratch runner over one, two and three miles and, just before the Auckland championships, was going well enough to beat the mile title-holder, Norm Ambler, off the same mark. Three weeks later, he kept his title by beating me easily; I just could not match him on the day. Nor could I catch Harold Nelson when I contested the three-mile title – he won in 14:31.'

Arthur's reaction to not winning when he felt he should have been capable of victory showed the change in him. It wasn't the response of someone training for life, but of someone with a resolute desire to compete well for his own satisfaction and gratification.

'These defeats exposed one of my main problems – I was hitting my peaks of performance at all the wrong times. I needed to find a method of not only building stamina for a lot of good racing but of timing my preparation so that I could be reasonably certain of being at or near my top form on those days when I needed to be. I had to learn to aim for and reach a peak at a pre-determined time and then hold it as long as was necessary.

'I was training up to twelve miles every day of the year, so what was wrong? The answer I gave myself led to the marathon-type training which has been the basic ingredient of all my schedules for the past 55 years. I found it by extreme methods. I ran staggering training distances, up to 250 miles a week, and soon found that, even if I flogged myself to exhaustion one day – to the point where I either walked or shambled the final miles – I would recover enough to continue easier work in following days and, a week to ten days later, would become markedly stronger.'

Arthur has no idea how many miles he ran while trying to find his solution because, regrettably, he has not been a diligent diarist and, for a couple of years, because of the financial needs of a growing family, he had a milk run on top of working at the shoe factory. This cut down the miles he could run. 'I'd get up at 2 a.m., do the round, get home for a shower and breakfast, cycle to work and then back home and get to bed about 6 p.m. after another shower and dinner. I always got about eight hours sleep. I ran only at the weekends during this time. The cycling and running around with milk bottles in my hands gave me enough exercise during the weekdays.'

Although Arthur was alone in his early days of experimentation, other younger runners became interested in what he was doing and he began to have company on his runs. One of the first to join was Lawrie King, who worked in the shoe factory with him. He heard Arthur trying to cajole a healthy-looking character into joining Lynndale and volunteered himself.

'My first reaction was that if he ran a mile he'd drop dead. How false that impression proved to be. Lawrie didn't have much time for training but he tackled it with the same intense enthusiasm that I had whipped up in myself. In his first year, he staggered home in 56th place in the Auckland cross-country. In his second year, he was third in the junior section, beaten only by two others who had joined my little pioneering school, Brian White and Tom Hutchinson. In 1945, they finished first and second in the New Zealand cross-country championship.

'That summer, Lawrie entered for the Auckland junior 2-mile track title. I told him to blow off his nervous energy – he was full of it – and he raced off like a madman. After one lap, he was seventy yards ahead of the field and everyone, probably including the other runners, was laughing at him. But, at the end of the race, he was still seventy yards in front.'

Lawrie was Arthur's first track success and he was proud of him for it, although it established him in the eyes of interested Aucklanders as a coach, a qualification he hadn't sought and didn't particularly want. But he had a growing band of runners who cheerfully tackled the extra training he piled onto them and he drew satisfaction from the enjoyment and benefit they discovered about long, steady aerobic running. Lawrie, incidentally, went on to run for New Zealand in the 1954 Empire Games after winning the New Zealand cross-country title and setting a New Zealand 6-mile record. His later life was marred by personal difficulties and he died comparatively young.

Meantime, the Lynndale club and Arthur had had a difference of administrative opinion and, in defiance, he started the Owairaka club's harrier section right on Lynndale's boundary and declared at the first club meeting he attended that, in four years, Owairaka would beat Lynndale, then the strongest harrier club in the country. Confident or crazy? It was typical of Arthur to put his money where his mouth was; he had a new-found confidence in what he was doing and, if others thought him crazy, that was their problem.

The scornful reaction was understandable because, at that initial meeting, Arthur was the only starter in the mile race and the only middle-distance runner in the club, apart from Bert Payne, with whom he was to become closely allied.

And, he recalls, 'I had six runners at the first harrier meeting – me and five who had never run before. But they were willing and I concentrated particularly on a youngster, Mick Stevenson, and turned him out to win his first major race, the Auckland junior cross-country championship, by 400 metres. He was a certainty for the national title but a week later he crashed at a fence during training and broke a bone in one of his feet. By the time he came back as a senior, the Murray Halberg era had begun and Mick couldn't do better than second in that company.

'As far as my threat was concerned, I was either inspired or determined or plain lucky. Without poaching from any other clubs, we built Owairaka's strength and, in four years almost to the day, we won the Auckland championship. Lynndale in those days was poaching good runners from other clubs to strengthen itself; I began not only with young runners who were not attached to any other club, but who had never run before. Lawrie King was a shining example of the ability that lies untapped anywhere you care to look. That success from out of nowhere added to the satisfaction I got from topping Lynndale.'

Arthur agrees that there were times when he thrashed his runners but, as the main guinea-pig, he thrashed himself harder. He ran distances of nearly 50 kilometres through the undulating roads and rough tracks in the Waitakere Ranges. These ranges are steep, thickly bush-clad, and the scenic roads and tracks rise and fall abruptly. The midday heat in the bush is intense.

'But I was determined to find out what the human body would take without cracking, so I frequently ran myself down to an exhausted walk. I always got home – somehow – and my track work improved. I realised I had the basic element of my plan at last. I was training for the marathon and marathon running enabled me to run faster on the track than I had ever run before. If that was good enough for me, why should it not be good for others?

'I made the discovery neither easily nor entirely accidentally. I had begun with a semi-schedule that combined distance with speed work and I just had to keep balancing the two elements against each other. I learnt that lack of the necessary conditioning made speed work useless; I could get one good race and then level off. So I altered the schedule and tried again; and as my condition improved, I found myself peaking too soon. I retimed the schedule again to try to slow down the accretion of speed. Essentially, every new point of reference I established involved a rearrangement and adjustment of my schedule.'

It sounds simple, but it took Arthur nearly nine years of training, experimentation, trial and error, sacrifice and hardship, during which he ran thousands of kilometres, before he felt that he had perfected the marathon-type training system he was seeking. He was so pre-occupied with this quest, he did little competitive running during those years, apart from marathons.

The marathon distance was the cornerstone of his schedules in which he delicately and precisely balanced sharp sprints, repetition training, hill work, medium-pace running, distance running, speed running and time trials.

'I don't have a record of the miles I ran while I was looking for the answer but I guess I must have covered about 30,000 miles (48,000km) or so. A typical week would have seen me run, say, ten miles on Monday, fifteen on Tuesday, twelve on Wednesday, eighteen on Thursday, ten on Friday, fifteen on Saturday and twenty-two to twenty-six on Sunday. It varied because I was trying all the time to find the right balance.'

Think about that 48,000 kilometres. It's roughly two and a half times the distance from Auckland to London; nearly 70 runs between Auckland and Wellington.

At the time, Arthur was charting his progress, but it was unfortunately not in a permanent form and all he remembers now of those remarkable years is some of the agony and much of the elation as he homed in on the winning recipe that was to propel him back into competition as a reborn champion.

4

marathon madness

IN THE 1940s the marathon was generally regarded as the sphere of lunatics and has-been athletes. To run under three hours was considered a world-class achievement and the Auckland provincial championship might attract only two or three contestants. They might be joined by friends having a bit of fun or by athletes adding to their training, but most of these extras didn't finish or even intend to finish. The marathon wasn't a race; the average speed was seven-minute miles or slower. Yet only 11 years later, Barry Magee won the 1960 national title in 2 hours 18 minutes, running at more than 11 miles an hour – well under six-minute miles – with none of the painful effort of the early marathoners.

The change was largely wrought by Arthur Lydiard, who brought to the marathon the benefits of proper conditioning and thoughtful, tactical running in whatever conditions prevailed.

'My running mileage was high at this time because I was experimenting to find the right distances for developing the stamina and physical endurance I knew were essential for sustained good performance. I started out by measuring off a mile on May Road in Mt Roskill and I ran up and down there twice a day for a time. Then I increased my distances, going out to Otahuhu and Papatoetoe and into the Waitakeres. I had to develop my ability to withstand heat, because in those days they started marathon races at midday and we'd have to run through the hottest part of the day. I'd run thirty or so miles up around the Waitakeres, deliberately choosing the hottest times. I'd jump a fence and sneak oranges or lemons to suck on the way.'

40

Arthur ran up to 400 kilometres a week – the equivalent of some nine-and-a-half marathons – and, unless he was totally stuffed, he never just jogged. I ran – jogged – his infamous Waiatarua course with him once. He was patient with my plodding progress up this long, winding hill to the Scenic Drive – from memory, the hill seemed about 200 miles long – then, as we neared what I thought was the top, he suggested we should pick up the speed. He accelerated round the corner; I forced myself to totter fractionally faster after him. Round the corner, the hill continued. But it was steeper.

Arthur had something of the same reaction when he first tackled the Waiatarua hill. 'It was then a loose gravel road. I got to the top of the hill and sat in the gutter wondering what the hell I was doing. But, the next weekend, I did it again and I climbed the hill no trouble. I'd found that I got a very quick physical reaction to those tough runs.

'No one tried to discourage me until years later, when the top coaches cast aspersions. By then, I was getting good results with my runners as well as myself and that's why they rubbished my methods. One of them told Barry Magee, "If I was you, I'd get away from Lydiard. He'll bloody kill you." Barry laughed them off – he was getting better all the time and eventually became one of the finest distance runners in the world.

'I have never killed off an athlete in all these years. And I had encouragement from one Jack Sinclair, a cardiologist and a New Zealand mile champion. Although he had some reservations about what I was doing, he was one of the guys who actually helped me in those early days. Another supporter was a heart specialist at Waikato hospital, who started jogging because he had had a heart attack himself. It was through him that jogging took off in Hamilton. The pathologist at that hospital told me that he had examined the bodies of many young people who had been killed in accidents, some of them still in their teens, and had discovered that many were already heading for heart attacks.'

This early physical degradation was not limited to New Zealanders; the same incipient heart disease was discovered during autopsies on young American soldiers killed in Vietnam.

The runners Arthur trained in the early days were all from a small area in the Auckland suburb of Owairaka, where he was living, and later from Tokoroa, where they came under the influence of John Robinson and John Davies, who themselves had been coached by Lydiard. Arthur believes the main reason they prospered was that, because he was a marathon runner, he was able to run with his pupils most of the time and see their potential and the effects the training had on each of them. They were, he recalls, without exception, sincere, dedicated and a pleasure to work with.

Years later, when Arthur was in Japan, he was asked what main quality he sought in his athletes. His answer was simple: sincerity. As he pointed out, anyone who coached and helped other people was giving up part of his or her life. 'I cannot afford to waste my time with fools,' he said bluntly. Arthur has never asked anyone if he can coach them; but he turns none away if they seek his help. It's when they show a lack of sincerity that he swiftly shows them the wrong side of his door.

An Auckland runner who was prospering under his tutelage once made the mistake of saying in a TV interview that Arthur was letting her down by not giving her his schedules. Since he was handling her closely, he took exception to this criticism and the runner went to another coach. Unfortunately, or perhaps not surprisingly, her progress went backwards and she returned to ask Arthur to resume her coaching. The door was closed.

Arthur's ability to place his runners at the distances that best suited them was based on his assessment of their individual basic speeds. His yardstick was the athlete's speed over 200 metres and, having determined that, it was simply a matter of ensuring their endurance was properly developed. His band of acolytes all mainly got together for long weekend runs, work and family commitments preventing more frequent collaboration. They developed a close friendship though, despite the competitive rivalry between them.

'I tried to make them understand not only how to train and what to do, but to understand the physiological and mechanical reasons behind what they were being asked to do,' he says. Remarkably, although he then had no scientific or technical knowledge of physiology or mechanics, he was uncannily close to the mark. His later association with experts in both fields confirmed that his layman's understanding of how the body functioned and reacted to the training he was applying was almost exactly right. And it is likely that the experts were pleased to have Arthur's practical confirmation of their theories.

For instance, his belief was, and still is, that the best psychology a coach can use with an athlete is to explain exactly why the training is fashioned the way it is and why each day's training is important.

'My boys could all work out together because their individual racing distances didn't matter. They all needed a high oxygen threshold, good speed development and an aerobic development to the utmost level. Their training differed only in the coordination periods.

'The various developments were sometimes approached differently. Murray Halberg had previously been trained by Bert Payne, one of the Owairaka club coaches, a fine sportsman and one of New Zealand's top rugby league referees. Bert had coached him to win the Auckland secondary schools' 800-metre title and asked me if I was prepared to take over from him because he didn't have the time to properly develop the potential he could see. Murray was then recovering from a rugby injury which had nearly cost him his life and had left him with an almost useless left arm because all the nerves had been severed. As a natural left-hander, he was having to learn life all over again. I couldn't run him far the first time I took him out because it was difficult to get him home again, but Murray had astonishing tenacity and the mileages and his fitness steadily increased.

'I can never forget our mutual elation the first time he was able to run a five-minute mile on a nearby road. He was then training a lot with Barry Magee and the stage had been reached where both were improving so well that we could not know who would be the better.

'I worked Halberg carefully while he regained full strength but the depth of his determination to not only live but to excel at sport was so amazing that within months I was confident enough in his ability to declare publicly that he would be the greatest middle-distance runner New Zealand had known and would begin cracking world records at the age of 27. I was right. He was 27 when he won his Olympic title and and began running into the world record books.

'About this time, I had stopped experimenting with human endurance. I was satisfied I had my recipe for building stamina and bringing an athlete to his peak, whatever his chosen distance, just when he wanted to reach it. Murray and Barry were my final test-pieces and how successful I was can be judged by their Olympic medals at Rome and their triumphs in Europe the following year. It had taken five to eight years, but that was the whole point of the system. Even so, some of the early results were startling – at the end of their first season, they were running New Zealand record times in training, Barry for six miles and Murray for the shorter distances, in which he was basically faster. They were setting these fast times on grass tracks, which were much slower than today's tracks.

'One test I set them demonstrated this astonishing progress. I told them my schedule required them to run two miles in 9:52. They gaped at me in disbelief – in those days a 9:18 two-miler would be world-ranked; Halberg had squeezed under ten minutes once but Barry never had. But my system had partly sharpened them and I told them they should be able to do it. They didn't believe a word of it but ran off. They clocked 9:40 and the following week ran 9:20. Then they believed me.

'The improvement may seem incredible, but they had worked on marathon-type training for ten weeks and had then transferred to hill running to add speed to their stamina to a degree they had not known before. They could now run faster than they believed was possible – when they heard their times, we were all dancing around on the track in delight.

'Later that season, Halberg signalled his arrival as an international force by running a 4:04.4 mile. This also showed that my schedules were finally right and that all the years of trials and frustrations had not been totally wasted. Murray and Barry and some of my other boys were hitting their peaks of performance when and where my schedules said they should and that was all that mattered. Barry's only problem was that, faced with actual competition, he suffered badly from nerves and flopped for a time before, as in Rome, demonstrating his flawless running style and stamina for middle and distance success. In 1955, the year I won my second marathon title, Barry overcame his nerves and won the national 6-mile title. Kerry Williams, who I was teaching by correspondence, was cross-country champion, Bill Baillie was my half-mile winner and Halberg won the mile – giving the system five New Zealand titles.

'I think maybe one of the greatest triumphs of young Halberg was his 12:11.4 three miles at Auckland's Olympic Stadium one miserable night. The ground was Olympian only in name. The track was short, its bends were too sharp, the surface was uneven and softer than runners would want. I believe only Murray had the fortitude to achieve that remarkable time in those bad conditions. His dedication to running was such that, although he was trained as a teacher, he worked as a labourer – sweeping up leaves in the Auckland Domain and doing work on the Auckland municipal golf links – to get himself fitter and to have more time for running.

'His extraordinary 3-mile run led to some deservedly grumpy media criticism of the local authorities for failing to provide better facilities for athletes who had already established themselves as world beaters. It is safe to say that, given a good track, Murray would have run a world record that night.'

In five years of travelling the world and racing in many competitions, Murray ran three world records and was beaten only three times. Arthur has always admired him very much for his purpose of will and his determination to overcome his disability.

Late in 1954, Arthur became embroiled in an argument with people who claimed that marathon racing was harmful. 'This,' he says, 'was a bunch of bunkum and I was joined in saying so by fellow coach Les Barker, a 50-year-old Auckland bank manager, who said he felt miserable all day if he didn't have his daily run of at least twenty miles before breakfast; and Dr Harold Moody, a former national shot and discus champion and 1950 Empire Games representative. Dr Moody said in a newspaper statement that he did not believe the limit of human effort had been – or ever would be – reached.'

Arthur, too, says the limit has not been reached although, again demonstrating his intuitive knowledge of human capacity, he forecast about four decades ago that the marathon limit would be around 2 hours 5 minutes. No one could run any faster for that length of time. In September 2003, Paul Tergat set the current lowest time of 2:04:55.

Arthur also said, 40 years ago, that he thought the limit for a mile would be about 3:40. Hicham El Guerrouj's world record stands at 3:43:13. 'Once you understand the physiology of it,' says Arthur, 'you can work it out easily. Perhaps you could get under two hours for a marathon on a downhill, one-way course with a tail wind, but you have to assess marathon performance on true marathon courses, which start and finish at the same place. Boston, for instance, is mostly run with a tail wind, except for a couple of years ago when we sent a very promising girl over and she faced a head wind and very cold temperatures. That was very bad luck and she hasn't been healthy since and hasn't run well. But the Boston record is only 2:07:15, set by the Kenyan Cosmas Ndeti in 1994.'

At the time of the dispute, Arthur was 37 and neither he nor Les Barker had ever collapsed in a marathon.

'I pointed out that I had medical opinion that my heart was the strongest part of my body. I was running six and ten miles faster than I could ten years earlier. Les had been running long distances for 28 years and had started full marathon races only six years earlier. I had also recently run a marathon with a 22-year-old who had not previously run more than six miles. We finished the run in under three hours and he showed no sign of distress. He had run the whole distance without apparent effort.

'But I did take exception to the official practice of running marathon races during the midday heat. They didn't know about hyperthermia in those days so marathons were started at 11 a.m. or noon, on the hottest days of the year, when the tar would be melting on the roads we were running on. We could train over the course in the cool of the evening in under 2:30 but in the hot sun we ran much slower – the tar sticking to the soles of our shoes had something to do with that, as well as the energy-sapping heat.

'The rare collapses in marathons were due entirely to that heat factor. The 1950 national title race had been run at Napier, one of New Zealand's sunnier corners, in 90-degree Fahrenheit midday heat, with the sun blazing down. When the field reached the turn-round at Hastings, it was apparent that few of the runners would return to Napier under their own power. Only five did – three running and two staggering and walking. One athlete ran unconscious into a fence and two just fell on the road when they lost consciousness.'

Arthur had already campaigned for a change to sensible late-afternoon or early-morning starting times. The Auckland officials were sympathetic, but the consistently pig-headed New Zealand Amateur Athletics Association (NZAAA) turned a deaf ear.

The debate was important, because the national championship was being run in Auckland two years later and Arthur was anticipating another debacle like Napier unless the time was shifted from the midday start.

'Les Barker, in backing me up, said undue distress in marathons was caused by organisers controlling a race they did not understand. He recalled what happened to Jim Peters at the Empire Games in Vancouver when he collapsed within sight of the finish line.

'They had water stations for New Zealand marathons but they were few and far between and the first did not come until the runners had covered five miles. My practice was to grab a bucket of water and up-end it over my head. The relief was effective and much better than drinking water, but I don't remember other runners using the method.

'As a perfect example of the muddled thinking we complained about, the first marathon I ran started from Carlaw Park in central Auckland and went straight up the steep Parnell rise and on out to Otahuhu in the midday heat. It took me three and a half hours to finish – I was cooked. Three weeks later, I ran 2:42 on a more sensible course. The officials were crazy in those days and knew nothing about the effects of heat and humidity.

'I may not have had much experience of running marathons but I knew all about running in the heat because I had trained in the heat of the day and I had the nous to hold back. It was equally crazy to have to finish the marathon on a steep downhill on tired legs.'

Arthur says he experienced courses even worse than the Carlaw Park event. One at Auckland's Western Springs took the field over steep hills towards the end of the race.

'A traffic cop who was following the race said afterwards, "Arthur, on those hills you were going two forward and one back." We started that race at 11 o'clock in the morning of Auckland's Anniversary Day, which is always one of the hottest of the year. It helps to explain why there were not a lot of marathon runners in those days. I was fortunate because my training had meant I'd developed a very good blood transport system, which was to stand me in good stead in various places around the world in later years.'

Arthur won the Auckland title in his first marathon attempt in 1949 and was second to the stronger-legged and more experienced Gordon Bromily in the New Zealand championship. He was about 100 metres ahead as he finished in 2:40:12, but Arthur finished fresher. 'He was tougher,' Arthur says.

Next year, one of Arthur's children had whooping cough and, for four or five months, he had many almost sleepless nights. Proper training was difficult and he ran second to Bromily again but won selection for the Empire Games, held in Auckland that year.

'I wasn't fit enough and couldn't get fit enough, running what I considered a poor race into 13th place. I was 34 years old. Bromily beat me again in 1951, I was fourth in 1952, but finally, in 1953, took my first national title. A pulled muscle interfered with my training for two months the following year and I ran second to Eddie Rye. I was invited to run a marathon in Korea but declined; I was not fit enough to represent New Zealand adequately and I felt a failure might reduce the chances of other marathoners getting overseas trips. I had the 1956 Olympic Games in Melbourne in mind. Eddie Rye went to Korea in my place and pulled out after fifteen miles.'

Arthur deals with this significant phase of his life with typical brusqueness. He skips over the fact that, in 1952, he had decided not to defend his Auckland title. The decision was understandable. He was 35, the family and its demands were still growing, he wanted to finish a holiday home he was building for them at Stanmore Bay, on the Whangaparaoa Peninsula, north of Auckland, he had not competed in any of that summer's road races and his training had been minimal.

What changed his mind was equally understandable. A runner named Colin Littler won an annual 18-mile road race in December in record time and also chopped four minutes off the record for a 15-miler. He had come off an excellent cross-country season and it was apparent that he was capable of a good marathon. He was shaping so well that someone observed that, even if Lydiard chose to enter the Auckland marathon, he would probably go down to Littler. In the way whispers do, this remark eventually reached Arthur's ears and he immediately decided he would compete after all and show any knockers they didn't know what they were talking about.

The race was less than two months away but Arthur had readied himself in less time before and he knew he could do it again. Conveniently, his Auckland home and Stanmore Bay were about marathon distance apart, which solved a major part of his training problem. He simply ran from his home up to Stanmore Bay on Saturdays, worked on the house and then ran back home on Sundays.

In their book, *The Lonely Breed*, Norman Harris and Ron Clarke commented:

> He amazed runners who chanced to meet him on the return trip, just a few miles from home, because he was running harder than they wished to, and he was not virtually out on his feet thinking only about collapsing on his back steps and sliding into a bath – he was thinking about buying some ice cream from the dairy near to his house, to thin out and cool his blood, and he was debating what he was going to do after that.
>
> His friends enjoyed the joke, which he himself had offered, that he wasted so little time that he wrote out his training

schedules in the toilet. Even they, after all this time, regarded him as something of a phenomenon with his apparently limitless drive and energy.

In addition to the demands of a young family, Arthur was still working at the shoe factory, doing his early morning milk run, keeping his home garden in prolific production, building his holiday home at weekends and still finding the reserves to train harder than anyone else. It was not surprising then that this human dynamo again won the Auckland title. Point proved; he had shown the knockers.

Arthur recovered the New Zealand title in 1955 and that ended his marathon racing. He needed money to establish himself in a business and that had to come first. Bill Richards took up the marathon gauntlet Arthur had tossed down, gaining Games selection with a 2:31:46 title win, which was the fastest marathon ever run in New Zealand until the Lydiard-trained Ray Puckett ran under 2:30 three years later.

Arthur's marathon times, after his initial Auckland title win in 1949 in a slow 3:30:07, were remarkably consistent. He dominated the Auckland marathon championship for five years, winning in 1951 in 2:56:42, 1952 in 2:52:19, 1953 in 2:52:35, 1954 in 2:55:07 and 1955 in 2:51:13. That he ran only to win and could have – and would have – run faster if the opposition had been stronger, is confirmed by the times he recorded for his two national titles: 2:41:29 in 1953 and 2:42:34 in 1955.

In January 1955, Arthur and George Gibson made an attempt on the New Zealand 20-mile record, which had been set by the then-national marathon champion Eddie Rye in Nelson the year before. They used New Lynn's Olympic Park and the conditions were good – there was no wind and it was a cool evening – although the uneven grass track caused jarring problems at times.

George, not long before, had been credited with 1:52:12 over a 20-mile road course and, as the younger runner, was expected to have a better chance at a new mark than Arthur, who was then 37 years old.

'But he started too fast, running the first lap in 76 seconds as he set a pace I wasn't prepared to follow. I ran easily over the first ten miles and, when I had my turn in front, I tended to keep George in check to conserve his strength. But he was showing real strain after 61 laps and began dropping behind quite fast before he gave up altogether on the 68th lap. I was surprised he had not been able to stay with me because I thought he had all the makings of an Olympic representative.

'I finished alone in 1:54:52.4, which was 47.4s better than Rye's Nelson time. I had a good background for the attempt and I covered the distance quite comfortably. By way of comparison with George's unwise early speed, the slowest lap was my 95 seconds in the 78th lap, half a mile from the finish, and I ran 82 seconds for the last lap.'

Years later, Arthur ran 20 miles in 1:51:7.28. His opinion was that a well-conditioned person could virtually coast for a year on light work without losing significant fitness. Through those years, he never coasted.

So Arthur was enjoying great success, but it didn't come easily. No one helped financially in those days. Athletics in New Zealand was still an amateur pursuit, so people had to go to work. It actually cost Arthur money to be a coach because, once he became successful, people wrote to him, phoned him up or came to visit him personally. They all wanted to know how he did it.

He comments: 'Most didn't go any further – when they found out the training they would have to do, they suddenly lost interest – but I still had correspondence to answer, toll calls and other expenses in helping those who did want to carry on.'

He mentions this with remarkably little rancour, although it must have been tough on his tight budget, but it was not in Arthur's nature to deny any genuine requests for help. However, he says he would never have been able to train anyone, if it had not been for Jean's selfless support. 'It emphasised what a wonderful wife and mother she was.

'I had never set out to be a coach – I didn't want to be one – but when these young guys began running with me and then winning New Zealand titles, suddenly I was one. And Jean was always totally supportive. But, thinking back, I guess it was all worthwhile. Maybe architecture would have given me more money, but would it have given me the same satisfaction?'

5

enter Murray Halberg

APPROACHING THE 1954 Vancouver Games, Arthur predicted the mile would come down to a duel between Roger Bannister, John Landy and Murray Halberg. He knew Chris Brasher was a fast early runner and that Bannister always turned on his best speed in the last quarter. He figured the two would work together and the pace would be cracked on from the start. Murray's best time of 4:04.4 indicated he would finish 40 yards behind the 3:58 of Landy, but Halberg had now become a much improved and far stronger runner.

Arthur relates: 'Landy had said he put no more effort into his 3:58 world record than he had been putting into slower races in Australia, but he had been exerting himself to the limit and had been averaging 4:02. He put his record down to the better track and conditions when he ran it in Finland. Landy seemed always to weaken during the mile and his last quarter was markedly his slowest, which is the sort of chink in the armour that I looked for when calculating tactics. It was hard to find such a weakness in men like Bannister and Landy, but I believed it was there – in their lack of stamina.

'Bannister had admitted he was beaten in the Olympic race by Luxembourg's Josy Barthell because Barthell had superior stamina. It was always my contention that any man can run a quarter of a mile in under a minute, but the test comes in doing four such quarters one after the other.

'As far as Murray was concerned, it would be a stayers' race and, if he could get a ten-yard lead in the last half mile, he would take a lot of catching. Bannister and Landy would be watching each other and that could be Murray's advantage.

'When I was asked if Murray had a chance of reaching 3:58, I said if he didn't do it in Vancouver he certainly would later in his career. Murray astounded me at times. He had the indomitable will of a champion and he was still nowhere near his best. He was then only 21 and I knew he would keep at it until he got there. He was faster at 21 than Bannister and Landy had been at that age. He had run 4:04 at his first attempt at a mile, but he usually ran tactically, without watching times. He had also run 1000 yards in 2:12, only three seconds off the world record, held by an American, in only one season of serious track training as a senior.'

Arthur had coached Murray to judge pace well and he had trained in every variety of conditions in Auckland, from the coldest and wettest winter days to the hottest and muggiest summer days. They had worked so hard on building Halberg's stamina that there were times when Arthur felt sorry for what he was putting Murray through. But the frail-looking body of the youngster had a core of steel and a will of iron.

Murray really became a force on the international scene in April 1954, when he ran away with the Benjamin Frankin Mile in Philadelphia. The 1948 and 1952 Olympic 800 metres champion, Mal Whitfield, and the first Franklin Mile winner in 1950, Fred Wilt, were in the field, but Murray-the-novice took the lead at the start and was never headed, winning in 4:10 on a heavy track, with Whitfield six seconds back and Wilt third. The only other runner, Horace Ashenfelter, who won the 3000-metre steeplechase at the 1952 Olympics, was last. Murray was 15 yards up at the quarter, 30 yards up at the half-mile, 50 up at the three-quarters and won by about 40 yards. The steel was beginning to show.

The win was followed by several invitations to run other races in the United States, but Arthur advised Murray to come home because hard racing would affect his preparations for the Empire Games in Vancouver in August. He was at the stage of his development where he needed hard training and little racing.

'They wanted to race him against Barthell, of Luxembourg, in Massachusetts, against the Kansas star Wes Santee at the

Coliseum Games in San Francisco and in the Boardwalk Mile in Atlantic City, but this was in the race promoters' interests rather than Murray's. He was only 20, only a year out from being a semi-invalid – and there would be plenty more chances for him to see something of America.'

According to press reports, Murray said he was scared stiff before the Benjamin Franklin Mile because it would be his first race on a cinder track and it was later suggested that he could have run much faster than he did, bearing in mind his 4:04.4 on grass in New Zealand. But, with none of the others able to produce anything resembling a threat, Murray won with little trouble. When he was asked what he thought of his opposition, he replied in typical Halbergese: 'I don't know. I didn't see them.'

As it eventuated, the Vancouver Games mile didn't go quite as Arthur predicted. Halberg and his fellow-Kiwi miler Bill Baillie formed a close attachment to Australian John Landy in Vancouver and they became a clique in counter to the stand-offish Englishmen. And when Landy gashed his foot severely in the Games village the day before the heats were to be run, Murray and Bill formed the idea that they would help John to win the final, if they all got that far. They did, but when Bill set the Landy aid programme in motion by racing to the lead at the starter's gun, Landy raced past him, going even faster, and the plan was ruined.

Bannister sat on Landy and outsprinted him in the closing straight. Murray finished fifth in 4:07.2 and Bill clocked 4:11. Both had to thread their way, with the other finishers, through the hordes of officials who crowded onto the finishing straight to slap Bannister and Landy's backs.

For Arthur and Murray, a critical corner had been turned. The coach and his star were both on course to become virtually unbeatable, partly due to Arthur's singular ability to analyse and exploit not only his own runners' strengths and weaknesses, but also those of their opponents.

Arthur has always regarded Murray as his star pupil and the man who inspired others to follow the Lydiard dictum. That's typical Lydiard humility. In *A Clean Pair of Heels* Murray described how his first coach, Bert Payne, passed him to Arthur because he felt he didn't have the time or the ability to develop the potential he saw in the teenager.

Murray said: 'I quickly found Arthur the sort of man to be naturally followed and listened to. He was a leader. He talked like one and he acted like one. My first impression of him was of a guy who didn't go halfway. You either did what he told you to do or you didn't. There were no shortcuts and he had no intention of wasting his time or yours on doing anything but what he said. But neither did he turn anyone away who was prepared to follow, even if they had no prospect of doing anything significant. The more I committed to and followed the development of his concept, the better everything turned out.' That first impression was the right one. Arthur is a shrewd, forthright man, a man of no nonsense. His manner and bearing come from confidence gained through success, yet he is a very simple, natural man. One of the boys.

'He has led a full life, almost a nonstop one, but only rarely does he bring out his inborn sense of humour. It is sometimes astonishing to discover, when he begins his story-telling and reminiscing, that he is a man who can make a laugh a minute out of life. Too often, he gives you the impression that there is no time for fun. Most of his stories centre round the formative years of what he refers to, I think with pride, as "his stable".

'Arthur is short, crag-nosed, weather-beaten, with a stocky, strongly constructed body. No frills. He is intensely practical, without wasting any words, which is what you would expect in a man who lives like a human dynamo. He is a man in a perpetual hurry. Yet behind it all he is really kind and considerate. When I went with him on his Auckland milk-delivery round, I noticed that he always put the empty bottles in their metal crates very gently and avoided over-using or revving his engine so that he was almost as silent as the people who were asleep all around him.

'Bill Baillie and I took over his round once to give him a break. After we had yelled up and down the streets in our usual boisterous way, shouting instructions at each other, with Bill sounding as if he was firing the bottles into the crates from ten yards' range, Arthur returned to do the money collection.

'One of his customers said, "You've been delivering here for a long time and Saturday was the first night I've ever heard you."

'"Oh," said Arthur, "that was the night Halberg and Baillie were on."

'Lydiard was just another name in the days when I first met him. Some people who knew of his methods said he would burn athletes out. That he would ruin more runners than he would bring on. He still has his critics today, but they only helped to make winning easier for us. I never thought Arthur was going to burn me out. I knew after the first few days with him that this was the way to run. Quickly, I could feel the benefits, the power coming. And I learnt the pleasures of running.

'I did not question him at all. I was pleased that someone like him thought enough of me to help me. I was lucky to come under Arthur's influence when I did.'

Halberg now sometimes wonders how, as a youngster, he followed a line of coaching that flew in the face of everything he'd been taught by Bert Payne. He remembers when Lydiard experimented by giving his runners honey and molasses to see how they worked. 'I can't say they did. They made me want to spew,' Murray says.

He remembers Lydiard's first running shoes, fitting skin-tight like a glove, and made long before such fancy footwear hit the wider market; Lydiard's abandonment of the traditions of eating steaks and drying out before competition; his gift of humour, which made his young followers eager to accompany him on two-hour runs. The only problem: 'You had to hang on at first because he always started at the pace he meant to maintain all the way. Arthur's reason – "there's no time to waste. Let's get this thing done".'

Murray recalls people telling him that training the Lydiard way wasn't good for him. It would give him an enlarged heart, he was told. And only recently he reflected on a comment made in Rome in 1960. He was in a taxi with Lydiard, Peter Snell and Joe McManemin, the New Zealand team manager, and as they crossed the Tiber on their way to the stadium for their finals races, Lydiard leaned across to him and said, 'Peter is going to be an Olympic champion before you.'

'And Peter was, by one hour,' says Murray. 'I'd always thought that Arthur had said that for my ears, but my brain kicked in recently when I started mentioning a double-edged sword. He had said it loud enough for everyone in the taxi to hear. Whether they did hear it I don't know, my focus was all on myself. Now, after 42 years, it occurs to me that the remark was possibly intended not for me but for Peter. I don't know if either Peter or Arthur remembers the moment, but it has fascinated me.'

Murray shares the virtue of humility equally with Arthur. In discussing the injury which nearly took his life and his battle to overcome it and turn himself into the kind of runner Bert and Arthur saw in him, he said with his typical casually comic slant on life, 'Having to run with my left arm and hand curled up and useless tended to help me on any anti-clockwise running track.'

Barry Magee says without hesitation, as do many others, that meeting Arthur and being trained by him totally changed his life. One aspect of that change reflected Arthur's talent for spotting an athlete's precise potential. Arthur recalls, 'Barry ran some classic track races against Murray Halberg, but I put him on to the marathon as his best event because there was one hill on my Waiatarua run, about three miles along the Scenic Drive from the left turn at Waiatarua, which is quite steep but full of turns and twists. It is very tempting, because every time you go round a bend you tend to think, "Ah, this must be the last one" but the climb continues on for much longer than you expect. It's always a struggle after you've come off the three-mile climb up from the foothills near Oratia. Your legs are really feeling it by then, but you recover along the Drive – until you meet that hill.

'Barry was always the guy who could take the hill on and keep going. He had tremendous natural endurance, which we developed further. His speed wasn't very exciting, but I anticipated he would become a very great distance and marathon runner. He was a tenacious, sincere and dedicated young man. He still is – except for the young bit. He's very knowledgeable and has become a very good coach.

'His marathon training in time turned him into a great three-miler. He began to chase Halberg and came close to beating him when they raced almost to a world record in Stockholm in 1961. They were only a hundred metres from the finish and we still didn't know which of them was going to win. Halberg just made it. The next year, Barry ran the fastest 10,000 metres in the world. He won the Fukuoka marathon in Japan several times. The Japanese thought very highly of him. I have often described him as a ballet dancer on the roads because of his beautiful, easy running.'

I once asked Arthur to rate his best and worst races. It made him think and he finally plumped for this answer: 'I guess the best races I saw were the gold-medal races Halberg and Snell ran in Rome because they verified all the training we had done and put paid to all the criticism we had received.

'The worst was probably Barry Magee's after he broke the New Zealand 10,000 metres record in training and then went to the New Zealand championships and ran like a bloody goat. He was just a bundle of nerves. That was why we put him in the 10,000 in Rome, so he could get rid of his nerves before the marathon. With hindsight, maybe it was a good thing that he lost that New Zealand race. I explained to the New Zealand officials that I wanted him in the 10,000 in Rome as well as the marathon. They said he wasn't a 10,000 runner, but I told them it was only to get him through his big race nervousness. As it happened, he didn't run a bad 10,000, considering he wasn't running to try to win it. He was just round the bend when they finished, about a hundred metres behind the winner. The next season, of course, Barry ran the fastest 10,000 metres race in the world for that season, which rather suggested the officials didn't have much idea of what they were talking about.'

Interestingly, both Murray and Barry Magee make a special point of the fact that they were 'given' to Arthur by other coaches. Murray had been fostered initially by Bert Payne, and at age 18 Magee was handed over as a junior after winning the Hamilton road classic, Round the Bridges. His coach, Gil Edwards, recognised Magee's immense potential and linked him up with Lydiard in what Barry describes as 'the most unselfish gesture any coach could make, to give away his most promising pupil'.

'Gil, who was club captain of the Wesley Harrier Club, had

been training me for two years and had given me what I thought were huge schedules of training for about four days a week, which was a lot in those days. I had suddenly come to the fore about this time. I got second in the Auckland cross-country championships, had won the junior Bridges and was fourth in the senior road race from Onehunga to Auckland, which was pretty good for a junior. Then I finished third in the Great Eastern Road, behind Colin Lousich and Lawrie King, I think, which gave me first junior place.

'I think this made Gil realise that he had some potential on his hands and he changed my life for ever by making this amazing decision that it would be good thing to give me to Arthur Lydiard. That is a rare thing for a coach to do. What he and Bert Payne did was the absolute opposite of selfishness, because the one thing coaches love is to train champions. I am immensely grateful to Gil.

'Arthur could see right away that we had potential. This was the stage when he only had local runners around him and had had a fight with Lynndale and said, "All right, bugger you, I'll start my own harrier club where I live". And he did and turned it into the number one club in New Zealand in only four years.

'Arthur was a little bundle of dynamite. A powerhouse of energy, ideas, thinking and application. When I was introduced to him, he said something like, "Son, if you're prepared to do the work, if you're prepared to run a hundred miles a week, I will coach you. Otherwise, don't waste your time or mine."

'I had never run more than fifty miles in a week before – and that was considered over-training in those days, when even marathon runners knew nothing about conditioning – but I must have mumbled something like, "Yes, all right", because I was round at Arthur's home the following day.

'I never dreamed then of becoming a marathon runner after seeing those who were staggering around on the road over the last ten miles, many of them never finishing – and there would be only twelve or so in the race. It was a whole different ball game from the marathons of today. It was enough to put you off for life and it took Arthur about three years to get me into running one.'

Barry was just 18 when his father died following an accident and Arthur then became a stabilising influence in his life. 'He never spoke much about my father, but he treated all his runners as if they were part of his family. The open-house policy that he ran created an incredible relationship.

'I had another major influence in my life, too. I was working then for Farmers department store and Graham Miller, who ran a grocery store right across the road, asked me why I didn't cross over and work for him. He offered me a pound a week more than I was getting – and bribery will get you anywhere. Arthur and Graham really took over as father figures at a critical time in my life. As well as a coach, Arthur became a friend, a confidant and a father and I have never lost that relationship.

'He is a man of honour and you always know where you stand with him – but I would hate to get on the wrong side of him.'

The telling element with Magee was that, through Arthur, New Zealand distance runners were being conditioned in a way that the rest of the world had either lost or had never recognised. 'I still believe the key is that everyone, from the 800-metre runner to the marathoner, conditioned the same way. We didn't do it together; Arthur just wrote down what he wanted and inspired us all to go out and do it. I did ninety per cent of my mileage on my own. We all did and just got together on Sundays. During the week, we would run from wherever we were working. We would sometimes get together for time trials but otherwise we worked alone. Inspired by Arthur.

'We trusted him. His secret was that he knew exactly how to condition us, how to give us the hill strengthening work and then combine that with speed work and slowly get us running faster and faster and then add the anaerobic work to sharpen us up for race time. This is the secret that half the world has moved away from again or are trying to do it in different ways. Even the coaches doing conditioning get their athletes to run five by six-minute reps, where we went out and ran at a steady state for thirty minutes. They try to break it down in sections and there is a major difference there. Our eight weeks of aerobic work made us, although other coaches insisted that it would ruin us.

I remember I was once cornered by a Western Suburbs coach, who said, "Lydiard's going to kill you, Barry. All of you guys." I think he was a hurdles coach. I think I said, "Let's wait and see." And at the nationals, we won the 880 yards, the mile, the three miles, the six miles and the marathon. Proof of the pudding was right there. We were the best conditioned athletes in the world and we had about a five-year start on the rest of that world. It took from about 1958 to 1965 for anyone else to catch on. What we did was unbelievable.'

Barry says that period of domination overflowed to produce the John Walker, Dick Quax, Rod Dixon, Richard Tayler and Lorraine Moller eras. They were all following the Lydiard principles, although coaches such as Arch Jelley tended to treat their athletes individually and somewhat differently.

Barry is now coaching for the Auckland club, working with 18-year-old juniors who do nothing like the mileage he used to do. Arthur's runners were conditioned enough at that age to be ranked in the top half-dozen in New Zealand cross-country when they became seniors at 19. 'I had never trained in the mud, I didn't like the mud but the others did. I got home at six o'clock at night and had no opportunity anyway to train for cross-country during the week. So my conditioning was all on the roads, which Arthur reckoned was better anyway because you could maintain style and rhythm better. I only raced cross-country.'

Magee recalls that, after any meeting of runners at Lydiard's house, he would be raised to another level of attitude when he left. He adds that hundreds of thousands of people around the world also owe a great deal, possibly their lives, to Lydiard through his promotion of jogging for fitness. 'You would listen to Arthur's machine-gun delivery to a group of rugby players or businessmen and you would see some of them turn pale. But twenty per cent of those guys went home and became joggers the next day. He had the ability to speak into their lives. I remember one of his lines was, "You guys spend more time on your cars than you do on your own bodies".'

My own experience of Arthur Lydiard is testament to Magee's words. I had only recently met Arthur when I attended a party with him and several of his runners at the home of one of Auckland athletics' finest administrators, Frank Sharp. The conversation inevitably got around to Arthur's constantly iterated belief that anyone could become a marathon runner. His boys were the evidence that proved him right.

'Even you,' he said to Frank and me, 'could do it.'

As a dedicated chain-smoker and studious drinker, I laughed. As a rather portly fellow, Frank laughed. Undeterred, Arthur invited Frank and me to join him in a jog from his Wainwright Avenue home to the New Lynn track one evening and, such was his charisma, Frank and I kept the date.

Frank had sandshoes to carry along his rotund little frame; I borrowed a pair of running shoes from the pile at Arthur's back door. The three of us ran off. More accurately, Arthur vanished down the road and we trailed after him. I believe the distance – shades of Jack Dolan – was some 6 miles and they were mostly miles of pure agony. But, because it was Arthur Lydiard who inveigled us out there and because he said anyone could do it, even we could do it, we did it. My borrowed shoes proved to be not quite my foot size or shape and blisters developed, burst and bled with relish. I knew Frank, too, was suffering. But we did it. And I, for one, because I was now in constant touch with Arthur, became a marathon runner by finishing the Owairaka marathon some three months later. I proved to myself that anyone can do it.

I include this story not because I am particularly proud of that effort – my time was under four hours but a lot of it was hell and I remember Bill Baillie running past me, lapping me quite early in the race, and giving me an encouraging slap on the back that nearly felled me – but because it illustrates the awesome power Arthur Lydiard has to make you do things you would not dream of doing otherwise. Like so many others, I could not let him down, even if I had no chance of ever being more than a plodder.

Barry says the Dublin 4 x 1-mile world record relay was achieved because Arthur chose the order of their running exactly right – Philpott first, Halberg second, Magee third and Snell fourth. 'The first time we hit the front in sixteen nail-biting, incredible laps of racing was only eighty yards from the tape.'

Magee raced Halberg hundreds of times over 10 years. He thought he had him beaten in the Gothenburg 5000-metre race in 1961; he was giving it everything he had and could not have run a better race, but Halberg swept past in the last straight and beat him by four seconds to take the world record. The same thing happened later in a classic clash on Eden Park, in Auckland. In fact, on the track, the road and in cross-country and over a variety of distances, Magee won only once, proving Lydiard's theory that it all came down to the basic speed element – determined over 200 metres – in the closing stages of a race. Halberg's basic speed was 24 seconds, Magee's was 25 seconds.

Barry's sole victory was a cross-country race at Auckland's Ellerslie racecourse, when Halberg fell off the pace about halfway through and Magee went on to win.

Arthur's stable ran their great middle-distance times on cinder tracks, which would be at least a second a lap slower than today's modern track surfaces. On cinders, runners lose drive because their feet tend to slip back fractionally with every take-off. Peter Snell, for a classic example, was such a power driver he left great holes in cinder tracks when he applied full speed, but in doing so he lost traction. John Davies once described how chunks of the track were flung up in his face when Snell hurtled past him. Grass, too, is slower by about a second a lap. When athletes started running on synthetic tracks, 5000-metre times went down about half a minute all around the world and the times for other distances showed an equally distinct drop.

Not every Lydiard pupil became a champion, but hundreds became what might be classed as 'second tier' runners, who gave the élite 'first tier' a vigorous run for their money and, under the stimulus of Arthur, performed above their expectations. Vern Walker, a 1960s middle-distance runner, typifies that second tier.

Vern hated racing over the half-mile and mile and did so only to sharpen up for the 3 miles or 5000 metres. 'I was almost flat out all the way over the shorter distances and my best times were only 2:01.4 and 4:16.5. But Arthur's aerobic system was just great when it came to the 3 miles. My best over that distance was 13:45.7. At the time, only the New Zealand reps were running faster. [As late as 1992 this performance – circa 1964 –

had been beaten by only seven other New Zealanders, as reported by P.N. Heidenstrom in *Athletes of the Century*.] I really believe, given my lack of basic speed, no other training system but Arthur's could have produced anywhere near such a time.'

Meeting Arthur, and often training with Barry Magee, fired Vern up, and set him on the right course. In 1958, he was running 3 miles in 14:50 and had been competing for two years. After flicking through Vern's diary, Lydiard predicted he would soon be able to run close to 14 minutes. 'I simply did not believe him. This was a quantum leap. It was like a Model T Ford suddenly almost becoming the Porsche of the track. But he was spot-on. Within eighteen months, I ran 14:04.6. Arthur suggested I train with Barry Magee, as we would be temperamentally suited. Again, he was right. My improvement was so sudden, that at times I think even Barry was surprised.'

Walker became a prominent second tier performer: third in a 3-mile New Zealand championship (behind Halberg and Magee); third in an Auckland cross-country championship (behind Baillie and Jeff Julian); first in the Round the Bridges road race in Hamilton (6 seconds outside Magee's record); second in the Victorian cross-country championship in Melbourne; third, to Magee and Baillie, in the Auckland v. Australia cross-country race; fourth in the New South Wales 10-mile cross-country championship in Sydney; first in the Queensland and South Australia state cross-country championships; third in the Onehunga-Auckland 'coast to coast' road race in 33:19 (Baillie ran 33:04); second to Gary Philpott in the 'Great Eastern Road Race' in Auckland.

Walker says: 'When you got to know Arthur, there was a jocular side to his character. Often, in a light-hearted way, he would hype me up. Referring to my red hair, he would often say: "You know, red-heads are good to train. They are always very determined."

'As with countless others, Arthur shaped my life in other ways. The disciplines attached to constant hard training rolled over into other facets of my life.'

Walker says all runners touched by the running gospel according to Lydiard owe him a tremendous debt. In turn, their feats created an enormous groundswell of public interest in the sport, and enabled second tier runners like him to get international competition. 'We often hung on to the coat-tails of the top runners and so were drawn out to times and performances we usually only dreamed of.' Vern says Arthur was 'an irrepressibly optimistic kind of father-figure. While his own marathon times were rather Jurassic, they were tops at the time. But any athlete should only be gauged by performances within his own era of competition. He was a leader of men.

'Like the great American evangelist, Martin Luther King, Arthur had a dream. And he has spent a lifetime fulfilling that dream – of running far in order to run fast. I have the greatest admiration for him. No frills, simple, with certainly no pretensions.'

6

the road to Rome

MELBOURNE HOSTED THE 1956 Olympic Games and Murray Halberg spent some time in Australia preparing himself. That his progress was on track was proved when, three weeks before the Games, he broke the Australian 2000 metres record in 5:17, the eighth best in the world for that year. But that fickle finger called fate intervened. Just before the Games, Murray took a bus out to a meeting 50 miles from Melbourne, picked up a chill from the air blasting through the open windows and, by the time he was to run the 1500 metres, was suffering from influenza. Typically, he told no one and it was never made an excuse for his failure to win a race from which he could at least have expected a medal.

Murray has since identified that event as the focal point of his career. He promised himself that, in the name of the Olympic flame burning above the crowded stadium, he would be back. He said nothing about his illness but blamed his loss on his failure to run with his head as well as his legs. He wasn't going to do that again.

Two years later, in Cardiff, it was his mental approach, in combination with Arthur Lydiard's, that allowed him to run away with the Empire Games 3-mile title in 13:15, knocking 20 seconds off the Games record. Arthur had postulated, accurately of course, that in the 3 mile or 5000 metre races, there was a critical point at which the properly prepared runner could take command. Analysis of his own training had told him that, if he prepared himself over one mile and six miles, he could produce a better 3-mile performance.

Lydiard had also determined that most 3-milers fell into one of two categories – the natural miler and the natural 6-miler. He calculated that the milers would be comfortable with the early pace but that the nervous tension of the big event meant they were inclined to go too fast too early. They would begin to blow up between one and three-quarter miles and two and a quarter miles, with three laps left to run. The 6-mile stayers would find the early pace difficult and, about the time the milers were beginning to sag, would be wondering if they could maintain that speed to the tape. Thus, at this point, three laps out, there would be a moment of general indecision and reluctance. And that was when Murray, conditioned as well as he was, would strike.

And, in Cardiff, when he did strike, having sat back in the field watching the leaders jostle at the front, it was immediately all over for the other runners, including the redoubtable Albie Thomas, Gordon Pirie, Derek Ibbotson and the Africans who were beginning to make themselves known in track circles. Murray recalls that, just as Arthur had predicted, the speed of the race slackened during the ninth lap. 'In fact, as the two types merged, I had the sensation that I was stopping on the side of the track and lying down while the others went on. During the lull, I recovered completely from the early speed [the first mile had passed in 4:18].'

Murray moved to the front on to Thomas's shoulder, steadied himself and then sprinted. He sensed the surprise of the others and the plan worked perfectly. He simply raced away from the field and hit the tape in Games record time as Thomas, who already held the world 3-mile record, led the rest into the straight. Two days later, Halberg ran 4:09.9 to qualify for the mile final, in which he finished, as in Vancouver, in fifth place.

Murray then joined an international team, which included Herb Elliott, Merv Lincoln, Pirie and the Portsea coach, Percy Cerutty, for a European circuit. Twice, he ran under four minutes for the mile. He also ran the world's best four miles and second-best two miles, only a second from the world record he was to break three years later.

So by 1960 his Olympic 5000-metre aspirations were looking good – he was coming back in style – and his chance of success sky-rocketed when Arthur joined the team of Halberg, Snell, Magee, Jeff Julian and Ray Puckett in Rome.

Arthur recalls: 'I went to Rome with my runners only because, through the initiative of Frank Sharp, the president of the Auckland Centre, the *Auckland Star* ran a fund-raising campaign for me. The appeal was given a great boost by a roll of new £5 notes which arrived on Frank's desk in a plain unregistered envelope. Nine months earlier, the same nameless donor had sent £100 in a torn envelope to help finance Jeff Julian and Bill Baillie to the Hellenic marathon in Athens. He had already sent £30. It was believed he was also the anonymous donor who gave £80 to Auckland swimmers in the national team that visited Australia the previous summer.'

With the money sent to Frank was a note: 'Seeing the boys [Arthur's runners] give not only their time and energies to the task but also subscribe to their coach's fund, I do not mind helping.' It was a fact that the athletes had dipped into their own pockets to help their coach – the cynic might see self-interest as a motive but, if it was, it was well served. It would not be surprising if the gesture didn't contain some tacit criticism of officialdom for failing to appoint to the track and field team the man who had provided most of its members.

In Rome, Arthur found accommodation three miles away from the training venue, so he 'ran or walked there and back twice a day and waited at the gate of their compound until they came out. The athletics team manager, Joe McManemin, was a great ally in gaining me as much access as he could.

'The New Zealand Amateur Athletics Association chief, Harold Austad, eventually asked me into the compound for lunch one day because the 1924 New Zealand Olympic Games bronze medal sprinter and later Governor-General of New Zealand, Sir Arthur Porritt, would be there and he wanted to present some of the Games medals, if possible to New Zealanders. Sir Arthur asked what I thought and I said if he wanted to give gold medals to New Zealanders he should make the presentations on the day of the 800-metre and 5000-metre finals because I believed we would win both.' (Later, Sir Arthur Porritt came to New Zealand on a visit and a function was held for him at the Ellerslie racecourse. He asked where Arthur Lydiard was, but he wasn't there because he hadn't been invited. Murray Halberg, who was among the guests, was fairly upset about it.)

Arthur sat with Murray through the Games opening ceremony. He was to run the next day and Arthur wanted him to save his legs from getting too tired. 'Murray was intent on getting a photograph of the cloud of pigeons when they were released from their cages in the centre of the stadium – but, before the official release, one of them got free and flew off. Murray immediately snapped it. None of the other birds escaped.

'One bloody pigeon,' he said disgustedly – and then completely missed getting any pigeon picture at all when the flock was released before he had his camera ready again.

Arthur's positive attitude when faced with what others see as problems, surfaced early in Rome. 'Peter had to run two heats, a semi-final and a final if he was to succeed. In the first heat he drew Roger Moens, the world record-holder. People said to me that this was unfortunate, but my reply was that I considered it ideal, as he could now test out Moens in a sprint to see how their speeds compared.' As it happened, Peter was able to give Moens a start and out-sprint him in the straight to win the heat. So they now knew that Moens was not as fast as Peter.

'Peter was beaten by Roger in the next heat but won his semi-final with an Olympic record. Moens then won the other semi in an even faster time to take the Games record back in a matter of a few minutes.

'I was not worried,' Arthur remembers. 'I knew that we had reached the point where Peter's stamina would be the deciding factor. There were only six in the final – the number was not increased to eight until the Mexico Games – and adidas gave gifts to five of the finalists. They didn't consider Peter a medal prospect, so they didn't give him a pair. So the other five runners went out on the track wearing nice new adidas shoes for the race, while Snell wore the plain white shoes I had made for him before we left New Zealand. I had added a small rubber heel to them because I was concerned about the cinder track and the jarring effect it might have on Peter's legs. He had run only once on cinders, in

Australia, and I knew that, with little or no protection, blood corpuscles could be damaged by the hard surface and could accumulate in the legs' capillaries, causing the muscles to get overheated and restrict blood flow. He needed the added protection I provided to get him through four hard races in three days.'

Peter won the final in record time by the barest of margins but, before the race, Arthur was in no doubt that, given a fair run, he would do it.

'When he mounted the dais in his plain white shoes, adidas officials immediately asked where he had acquired them and he told them I had made them. They then asked me why I had added the heels and I explained it was to help Snell on the hard track since we ran on grass in New Zealand. Peter had got through his races without leg trouble, which I was very happy about. Prevention is always better than cure.

'Adidas subsequently developed what they called an interval shoe with a rubber wedge on the heel.'

If Snell's success was unexpected, it wasn't alone. The day before Murray Halberg had cruised through his heat of the 5000 metres, letting the others do the running and eventually qualifying second behind Dave Power. That night he'd gone to sleep unworried about his immediate future.

As the 800-metre runners lined up on the track, the 12-strong 5000-metre field assembled in the holding room. As they walked out into the stadium, Murray learned the unbelievable had happened. Peter had shattered the field – and the adidas officials – by winning in 1:46.3.

It was all the encouragement Murray needed. He started the race at the tail of the field and stayed there until the eighth lap, when he put part two of Arthur's plan into action, moving up into second place. And that's where he stayed – briefly. Then, with all the strength he had, he accelerated away to claim gold. The field closed in on him over the last lap, but Halberg was well beyond their reach.

As Arthur noted with his customary reticence, it was a good win. Snell and Halberg had done no more than he expected, and even if the eyes of the rest of the world were popping out, Arthur was simply accepting of the outcome.

Five days before the marathon, Arthur took the team over the course so that the trio of Puckett, Magee and Julian could get the feel of it. 'Our driver turned up in an asthmatic Fiat and Ray, Barry, Jeff, Murray Halberg, Joe McManemin and I somehow jammed into it with the driver. The tour took so long because of breakdowns and trouble with the police that we could have run the distance faster.

'The cops took frequent exception to the number of us crammed into the Fiat – they were supposed to have only two people in the front – but Joe soothed them with gifts of New Zealand fernleaf brooches and by taking their photographs.

'At the ten-mile mark, we were stopped by the sight of two bodies on the roadside, the aftermath of a collision between a truck and a scooter. And, at another stage, we all had to pile out and push the car half a mile up a hill because that was the only way we could get to the top and down the other side. The car finally seized up completely in the middle of Rome when we were on the way back to the Games village. We said goodbye to the driver and took a taxi the rest of the way.'

Getting to see the race itself was a different experience. The course for the marathon, which began late and ran into the night, was closed, so Arthur and Murray decided to find a bar close to the course and watch in comfort. They watched the race start from the bottom of the Capitol Hill steps and then searched in vain for a bar. Finally, they went back to Arthur's hotel, but they couldn't get any news of the marathon there so went to the finishing point near the Arch of Constantine. As darkness closed in, brief snippets of news told them only that Barry was running well.

How well, even Barry didn't know. In the gathering darkness of the streets, lit only by flaming torches held by soldiers, he had no idea who was ahead of him or how many there were. He, Puckett and Julian ran, as Magee recalled it, fairly sedately for 10 kilometres and he reckoned they were somewhere in the middle of the 70-strong field. Then Sergei Popov, who had run the world's fastest marathon, led a bunch past them. Barry and several others promptly tacked themselves on to this group. They numbered ten, then nine, eight, seven as others drifted back. Puckett was the first New Zealander to slip behind, and then Julian faded as the Popov group pulled in other runners.

Barry figured he was in the top ten at the 25-kilometre mark and he was feeling relaxed and handling the pace well. By 30 kilometres, they had passed the top-favoured British champion, Arthur Keily, and Barry reckoned only he and Popov were left. Ten kilometres from the finish, Popov veered into a drink station and Barry accelerated away from him. He could now see press photographers' flashes going off some 600 metres ahead, so he realised there was at least one runner ahead of him. He had no idea where he was placed. He knew he wasn't winning, he knew he had passed a lot of runners, but that was all he knew.

Barry learnt later that from the 30-kilometre mark, he had picked up half a minute on the only two who were still in front of him, Abebe Bikila and the Moroccan Abdesiem Rhadi ben Abdesselem, who stayed together until the barefooted Bikila sprinted to the end. But it was some time after Barry finished before he discovered he had come third – a New Zealand hockey player fought through the milling mob to slap his back and tell him he had a bronze medal – in a New Zealand and Commonwealth fastest time of 2:17:18, only just behind Bikila, whose 2:15:16 was the new world's best. It was yet another convincing demonstration of the Lydiard system's effectiveness. Julian finished 18th but Puckett had a bad race, finishing in 51st position with a time of 2:37:36. Puckett always seemed to have problems when travelling, and was especially vulnerable to any stomach bug going around. He picked up a gastric problem on the way to Rome and he was still weak when he ran the marathon. His time was nearly 20 minutes slower than his PB of 2:17:39. He would represent New Zealand again at the Tokyo Olympics and this time fare slightly better, finishing 27th, but the first New Zealander home.

Earlier in the Games, Murray had run both the 5000 and 10,000 metres and later said he felt flat and uninspired in the second race. The three Englishmen in the field shadowed him so closely that they clipped his heels and he peevishly told them to push off. He didn't see them again. With about four laps to run, his attitude changed. He saw the Pole Zdzislaw Kryzszkowiak in front of him and decided he wasn't running too badly after all.

Then the American Max Truex caught up with him and he decided he must actually be running badly, because no American had ever run a good 10,000 metres. So he stirred himself, burnt Truex off and astounded himself not only by finishing fifth but by running within a second of his best New Zealand time. It was typical of media reaction that, in New Zealand, Halberg's fast fifth was seen as something of a failure when, in truth, it was a class run. Barry Magee ran the same event purely as a warm-up for the marathon two days later and, as Lydiard said, to settle his big-race nerves. Obviously the stratagem worked.

Arthur was not a great diarist or keeper of records, which means that much that he has seen, learnt and created is locked away in the seclusion of his mind. This, in time, may come to be seen as a tragedy, but it is another indication of the privacy and humility of the man. What few diary notes he kept, around the times of the 1960 Olympics and the 1961 world tour, don't give much away to the reader, except to reveal his interest in seeing the sights around him and his ability to utterly understate. Consider these cryptic, far-from-Pepysian comments – and they form almost all the entries in his 1960 diary:

13/8/60. 10 a.m. arrived in Rome. Pension Fabrello is an old building, 150 years to be exact. Seems a homely place and I had a good meal to start with. Took a run out to Olympic camp by bus but it was 9 o'clock before I arrived so didn't bother to ask to go in.

14/8 – Went out to camp and saw boys. They appear OK. I spent quite a few hours there. Walked back to the hotel then to the Parthenon (sic)... went back to camp but had not put my pass in and couldn't watch Snell train.

15/8 – Went to training track at 9 a.m. Most wonderful tracks I have seen. Walked to Games village and back. Again walked there and back for afternoon training session. Saw 'Roman Holiday' at night.

16/8 – Again, day taken with training. Very tired and and went to bed early.

21/8 – [after Halberg's training session] Halberg did well.

23/8 – Peter ran well, 3/4 mile in 2:58.2. Sick of lonely evenings in Rome.

31/8 – Peter ran at 11 a.m. and ran well 1:48.1. Very easy. Murray also ran easy to qualify. Peter ran in afternoon; ran second to Moens, still ran well. Quite pleased with results.

1/9 – Peter won semi-final in 1:47.2. Good performance. I believe he has the field covered. Only one of tomorrow's finalists to do it easy.

2/9 – Peter and Murray both took gold medals. Everything went according to plan, except Peter's sprint. Looking forward to the marathon and 10,000 metres. Late leaving. Pretty tired. Snell's mental approach to the race and lack of nervous tension were remarkable. His big time temperament is better than Halberg's.

5/9 – Went over marathon course with boys.

7/9 – Stewarded Norm Read on 50-kilo walk. Got fouled up and had to walk and run 25 miles. Arrived at camp at 8.15 very tired.

8/9 – Murray didn't have it [in the 10,000 metres], tired in middle stages but still ran a good race.

10/9 – No chance of seeing marathon. Had to wait tensely at finish. Very pleased with Magee. Has vindicated my faith in him as a marathon runner. A very fine performance.

Lydiard and his boys moved on to England and Ireland after Rome. Snell ran at Santry on 22 September, but a day earlier Arthur had recorded that they had a Guinness in a Dublin local before bed and on race day wrote: 'We appear to be overfed, the meals are simply wonderful. Peter ran a good race for first place but seemed tired.' The next day he recorded, 'Peter and I ran 8 miles in morning, feel better for it. That night: Peter ran 5th in 1 mile, 4:1.5; quite good, everything considered. Now 1.30a.m. and off to bed.'

Back in England, Lydiard visited Oxford – and bought an evening suit for 11 pounds 15 shillings. His diary note on the White City meeting read, 'Peter ran impressively though didn't break record'.

7

no meeting of minds

OVER THE YEARS, people have often wondered how Arthur and that great but eccentric coach, Percy Cerutty, got along. The most accurate answer I have ever been able to give is that they didn't, because they met only three times and Arthur's recall is that they never discussed coaching philosophies, even though they had much in common. Murray Halberg spent a weekend at Cerutty's Portsea training camp in 1956, ran along the beach with an 'angular' Herb Elliott, then an unknown, and was impressed by Cerutty's animated demonstrations of his theories. 'His dramatic caperings were so intense that it didn't seem strange at all when one particularly graphic illustration of athletic ability ended with Percy a crumpled heap in one corner,' Halberg recalled in *A Clean Pair of Heels*.

The first Lydiard-Cerutty meeting was in Rome, in the Olympic changing rooms. Halberg and Snell had both won their races and left the complex.

'I found him very affable and an easy person to get along with,' Arthur remembers. 'The second time, we were in London for a White City athletics meeting, at which we both had teams of runners. I had been out for an early run in nearby Hyde Park and, when I returned, Percy was at breakfast. Believe it or not, he was enjoying a typical English meal of sausages, eggs and bacon.

'I asked him, "What happened to the dry oats, nuts and so on that you write about?" He just went on eating.

'I offered to take him to Trafalgar Square, where there was to be a gathering of the athletes, as I had hired a car to get me around London. Those were the days when I used to drive fast and I remember Percy's white-knuckled grip on the door handle all the way.

'When we reached the square, I said I would take him back again after the meeting. He replied that it was no wonder my athletes ran so fast, the way I drove – and politely declined my offer.

'The third time was at the Perth Commonwealth Games. The Karangahape Road business community had paid for me and my wife to go to the Games so that I could continue preparing my runners. Percy at that time was advertising a line of men's underclothing, called Sincerity. Percy told me he was to do the advertisement with a young man who was currently Mr Australia Body Building Champion. This guy was supposed to lift some weights, but he couldn't get them off the floor, so Percy moved him aside and proceeded to lift them himself. By then, he was getting on in years.

'Later, Percy and I were having a few drinks in a bar where a pianist was doing his best to entertain us. Percy got up and put a few dollars into a jar on the piano top. I realised at the time he was a man with a kind heart, a giver not a taker. As long as he was influencing middle-distance running there, Australia produced some of the world's best. Since he departed from the scene, there has been a dearth of great Australian middle- and distance-runners.

'I never managed to discuss training with him, but I knew him as a kind-hearted and decent guy who loved his sport and was prepared to help anyone with their training and health problems.'

The sadly defunct *Auckland Star* brought Percy to New Zealand for a brief lecture tour during which he astounded people with his demonstrations of running, which included spectacular bounds, much as Murray Halberg had witnessed at Portsea. I was interviewing him in his hotel when he startled other guests in the lounge by leaping to his feet and hurdling some of the tables. He was showing his technique for holding the pelvis forward to achieve leg drive and stride length. He was, like Arthur, a small, wiry man with tireless energy.

Students at Auckland University used to have an annual race from side to side of the steep Grafton Gully in the days before a motorway was carved through the dense bush. Percy took them on, and displaying much the same all-out determination that is the mark of Arthur, he beat the students, most of them less than half his age, and he did it handsomely.

During his visit, he made the comment that only six runners had broken 28 minutes for 6 miles and emphasised that two of them were Australians and none was a New Zealander. Arthur, as might be expected, leapt to take the bait.

'I said to Murray that this was a bit of a snide remark. We knew there was a 6-mile race scheduled for the grass track at Manurewa. It was nearing April and the nights were becoming cool, but we decided this was a good time to set the record straight.

'Before the meeting, we put Murray in a hot bath, pulled him out, dried him up and put olive oil on his body to keep the heat in. We wrapped him in his tracksuit and a blanket and drove the fifteen miles to the track. Just before the race was to begin, when we got him out of the tracksuit, he was still so hot the steam was rising off his body. He ran 27:52.2 that night, which happened to set a New Zealand and British Commonwealth record. We knew all along he could do it, but it depended that night on three factors – keeping his muscles warm, getting his pulse rate up, which the excitement of the race took care of, and some careful stretching. The important thing was that he wasn't standing around in the cold night air for too long.'

Cerutty's response to this rapid answer to his challenge was to say nothing at all.

Interestingly, although Cerutty coached the great Herb Elliott and several other notable Australian runners, he was never sought overseas for his undoubted knowledge and talent as a coach. But Arthur certainly was. The Rome Olympics had catapulted him onto the world stage in spectacular fashion. Suddenly, everybody wanted to share him and his gifted runners. His training system came under intense international scrutiny, evoking a variety of responses. Some were deeply impressed, some wrote off the Rome triple-medal success as a one-shot stroke of luck, some discounted the training method, preferring to believe the medals were won by a fortunate combination of superstars. The 'superstars' found this notion and any other criticisms ridiculous and they were about to dash them into the dust.

8

Europe, here we come

IF PROOF WAS still needed of Halberg's ability after Rome, he proved it in January 1961 when he slashed nearly 12 seconds off the world indoor 2-mile record in Portland, Oregon. Arthur had told him before he left New Zealand that he should give it everything he had and make sure he came away from the United States with his name made famous. He did all of that.

'The plywood track, which measured only 220 yards, didn't make for fast running, but it suited Halberg's short, fast, choppy stride,' Arthur says. 'He led all the way, through the half-mile in 2:06 and the mile in 4:13 and finished in 8:34.3, only seconds away from Albie Thomas's world outdoor record. He finished about half a lap ahead of the fine Hungarian runner Laszlo Tabori and almost lapped the great American Max Truex.'

It was a wonderful hint of the great running that was still to come from Halberg as, later that year, Lydiard launched his greatest attack on the northern hemisphere's runners. Before he opened fire, he predicted it would be a success. Murray was now training at a faster pace than he used to race at and had covered a trial three miles in 13:31 without the least effort – in March, he'd won the national title in 13:32.2. Peter, in wet and blustery conditions, had run a 3:03 three-quarter mile and Barry, the marathon runner, had covered the same distance in 3:08. They were startling times.

Arthur explains about the build-up: 'We had learnt from the Rome Games that Murray had been short of racing when he tried the 5000/10,000 metre double and we were not going to make that mistake again. On top of the trials, the preliminary tour races we had arranged would make sure of that.

'Bill Baillie was originally to be one of my team but he was offside with the officials again and they replaced him with a half-miler, Gary Philpott. Les Barker, who coached Gary, had timed him at under 1:20 for 660 yards, so he was in good shape.

'The tour, apart from the individual achievements, was probably most remarkable for the 4 x 1-mile relay world record the boys ran in Dublin despite having almost no miling experience.'

Philpott and Snell were half-mile and 800 metre rivals in Auckland and, not too long before the tour, Snell injured himself during hill training. He was wearing sandshoes instead of his running shoes when he went up the very steep Bullock Track near Western Springs and suffered a stress fracture. His leg was placed in plaster and he and Arthur were sitting in the stand at Sarawia Park in Newmarket watching a sports meeting early in the season when Les came along and asked, 'How are you doing, Peter?'

Peter said, 'OK, Les,' because he was cycling and swimming with his leg in plaster, trying to do as much as possible to maintain his fitness.

'It wouldn't matter anyway,' Les said. 'Gary would beat you.'

Les had convinced Gary that he could beat everyone he raced against. After that crack, Peter couldn't wait to get the plaster off and get back on the track and take on Gary again. He was back to full fitness rapidly and won the Auckland and national titles that season. Gary saw only his backside ploughing away from him.

But Lydiard rated Gary a very good 800-metre runner, who was just unlucky to have Snell running at the same time. 'My recollection is that, in all the times they raced, Gary beat Peter only once, but he was a very fine runner who would have made a much bigger impression but for the huge shadow of Snell. Coincidentally, Murray Halberg and Barry Magee, although they were training companions, were fierce competitors whenever they met – they must have raced each other scores of times and, although Barry beat Murray only once, it never stopped him from trying.'

Arthur also forecast that the European tour, on top of the Olympic medals, would make New Zealand the Mecca for the world's top athletes for at least the next two or three years. Once again, he was right. He also said it would place the administration of the sport on a firm financial footing, for the first time, if the right decisions were made.

'In the past, we had had to accept the second-best, fourth-best or even sixteenth-best athletes coming here, but now we had athletes who the rest of the world's champions would want to beat and they would have to come to New Zealand to do it.'

Those tours, which Arthur and his supporters were able to organise thanks to the generosity of business sponsors, proved that athletics at an international level can provide both entertainment and money. It is a shame that New Zealand can no longer host such events, partly because the magic of Arthur Lydiard was allowed to vanish in a puff of bureaucratic smoke.

Arthur was only able to go on the European tour because of the support of Ray Puckett, to whom he remains grateful. 'While I was in Europe, Ray took over my Remuera milk round. He took a month's leave from his regular job and every night left his Papatoetoe home at 11 p.m. and did not get back until 10.30 the next morning. He discarded his training and gave up all hopes of contesting the Korean marathon, in which he ran in 1959. He did this as a way of repaying me for guiding his training – while he was preparing for the Commonwealth Games marathon, I ran with him on nearly all his long, lonely runs. He was helped on the milk round by other athletes and when I came home from the tour and was asked which I thought was the greatest performance on the trip, I suggested the performance of the athletes who completed my round in three hours. I never managed that.'

By the time Arthur and his team reached London, the coach was confident Murray would have a world record before the tour was over.

'I believed he had never been in better form. On the way over, we had stopped at Stanford University in California and he had run the field into the ground in winning a mile race in 4:08.9. He followed that with a mile in 4:03.4 in Gateshead, in England, after shaking off an illness, and both were great preparation for his attacks on the longer distances ahead.

'Barry was equally impressive. I had been hoping he would add some international track laurels to his road and marathon record and he did not let me down. He ran 2 miles in 9:02 in California and then ripped the field apart in the White City 3-miles in London, running 13:18, eleven seconds faster than his previous best and only strides away from the world record.

'Peter and Gary both ran in California and Gary looked the more impressive. He eased over 440 yards in 48.5, despite being disconcerted at the beginning by the 240-yard length of the straight on which the race started. Peter followed the field in the 880 yards and broke away in the last 100 yards to win in 1:52.2. But he proved the race had been good for him by running 1:48.8 at the White City meeting. Since these were their first real tests in three months, the future was looking good. I was delighted.'

The New Zealanders were green with envy over Stanford University's facilities – acres of ground containing swimming pools, stables, a variety of courts and not one but two cinder tracks. The main one was in a 100,000-capacity football stadium.

A promising itinerary was taking shape, with the World Games in Helsinki on 5 and 6 July, Cologne on 12 July, Dublin on 17 and 18 July and Stockholm on 25 July. It meant plenty of racing – and plenty of travelling – not that Arthur was worried about that aspect.

'But I found that, unless you have a mathematical brain, you can become confused by the time zones. When you land at an airport, you don't know whether you should be heading for bed or starting out on the day's engagements. And food was proving a problem of the jet age. Not the lack of it – the excess of it. On our flight out of Auckland, starting at 5.30 p.m. and ending in San Francisco at 5.30 p.m. the same day, we had three breakfasts, two lunches and one dinner.

'Then, on our flight from the US to London, we had uninterrupted daylight, which can lead to total confusion. Three hours before we reached London, we were served breakfast.

When we arrived, we were served breakfast. We couldn't face it. We high-tailed it to bed to try to stabilise our systems before the White City meeting.'

Arthur remembers that Gary Philpott was very quiet in the early stages of the tour. 'He didn't say much and he didn't mix in too well. He was very reserved and in-turned. His first race in England was at 800 metres at White City in London and I realised that Les Barker must have told him he could win the race, because he charged to the front at the gun and led all these Russian, German and other gun runners for the first 600 metres. Then they all swept past him like a bunch of rockets and Snell went on to win.

'I later saw Gary leaving the ground. He was looking very depressed and dejected. His shoes were hanging from his hand and his head was hanging from his shoulders. I asked him where he was going and he said he was going back to the hotel.

'"Like hell you are," I said. "Wait here a minute."

'I had earlier met an attractive young lady who was secretary to one of the sports promoters and I knew she owned a nice sports car, so I went to her and asked what she was doing that night.

'"Nothing," she said. "Why?"

'I pointed to Gary. "See that guy," I said. "How would you like to take him to a nightclub tonight. Give him a good time. I'll give you the money for it."

'Gary was a good-looking youngster and she said she'd be happy to do that, so I took her over to Gary and told him, "This young lady wants to take you out tonight. She's going to take you to a nightclub."

'I didn't see Gary again until about 11 o'clock the next morning when he came in from training and changed. I asked him where he was going and he said he was meeting the girl again. He was as happy as Larry. After that, he was as good as gold, one of the boys. He still remembers the young woman's name.'

The team went to Helsinki for the World Games and Snell and Philpott were placed in the same B-grade 800 metres. The organisers were plainly among those who thought Snell's Olympic 800-metres victory was a quirk.

'I got that changed and Peter won the A-grade, Gary won the

B-grade, Halberg won the 5000 metres and Magee won the 10,000 metres. Between us, we cleaned them out. The Australian Dave Power approached me then and asked if I could help him. I asked him what the problem was and he told me his 10,000 metres runner, who at that time was one of only six men who had gone under 28 minutes for 6 miles, wanted to go home. He had a wife and young daughter in Sydney and was worried about his finances and the mortgage on his house and couldn't concentrate on his running. I asked Dave why he didn't talk to his team manager.

'Dave said, "He's a bloody no-hoper. He's never been overseas before and all he wants to do is go sightseeing." I talked to the Athletics Federation people about this guy and they said they'd give him a thousand American dollars to stay on and run. When I told Dave, he then asked if he and Pat Clohessy could join us for the rest of our tour of Europe. He said their manager would be glad to get rid of them so he could carry on sightseeing. So they went to Germany, Ireland and Sweden with us.'

By the time the team got to Dublin, where the four New Zealanders tackled the 4 x 1-mile relay, Gary had improved dramatically. He'd never raced a mile before, but he ran this one outstandingly. In Arthur's words, 'he gave it everything he had'.

'I don't know how Baillie would have gone in Gary's place in the relay. Bill was a tough nut, but Gary on that demanding occasion did really well.'

One outcome of the tour was that Clohessy got onto the Lydiard programme, which had a big influence in Australia when he became one of their leading coaches. But, adds Arthur, 'Clohessy was not only a good runner and a good coach, he was also a bloody good poker player. I found that out on the tour.

'In Ireland, we stayed in a boarding house. This was long before the days of big money and fancy hotels. The landlady asked for my name and when I told her she wasn't too enthusiastic. "What sort of name is that?" she asked. "English?" I said, "As a matter of fact, it's Anglo-Saxon."

'Then she asked Pat for his name.

'"Patrick Clohessy," he said.

'"Aaah," she said, "that's a fine name," and made him Irish

coffee. Pat didn't like it and poured it down the sink without letting her see.

'I told the woman, "Pat really loved that. Give him another one." That'll teach him to be good at poker, I thought.

'Later we visited Santry Stadium, and we saw there was a bloody great hole where the velodrome used to be.

'What happened there?' we asked.

'"The IRA put a bludy boomb under it," we were told. The bomb had blown out all the windows in the street as well as wrecking the velodrome.

'I was also taken to a park full of statues with all their arms, legs and heads smashed off. What happened there? Another "bludy boomb". Surprisingly, Nelson's Column was still standing in O'Connell Street. I couldn't believe it but, later on, I read that they'd blown that up, too.

'My sightseeing guide backed his car into something and was going to get out to look at what had happened, but his wife said anxiously, "No, don't get out. Don't look. Just drive on." There were a lot of scary people about in Dublin and my guides were very scared people.

'I was walking down O'Connell Street one morning, carrying a couple of buns I'd bought. I'd taken one from the bag when an old woman came up beside me and said, "Give us a bite." I put the bun back in its bag. "Oooh," she said nastily, "you're mean. You're mean." Dublin was so poor they fed their one-armed bandit machines with Irish pennies. If you won the jackpot, you might be lucky to get two bob back.'

Halberg was sure he could have scored his 3-mile world record in Dublin that July, but neither he nor Dave Power could hear the lap times during the middle of the race. The timekeeper just didn't call them loudly enough. Halberg said he thought they were running so slowly the timekeeper had given up their lap calls. He said if he'd known the time, he could have gone much faster over the last half-mile. He certainly finished as fresh as a daisy. As it was, he missed the world time by 0.8 seconds, finishing in 13:11.6.

His run was hailed by sports writers at the meeting. *The Times* man wrote:

We were treated to one of the sights of an athletics enthusiast's lifetime – Halberg in full cry, the brave fighter and magnificent runner unleashing all his resources. Failure is sometimes more magnificent than success. It certainly was so on this occasion.

Halberg dazzled, almost frightened us, with a last lap of incredible courage in 55.3s. He did not hear the lap times being called out after the first half-mile, otherwise he would certainly have beaten the world record. It was typical of Halberg that he could go over to the main stand and apologise for his 'failure' but also typical that his coach should add, 'Even though Halberg did not hear the time, I'm surprised he did not go away earlier, since he was so strong.'

The correspondent called Halberg's finish the most amazing final lap sprint he had seen in a 3-mile of that class. 'He went down the back straight like a half-miler and coming off the bend it seemed almost unbelievable that he could produce still more drive towards the tape.' One Irish journalist described Halberg as 'sprinting like a madman' and the *Daily Express* reported Halberg spurting as if he was at the start of a quarter-mile test.

Arthur returned to Ireland years later, this time with a Danish team he was training, and they scored a historic first win against another country by cleaning up the Irish.

Again, it is intriguing to read Arthur's diarised comments on the tour. The first entry follows their Palo Alto races: 'The boys ran well, considering these were their first races; Philpott 48.5 in 440, Snell 1:52.5 in 880, Halberg 4:8.9 in mile and Magee 9.02 in two miles.'

After the White City meeting four days later: 'Magee surprised the Englishmen by winning over three miles in 13:17, Snell won the 880 in 1:48 and Philpott was fourth.'

In Jyvaskyla, in Finland, on 7 July he wrote: 'Halberg realised an ambition and broke world two-mile record in 8:30. Had to do it on his own. Could do quite a bit better.'

The team went back to Dublin for their record 4 x 1-mile relay run at Santry Stadium. Arthur's diary entry recorded the lap times and added: 'Great night.'

On 25 July, in Stockholm he noted: 'Halberg ran a world record three miles in 13:10.1, with Magee right on his tail in 13:11.4. Went out in the evening and had a few drinks to celebrate. To bed at 1 a.m.'

The success of his athletes at the Rome Olympics meant Lydiard's influence was to spread far and wide, and as is so often the case in athletics, coaches around the world began to borrow from him and others, to develop a mix-and-match philosophy. Certainly this happened in Britain.

Ron Hill, the 1970 Commonwealth Games marathon champion, remembers Lydiard's influence as 'the long run on a Sunday morning. I was self-coached and I experimented with a lot of different methods before I settled on one that brought me some success. I met him once at Wheeling in West Virginia. Great guy, liked a beer and a chat.'

Colin Young, who coached Mel Batty to a world 10-mile record in 1964, mingled the philosophies of Lydiard, Percy Cerutty, Emil Zatopek and Jim Peters. 'Not a bad mix there,' he says. 'Basically, the more it hurts the better it is.' A comment Arthur does not entirely agree with. His mantra is 'Train don't strain', and he has always preached training to a point of pleasant tiredness.

The long runs and the hill sessions beloved by Lydiard were an essential part of Batty's methods when he took up coaching and advised Eamonn Martin, who won the Commonwealth 10,000 metres gold medal in Lydiard's home town in 1990. Batty also remembers meeting Peter Snell when they both ran in the 1962 Commonwealth Games in Perth. 'We swapped track suits,' he remembers. 'I wanted his because he was an all-time great runner. Why he took mine I'll never know. It wouldn't have fitted him anyway because he is much bigger than me.'

The Lydiard influence was also seen in another British runner, the buccaneering David Bedford, in the 1970s. Bedford, now race director of the London marathon, was famous for running 200 miles a week in training, a regime which took him to a world 10,000 metres record but not to any of the major race titles. His coach Bob Parker remembers: 'I really borrowed from three people: Arthur Lydiard for the long runs and hill work, Percy Cerutty for the sand dune running and Emil Zatopek for intervals on the track, getting David to run in army boots! I met Arthur once when I went to New Zealand. He was a lovely bloke and a very good trainer.'

Ireland, too, took notice as the Lydiard system spread round the world like a beneficent plague. Perhaps an ideal summary of that spread emerged just recently in an e-mail from 33-year-old Dubliner Colm O'Connor:

'Arthur, you are my absolute hero, simple as that,' he wrote, explaining he had given up football training, had started to run and now wished he had read Arthur's books years ago. 'Read your bible and that's it. I'm totally converted. I love to run because I now totally understand what I'm trying to achieve … I ran 2.06 at 800 last year with terrible preparation, so I would hope, with my aerobic threshold on the up and up, that I will blow that time away.

'By last count your books had gone through 49 hands, from soccer players, Gaelic footballers and hurlers to runners, and all say the same thing: Wow.'

9

publish and be damned

THE WORLD IS full of people always prepared to jump into print or get themselves on television to air their opinions on just about any subject that is likely to crop up. Arthur Lydiard is not one of these people. He would comment if he was asked to, but only if he felt he had a contribution to make; that was his limit. One of the rare occasions when he did speak out was in October 1960, when he had a whack at the Government for failing to follow the example of virtually all other nations by giving state aid to the promotion of sport.

'I said this would strike a decisive blow against delinquency. I pointed out that New Zealand didn't have one sports stadium or building provided by the state, yet it was virtually wasting millions on compulsory military training [CMT] for a net return of little more than a few obsolete trucks. I was also annoyed that they were building more prisons than sporting facilities and that the facilities many of the schools had were not being used.

'Governments all around the world had long ago recognised that sports built clean minds, clean bodies and healthy citizenship. If even half the money spent on CMT had gone into physical training or the promotion of sport, it would have been returned two-fold in the form of physically and mentally fit youth.

'I said that New York's Madison Square Garden and London's White City Stadium were two examples of arenas that worked for all sports and all New Zealand cities should have similar centres supplied by the state because our sports bodies were not big enough to do these things for themselves.

'State backing had been the reason for the astounding revival of sport in Germany, which had not only sent a big team to the Rome Olympics but also paid the full expenses of several hundred German youths who attended as spectators. I compared that with our voluntary workers in sport having to go cap-in-hand to the public all the time, running raffles and bludging for donations, merely to get enough money to survive, let alone expand.

'Our delinquents were delinquents because they had nothing else to occupy their minds or their bodies.'

Arthur cited a classic example of New Zealand's sports difficulties: the national gymnastic organisation had to pay £93 in duty to bring a trampoline valued at £46 into the country and then had to fight for three years to get the duty refunded.

'My argument was that the reform of delinquents should not start in the Borstals we operated in those days, nor should it begin with education or religion. The starting point should be to organise them into club activities and keep them so busy and fit with worthwhile activities that they never had the time or the inclination to go off the rails.

'We now have support for some athletes and sports but we need to keep systems going to develop the good athletes in any sport to their full potential. But today they are still building gaols and they are still leaving too many kids to their own devices so they get into trouble. It only needs someone to organise, say, a game of cricket in a street and all the kids would want to play in it. We lack motivators and role models who can actually reach to where the kids are most at risk.

'When a Finnish athlete won the Olympic gold medal throwing the javelin, for a long time, everywhere you went in Finland, long sticks were flying all over the place as the kids copied their new hero. The same thing happened here in the sixties when Snell, Halberg and the other boys were winning everything – kids were running all over the country.

'People who saw what I was doing with athletes and heard what I was saying about fitness began the jogging boom. The motivation was simply what I was saying about cardiovascular efficiency as a means of avoiding heart problems. Finding motivation for young people is just as vital.'

Arthur quite fairly points out that only the generosity of private companies – Winstone Ltd, Agfa and Rothmans – kept him in New Zealand after the Rome Olympics and enabled the country to capitalise on his athletes' drawing power by providing the backing for major international sports meetings. What he said in 1960 was listened to and acknowledged for its good sense, but there was little evidence that it was acted on.

But Arthur was by now well used to negative or indifferent reactions and he wasn't much bothered if no one picked up his challenge. He'd offered his thoughts, he knew they made sense and he had more important things to do.

He fell foul of the NZAAA again in 1961. 'I was writing a regular column for the *Auckland Star*'s *8 O'Clock* sports edition and I had entered for the Owairaka marathon in early December. The day before the race, the chairman, Harold Austad, issued a statement in Wellington saying that I could only run in the event if I immediately stopped writing for the newspaper. If I continued, he said, I would "offend my amateur status". The NZAAA administration committee had met to discuss my status at the request of the Auckland centre, but I still hadn't been advised personally of this ruling on the afternoon before the race.

'The decision was based on a new International Amateur Athletics Federation rule, which said no competitor could write, lecture or comment for payment in future without prior permission and then only if writing, lecturing or commentating was his or her main career. Austad said that, while the rule had operated since the previous Friday, the NZAAA would give a period of grace of a week or two to obviate hardship. This "grace" period was effective in the case of another *8 O'Clock* athletics writer, my pioneering pupil Lawrie King. But it didn't apply to me or to Ralph King, a brother of Lawrie, who was also a sports writer. Lawrie, Austad said, had applied for permission to write and Ralph and I had not.

'I can't remember exactly what happened but, since I ran in every marathon for which I entered, obviously I ran in that one. And I went on writing for the *8 O'Clock*. If it was an Austad bluff, I called it.

'I started another controversy when, speaking to the Hutt Rotary Club, I criticised the Customs Department for barring the importation of equipment needed for an Auckland gymnasium while, at the same time, allowing seven hundred dollars worth of wine to be imported for the touring French rugby team. My argument was that there was a lack of encouragement for people to take part in sports that didn't turn the turnstiles. I made a plea for some of the gambling money the government was raking in to go to physical culture organisations. I accepted that horse racing was an industry which would die if they took the TAB away, but contended that dog racing would flourish if they put the TAB on the dogs and athletics would flourish if they put the TAB on track and field. In my opinion, all the gambling monies were being spent the wrong way. That money should have been spent on making sure the youth of the country were steered in the right direction. I don't know what the situation is these days; I can only hope that it is better.'

I remember the French wine. I covered the rugby tour as sports writer for the *Auckland Star* and all the touring journalists were allocated a bottle or two with every dinner. It was, as I recall, a very rough and tongue-loosening vintage.

Meantime, Arthur came back from the great 1961 tour with a new problem on his plate. The solution to the problem was, eventually, going to be bad news for New Zealand.

10

going or staying

WHEN ARTHUR RETURNED to New Zealand after the 1961 tour, he was seriously considering an offer of a contract from the Amateur Athletic Association in England to coach there for five years. The all-expenses appointment, with its good salary, was highly tempting, not least because he believed English schools, with which he would be working, were the best in the world. In the event, he turned it down, hoping to stay in New Zealand.

'The offer was one of several I received on the European trip. I was quoted at the time as saying that the team I took to Europe did not contain potentially the best runners in New Zealand; there was talent as good or better which had not even been touched. I guess there were people who accepted that I was right and wanted me to help to find these athletes.

'At the same time, it was reported that the NZAAA was investigating ways of keeping me here. Harold Austad said the discussion began after several members of the public had asked what the association was going to do about my overseas offers. Some had suggested a fund to keep me at least until after the 1964 Olympics. What the NZAAA talked about was a secret but Austad said later it would be "wonderful" to keep me in New Zealand. However, the upshot of whatever they talked about was, to put it simply, nothing.'

The spate of letters to newspapers calling for official action to keep Arthur in New Zealand should have emphasised to even the most disinterested officials how highly the country thought of Lydiard. One letter writer asked: 'Are New Zealanders and the Government going to allow him to turn out athletes in another country with all the attendant glory and publicity? New Zealand cannot afford to lose him. The publicity value alone is tremendous.' Another asked: 'Why must Mr Lydiard run a milk round? Is there no other position available that would be more suited to his outstanding ability as a coach?'

A writer who referred to the brain drain that is still a hot topic in New Zealand today said: 'I am horrified to see that the man who made their [the four-man team Arthur had in Europe] performances possible – the man who trained them and can train other young New Zealanders – may be allowed to leave the country unhonoured and unsung. Why cannot we be big enough to create employment at a worthwhile figure for him? Why must he go the way of all our outstanding scientists, artists and students?'

Two correspondents called for an immediate lead from the Auckland Athletic Centre to find Arthur a post locally.

'Fair Deal' (they still published anonymous letters in those days) complained: 'There is something strangely incongruous about the way in which, on the one hand, the whole country (including the Prime Minister) is heaping well-deserved praise and congratulations on the New Zealand athletic team and, on the other hand, the position is allowed to continue that coach Arthur Lydiard will be forced to accept a post overseas in order to devote his full time to the sport.'

Another: 'I feel that we would be failing in our duty to our youth if we were to allow Mr Lydiard to be lost to us.'

One correspondent took a different and original view: 'It seems that the Government is as parsimonious with its praise as it is with its money. Isn't it marvellous that our political parties will spend millions upon millions of pounds every year on medical services yet never think of spending a tiny fraction of that amount on trying to ensure that we don't get sick in the first place. It's a pity we haven't got several hundred Lydiards for I'm sure that if we did we'd need just that many fewer doctors.'

The support from the ordinary people was gratifying but sadly made little practical difference.

The Mt Albert MP, Warren Freer, suggested that Arthur

should be offered a full-time and 'adequately paid' post as a youth athletic coach with the Department of Internal Affairs' physical welfare branch. Like a number of other official attempts to keep Lydiard in New Zealand, this one fell on deaf ears. Arthur, on the other hand, had to make a decision about the future. As well as the handsome English offer, he had proposals on the table from Canada, the United States and Europe. Obviously, he couldn't go back to a shoe factory and carry on part-time with his unpaid coaching work. The world was at his feet and he could not afford to be sentimental about his homeland when it appeared to be the one country that offered him nothing.

At the time, one of Arthur's dreams had been to acquire some land just north of Auckland in order to establish a residential training camp, under his guidance, for New Zealand and international athletes. There is no doubt that many of the world's aspiring runners would have made a beeline to such a facility. The cost at that time would have been insignificant – Arthur was not a man for grandiose schemes and his camp would have been comparatively Spartan in keeping with his philosophy. The investment would have paid dividends by establishing New Zealand as the world centre for middle- and distance-coaching for as long as Arthur cared to keep going. The fact that he is still, forty years later, an enthusiastic coach of youngsters – and is still turning them out as winners – suggests that the scheme could have seen out last century and carried on. Those who enjoyed the raging success of the New Zealand track meets after Rome will be able to envisage the meetings that could have taken place if international élite athletes were actually living and training here. As it is, many such runners do come to New Zealand for off-season training, but they are scattered about the country and are not in competitive mode.

Back home from the 1961 tour, Arthur publicly accused Russia of ducking New Zealand athletes and avoiding middle-distance and distance events – despite the fact that, like New Zealand, Russia's prime athletic interest was in races from 800 metres to 10,000 metres.

'Many European countries wanted our top athletes to run at their meetings, but the Soviet Union had lowered a curtain of silence as far as our boys were concerned. Their attitude was demonstrated when the world record-holder, Vladimir Kuts, rated Murray's chances of breaking the world 5000 metres record as zero. Kuts ranked East Germany's Hans Grodotzki and Poland's Kazimierz Zimny ahead of Halberg. I wanted a middle-distance match between Murray and Pyotr Bolotnikov to see how good my boy was. At the time, we could have fielded a team of six capable of running all the distances up to the marathon.'

At the same time, the great distance runner Jim Peters was boosting the New Zealanders, praising them for their ability to produce three Olympic medals despite what he called 'an appalling lack of facilities'. At the time, New Zealand had only one cinder track. Peters also made much of the fact that Arthur managed the New Zealand team in Europe, saying this was a lesson for Britain, where the man who accompanied a team was always an official and never a coach. It was a lesson New Zealand had only just learnt.

Peters also rated Barry Magee's 3-mile win at White City Stadium, in 13:18, within striding distance of the world record, as the most significant victory in top athletics for a long time, because Barry was a marathon runner and his previous 3-mile best was outside 13:30.

Later, when Arthur was coaching in Finland, he had some more positive dealings with Russia, travelling there several times at the invitation of their top middle- and distance-coach, Andrei Khorobkov. On one occasion, the Kenyan Kip Keino, who later ran world 3000 and 5000 metre records and won the 1968 Olympic 1500 metre race, was also there. 'We were talking outside the stadium in Leningrad until he said, "I've got to go, Arthur, it's time to get ready for the race."

'He turned to pick up his bag but someone had swiped it and he was left without his running gear. We found some gear and shoes for him and he won the race anyway – in someone else's shoes.

'Another time, I was invited to take the Finns' cross-country team to Russia. We went down to Kislavosk in Georgia, stayed in a nice hotel and were looked after by some wonderful people. The food was great. We went to a cabaret in the hotel some nights and, as soon as we sat down, we were given chocolates and vodka; we were recognised as strangers and this was the warm way they welcomed us. When the music started, all the men got up and started Cossack dancing while we and the women watched. As soon as one dancer left the floor, another one stepped out. It was an interesting aspect of Russian society.

'My interpreter and I were approached by two young girls, with glasses of vodka. I asked what they wanted and the interpreter said they wanted two of the young Finns to go with them. I said that would be okay, telling the Finns to be sure they were back for training early in the morning. They went outside and were back in five minutes. I asked them what had happened and they said the police had arrived and taken the two girls away. I don't know what they were but that was the end of it for the boys.

'I'd been out somewhere one morning and, when I returned, the head man at the hotel, who always wore a cap like a railway man's cap, was sitting at the top of a long table with my runners down one side and hotel staff members down the other. Apparently, a couple of photos of nude women had been found in one of the boys' bedrooms – that's something that the Finns don't bother about but the Russians took it very seriously. We managed to iron it out without any real trouble.

'The Finns ran in the cross-country championship but they didn't do very well. They weren't trained for it. But it was a worthwhile experience. We were supposed to stay three weeks but somehow the atmosphere wasn't right so I took my boys home early. I don't think the Finns were too happy about our early return but I thought it was pointless to stay on. We were running up in the mountains on icy snow and in very cold conditions. Not that Finland was any better as far as cold was concerned, but the snow was softer, safer and easier back home.'

Arthur went to a cinema while he was in Kislavosk and was sitting next to his interpreter, who was the head of all the universities in the Soviet Union.

The eccentric but successful Australian coach Percy Cerutty, seen here with Murray Halberg at his Portsea training camp.

The clock showed 2:19:4.0 as Barry Magee cruised through the tape at the end of the 1960 Asahi international marathon in Fukuoka, Japan.

Arthur's boys, Jeff Julian (left) and Bill Baillie (right), with Finland's Eino Oksanen between them, in the Hellenic marathon in Athens. Baillie had beaten Julian in a trial to decide who went to the event, but by such a tight margin that both were sent. Julian finished second in 2:27.

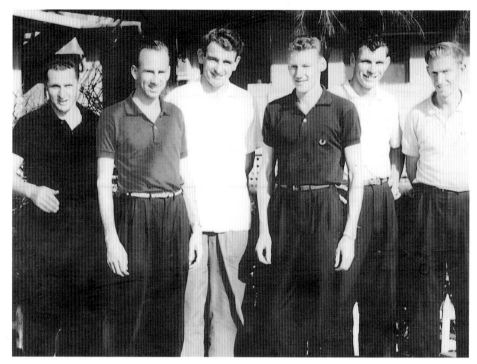

The superb 1961 touring team in Manila with New Zealander Lou Brunetti, who was teaching English there. From left, Arthur, Barry Magee, Brunetti, Gary Philpott, Peter Snell and Murray Halberg.

Arthur gets regal treatment as the guest of the Vaux Brewery in Gateshead in 1961.

American Dyrol Burleson, one of the great American middle-distance runners of the 60s, beats Murray Halberg and Bill Baillie, both showing strain, in the 1500 metres at the 1961 Agfa meeting in Auckland. Arthur's revenge came 16 months later when Peter Snell ran 3:56.1 to beat him in a Los Angeles mile.

Peter Snell striding out during training a week before breaking three world records in 1962.

Auckland's 1962 Agfa Games at Eden Park produced brilliant running. Here Peter Snell and American Dyrol Burleson charge through the tape almost together. When Murray Halberg (arm left) challenged, he blocked Snell and Burleson won in 4:05.6.

The tight corners of board tracks were awkward for Peter Snell's big stride, but he cracked records every time he raced on them. Here he wins a half-mile in 1:49.9 at the Japanese indoor championships in 1962.

Arthur defies the Finnish cold but his pupil doesn't as they train in snow.

'Soon after the film started, everyone began pissing themselves with laughter. I had no idea what was so funny so I asked my interpreter. The film was at the point where the couple are about to get married and are looking at a store window full of whiteware because they want to buy a refrigerator. When they go into the shop and ask how soon they can get the fridge, the assistant replies, "In about three years", and that's what they were all laughing about. It was a time when the Russians were very short of home equipment. I doubt they're any better now that the Mafia have taken over.'

Arthur visited Leningrad a few times because the Russians had been influenced by the first book we co-authored, *Run to the Top*. They'd printed hundreds of thousands of copies of it – for which they didn't pay a rouble in royalties because they didn't then belong to the copyright convention so just copied off anything they fancied. Khorobkov told Arthur they used his training for all forms of sport, including the Winter Olympic events, at which the Russians did very well.

In 1962, a rare event occurred. Arthur finally got one of his predictions wrong. He forecast that the mile at the Perth Commonwealth Games would probably be run under four minutes. 'But Perth's powerful wind put paid to that hope,' he recalls. 'The race instead became a windswept classic in good and bad tactical running.'

The good tactics were those of New Zealand's favourite, Peter Snell.

'Peter stayed back in the field because we knew that if he forced the pace out front he would lose – there were five sub-four minute milers in the race all waiting for Peter to make that mistake. But one of the first things you learn in track racing is not to hit the front if there is a strong wind. Bruce Tulloh forced the pace by leading for one lap and look what happened to him – he ran one of his slowest miles.

'Overseas commentators and coaches criticised Peter for not risking this, but I wonder how they would have advised him if he had been their runner. He was under no obligation to provide a fast time any more than any other runners in the race. His obligation was to win for New Zealand and help his team-mate, John Davies. I had told John to wait until he felt the wind on his back before making his break. The wind was blowing right down the front straight and he held off until 350 yards. If there had not been a wind, he would have gone a hundred yards earlier, at the bell.

'Peter, great athlete that he was, helped John by going up to his shoulder when John burst through. This made it difficult for Rhodesia's Terry Sullivan to go round the two of them. Peter was two yards in front of John at the finish and John was 15 yards up on Sullivan and 25 yards up on the Australian Tony Blue. I could only suggest to the critics that it would have been a great race if an Englishman or an Australian had won it in Peter's time of 4:08. But the only man who could push Peter was John Davies.

'The 6-mile was also slow but no one criticised Canada's Bruce Kidd for that. The same thing happened in Murray Halberg's 3-mile. No one was prepared to go out front and do anything. Murray was alone in the race. The English had two men, so why was a lone runner expected to make the running for other teams?

'I commented at the time that if fast times were needed and world records wanted, then it looked as if New Zealanders were going to have to push other New Zealanders into making the pace.'

The records show that Murray used the tactic of shadowing the runner he most feared, the up-and-coming Canadian Bruce Kidd, and virtually forgetting about everyone else. Kidd was in front at the bell, with Murray on his shoulder, and the New Zealander accelerated away down the back and recalls finishing with a smile on his face.

Arthur said the Perth track had a lot to do with the racing. It varied from day to day and it worried him. He took the New Zealand hurdler, Avis McIntosh, down to study it before the racing started. At one place, she could not get her spikes into the cinders; at another, where the track had been watered, she sank in easily and lifted a piece of the track away on her shoes. 'I asked if the track could be watered for the first day and it was, but the weather turned dry and the 6 miles was run at the end of the day when the track had dried out completely.'

Bill Baillie was in fine form when the New Zealanders arrived in Perth but, during a final two-mile trial with Murray, he faltered with only 200 yards to go. He had injured a thigh muscle and missed out on an almost-certain medal because, despite daily physiotherapy, he had to run the 6-miles with the thigh heavily bandaged. The original plan was to run him in the mile or 3-miles, but Arthur shifted him to the six because the pace would be slower.

'Bill Baillie's breakdown was heart-breaking for all of us,' Arthur says. 'He was as fit as Murray, who was the best-conditioned athlete in the world at the time. His injury didn't seem much, but it was deep-seated.

'I had copped a bit of stick for saying I was coaching the Australian Dave Power to beat Murray and Barry in Perth, but I didn't consider I was being unpatriotic. I was merely being a coach and, for me, there was a meaning in the words "brotherhood of athletics". I saw amateur athletes as fit men competing against each, and with each other, to enjoy racing. Those three men were the best of friends after their summer in Europe where they all helped each other, but that didn't mean they'd let the other man win. It's not a dog-eat-dog, win-at-all-cost game, but true athletes always run to win.

'I was also helping American coaches to learn our style of training and, in turn, the Americans were teaching me some of their track secrets. I believed knowledge should be shared between countries; I had the same outlook as a scientist who thinks all scientific knowledge should go into a common pool from which others can draw. I still have that view and I still help anyone who asks for help.'

As an indication of just how freely Arthur spreads his knowledge to anyone who asks, I quote from a recent article in a magazine by American marathon runner Kathrine Switzer:

I had the pleasure of dining with Arthur at his home last March. He's still feisty, grumbling about those who tinker with his training methods to try to cut corners, and annoyed as hell over his artificial knees, which have reduced him to a sort of speedy shuffle.

But the phone rings incessantly from all over the world and Arthur barks a few words of direction, clearly, absolutely, no hmmms or maybe-you-should-tries. Bang – he hangs up. I have this image of people in Italy and Japan and Portland, or on their cellphones calling as they are lacing up, or a coach who is standing trackside verifying the tempo before his charges all assemble.

Arthur's house is always filled with young people, too. They use his home as a training base and his presence as a directing touchstone. It's totally informal but it works. Tonight, two teenage girls – swimmers! – and their father/coach join us for dinner. After applying Arthur's methods to swimming over the last few years, they have today won each of their qualifying heats in record time. One of the girls has set a national record this afternoon and is going for another the next day. They are not nervous in the slightest about their finals. 'Why be nervous?' they said. 'We're ready.'

One of the girls was Jane Copeland, the daughter of swim coach David Wright. Wright and Arthur collaborated for almost a decade to ensure that the Lydiard schedules made a successful transition from ground to water. Jane is now on a swim scholarship in the United States, and the Lydiard-based swim schedules are in a book, *Swim to the Top*.

Back in 1962, though, Arthur's own stable of runners was about to put a bomb under New Zealand track racing. Oddly, the fuse was lit by a New Zealander whose name has vanished in the fog of forgetfulness.

11

Snell and the golden years

FLYING HOME FROM Rome in 1960, Arthur sat alongside a New Zealand businessman, whose name now escapes him. He regrets this because the man said that, after Arthur's successes, many international athletes would want to come to learn from him. He suggested New Zealand should find a sponsor and run international meets and added that, if Arthur couldn't find a backer, he would be prepared to step in.

As Arthur says, 'He may not have been aware of it, but he was the trigger for the finest period of track and field New Zealand has enjoyed at home. Agfa's managing director, Steve Ashby, was interested in letting the world know what was going on and as a result of meeting with him, we got the athletes and the sponsorship for the 1962 Agfa Games in Auckland and we did the lot, with the permission of, if not much help from, the NZAAA. They were highly successful meets, out of which we personally got nothing but the satisfaction.

'Peter was running very well for those meetings and I arranged with the Wanganui Athletic Club for him to run a mile on their grass track at Cook's Gardens. Unfortunately, a club official fed a story to the press that I had told him I believed Peter would run under four minutes because he had run 4:01 in the South Island and it was logical to think he could go under four.

'The fact that it got into the papers pissed Snell off, because it was putting pressure on him that he didn't welcome. In the event, it didn't matter much. Snell ran a world record 3:54.4 that night, leading home a first-class field of runners who were much more experienced in running miles than he was.'

Peter was something of an anomaly in the Lydiard stable. Arthur used a basic speed over 200 yards to determine his athletes' best potential and it always worked, except for Peter. His basic speed wasn't great and the fact that he became the world's fastest half-miler and miler came from different factors – a combination of the endurance Arthur developed in him and his amazing natural strength. At Mt Albert Grammar, he was only the third-ranked 800-metre runner. He was beaten by a boy called Michael Macky, who Arthur wished had gone on with his running because he would easily have made the Rome Olympics. He was faster than Snell and Arthur trained him to be the New Zealand junior mile champion and break Murray Halberg's junior mile record.

Arthur recalls that when he had his holiday home at Stanmore Bay, they would train over a 26-mile course which went away up through the township of Silverdale and came back through the hot pool district of Waiwera, a route that included some fairly big hills, and Macky, at 19, ran it in under three hours on a steaming hot day. 'Disappointingly, when he left high school and went to university, he joined a pop group and that was the end of his very promising running career.'

It was Macky, though, who finally put Arthur and Peter together and created the partnership that rocketed them both to world recognition. Snell recalls how Macky cornered him and asked if he had met Arthur. Snell said no; in fact, he had had two earlier encounters with the coach, but they had been brief and not meaningful.

'Well,' Mike said, 'after this you have to.'

'At that third meeting,' says Snell, 'Mike did all the talking, which was pretty much his custom anyway and, at the end of it, without Arthur asking me or my asking Arthur, I'd agreed to be coached by Arthur and he'd agreed to coach me.'

Macky and Snell both lived in the school-house at Mt Albert and they would go to Arthur's home on Sundays for their long runs, with Jean following in the car, and Snell was the one most likely to drop out and get in the car. Arthur adds, 'Mind you, he was only 15 at the time.'

Back to 27 January 1962, a magical night in Wanganui, made all the more memorable because of the atmosphere. It was a remarkable evening, calm but with thundery black clouds brooding over the city. A capacity 15,000 crowd jammed into the Gardens and the air was filled with a constant seethe of expectation. The spectators were so emotionally charged that, after the race, many came down to the arena, where they plucked handfuls of grass from the track to keep as souvenirs of one of the most astonishing events in New Zealand athletics. It wasn't only the time that was sensational, it was the chaotic scenes which followed.

Arthur's view of the race: 'Peter took only 0.1s off Herb Elliott's record but it was on a track probably four seconds slower than Dublin's Santry Stadium where Elliott ran his record. Peter was 5.2 seconds faster than Elliott's best grass track mile. He had to take the lead earlier than we intended because of the slow start – a 63-second first lap. Albie Thomas, who had paced Elliott to his record, finished third in Wanganui. And, of course, Peter had never before run a full-out mile.

'The race ended in confusion. For ten minutes, it was thought he had merely equalled the record, which was shown in the programme incorrectly as 3:54.4. Someone finally told the Wanganui officials that Elliott's record was 3:54.5. The tough little Englishman, Bruce Tulloh, who was the only one to challenge Peter after half the race was run, had to wait fifteen frustrating minutes before he learnt that he had cracked the four-minute barrier for the first time. He ran more than five seconds faster than he had ever run before. He had actually raced to the lead with only 385 yards to go but Peter, when he sprinted, was 20 yards clear in a handful of strides. Bruce finished 25 yards back and Albie was another 20 yards behind him.'

Officialdom managed another gaffe. Steve Ashby, the sponsoring Agfa's managing director, Auckland centre's Frank Sharp, a ticketed journalist and Arthur were ordered out of the middle of the ground, although Frank and Arthur were both official timekeepers. The overzealous man involved said later he didn't know who they were and he was only trying to clear the ground so the meeting could continue. Probably, by this time, 99 per cent of the crowd had lost all interest in any more events – they could only be anti-climactic.

Peter went down to Christchurch a week later and, on the grass track at Lancaster Park, ran world records for the 880 yards and 800 metres, which still stand as New Zealand records, testament to the subsequent decline of New Zealand athletics. Arthur, as his coach, was there. But he had to pay for his own air fare and accommodation. Even though Lydiard was now the internationally acclaimed coach of internationally revered runners who were making the NZAAA unexpectedly large profits, officials there did not think of putting their hands in their pockets to help him along. If he wanted to be there, he had to pay for everything.

'The race was another fantastic solo effort by Peter. Barry Robinson, a well-performed 400-metre specialist, was supposed to pace him through the first lap, but went out far too fast. Peter called to him to wait but Robinson didn't, so Peter in effect ran the entire two laps without pacing aid or any competition. The other runners in the race, including three top Americans, were just entering the finishing straight when Peter hit the tape at the other end.'

Incredibly, despite the gut-busting effort of running the world's fastest half-mile completely on his own, Peter was able to stop, watch the others come in and fall about and then trot off on a victory lap to let the Lancaster Park fans see him.

One hilarious reaction to Snell's world records emerged out of Australia. The Auckland journalist who acted for the Sydney *Sunday Mirror*, the late Robert Gilmore, sent off a brief piece and a photograph, which the *Mirror* splashed on its front page under the title, 'He's The New Wonder Man'. The caption below said: 'Peter Snell, New Zealand's wonder runner, shows the smooth style that helped to break three world records in eight days.'

Nothing wrong with the wording, but the picture was of Arthur, taken when he was 44. Gilmore apparently had acquired his picture surreptitiously, from the *Star*'s photo library, without checking it with anyone. To make matters worse – or perhaps more ridiculous – a story inside on Herb Elliott's hopes for a comeback and perhaps a clash with Snell carried a profile shot of 'Snell'. In fact, it was a profile of Arthur.

As Peter later commented, 'My reaction to seeing myself

depicted as weather-beaten and squint-eyed from peering into the sun was to split my sides laughing for five solid minutes. I've laughed frequently since.'

Peter's early experiences of Arthur were recorded in his 1965 biography, *No Bugles No Drums*. He was at Mt Albert Grammar and had just startled himself by winning a half-mile race in 1:54.1.

> I was an enthusiastic pupil. One of my first work-outs with Arthur was with Murray and others doing 220s. After, I think, three or four of these, I pulled out and said to Arthur, 'Well, these are fairly easy. Should I do them any faster if I feel like it?' Murray overheard this and his eyes nearly popped out. I think it irritated him more than a little. He was running them flat out...
>
> I had great respect for Arthur. I addressed him politely as Mr Lydiard until he told me curtly that his name was Arthur... I leaned on him heavily in the beginning and I was particularly anxious to please him with my progress.

Recently, Peter reflected on the way in which Arthur influenced his life: 'In the beginning, Arthur offered a vision beyond my wildest dreams. This vision motivated me to organise my life and strive to make his prediction a reality. On the way, he provided direction and encouragement, without which my Olympic achievements would not have been accomplished. His competitiveness, work ethic, honesty and integrity were qualities I admired and tried to emulate.

'Arthur's indirect influence is three Olympic gold medals. Having them has enhanced my life in many ways, and provided an enduring sense of achievement.

'In an attempt to understand why Arthur's training methods were so good, I became interested in exercise physiology and pursued a scientific career. Currently, I spend time explaining to skeptical coaches and sports scientists why "Lydiard training" works.

'Finally, Arthur unwittingly influenced my choice of a mate. After moving to Dallas to take up a post-doctoral fellowship in

1981, I met my second wife, Miki. She was a co-founder of a Dallas track club that Arthur visited each year to conduct a week-long running camp and that was where I met her.'

Meantime, Arthur's two-jobs' financial struggle was over. He was able to quit being a shoe factory foreman by day and a milkman by night and a coach and runner somehow in between through the helpful intervention of Auckland entrepreneur Gordon Dryden, who, in 1962, arranged for him to join Rothmans. This ended two years of what Arthur casually called 'a life that was more than hectic'. Rothmans also employed the great cricketer Bert Sutcliffe, New Zealand's champion All Black fullback Don Clarke and, later, Peter Snell. Arthur is constant in his appreciation of the sponsorship he was given by Rothmans and, later, by Winstone Ltd. It should be added that they were equally grateful for the work he did for them.

'Far from promoting the very antithesis of healthy lungs, my Rothmans' connection meant that I actually stopped people from smoking. I could say what I liked about people not smoking and I frequently did. Rothmans realised that, through me, they would help the kids, who weren't going to smoke, but, if their parents smoked, they'd be likely to turn to Rothmans. In fact, they went from 20 per cent of the market to more than 80 per cent in one year, when I was going round in their colours, saying, "Don't smoke".

'They were clever businessmen – their CEO, Ken Simich, was a very genuine person who saw that helping sports would also help his business – and they were more interested in shifting smokers' allegiances than in encouraging more people to take up smoking.'

At the same time, a number of big cigarette companies were heavily into sports sponsorship in New Zealand, but over the following years pressure against the tobacco industry mounted and such businesses were eventually completely barred from sponsoring sport. Whatever might be said against these companies, for a long period in New Zealand, track and field and tennis, in particular, were grateful for their backing.

Arthur says, 'We carried on with coaching my runners and organising international meetings with sponsors with such success that Lance Cross, a delegate at an NZAAA meeting, told me someone got up and asked, "Who's running athletics in this country? Is it us or Lydiard?" I was doing all this for nothing and I might have expected at least a small compliment and perhaps some help, rather than that kind of comment.

'Later on, when John Walker ran a sub-four minute mile at Mt Smart Stadium in Auckland, he drew 30,000 people and the guy that organised it got ten per cent of the gross gate. We packed the same number into Western Springs years earlier to see Snell and other internationals race a world-record mile and, later, a world record 1000 metres, on what was normally a cinder track used by midget cars – and nobody was paid for anything. What is mystifying is that the administration seemed happier to pay some entrepreneur ten per cent of the gate for organising a meet than to have me and my supporters do it for nothing.'

About now, Lydiard's influence on the world of middle-distance and distance running was to take a major step which was going to rob New Zealand of an asset it didn't appear to appreciate it had. Again, it wasn't Arthur who set the ball rolling but someone – with a lot more perception than the NZAAA hierarchy – who, luckily, arrived at exactly the right moment.

12

hello, America

ARTHUR REMEMBERS THE man who was the catalyst that changed his life. A leading United States coach, Forrest Jamieson, representing the American Peace Corps, came here on his way from the States to Indonesia. Shot put champion Les Mills introduced him to Arthur, and they went together to watch the running of the Auckland 10-mile championship on the Auckland waterfront, where six of the field ran under 49 minutes. Jamieson had never seen anything like it in his life and when he learnt that they were all trained by Arthur, he phoned Bill Bowerman, the University of Oregon coach in Eugene, and told him about all these New Zealanders who could run so fast.

Arthur recalls: 'Bowerman wrote to me, explaining that he was a good sprint and field events coach but he wasn't very good at middle- and distance-training. He felt inadequate in that area and asked if I could help. I was happy to and sent him my programme. He took on all aspects of my training for his sprint team, including 15-mile forest runs, which was a long way for a sprinter, and hill training on a golf course, which was a totally new sprint training approach. I was later shown the hill, which was about 400 metres long. Bowerman trained his sprinters up the hill and on a loop around to the bottom again and they would do this about twelve times. His athletes included the 400-metre champion in Rome, Otis Davis, the great Steve Prefontaine and Bill Dellinger, who ran second behind Murray Halberg in the Rome 5000 metres. Prefontaine was a certainty for an Olympic gold medal later on, but he was killed in a road accident before he could show what a truly wonderful runner he was.

Bowerman also later coached four of his team to break our 4 x 1-mile relay record.

'I had met Bowerman for the first time in Rome. He had established a high reputation as the Oregon coach at a time when I wasn't much more than a nuisance to the administrators here in New Zealand. When I got to Rome, I was lucky to get in the gate. Bill, of course, was more than welcome.

'Oregon has two universities and there was strong rivalry between them. Bowerman's immediate success with my training system gave him an edge. The coach at the other university, Oregon State in Portland, learnt what Bowerman was doing and began using my methods too, but he then moved to Champagne, Illinois, and took our methods there. Another runner at Champagne subsequently moved down to the university in Florida, where Geoff Galloway and Frank Shorter were among the runners based there. They also turned to my training and Galloway and Shorter both made the American team to Tokyo, where Shorter won a gold medal.

'By this time, I had set up a correspondence facility, operating with a small portable typewriter, which I carried around the world and replaced only in 2002 when it was finally fatally damaged. I bought another portable for forty dollars. Among my early correspondence pupils was Pat Clohessy, who was studying at a Texas university. He went on to win the USA indoor three-mile championship.

'Then Billy Mills, who was educated and trained at Kansas University, moved to Houston, where Pat was. They met and Pat got him onto my training methods. Billy went on to win the 10,000 metres at the 1964 Tokyo Olympics. Pat wrote and told me all about Billy before I went to Tokyo for the Games, so I already knew a lot about him when I met him there. I asked him how he managed our training. Billy said he had tried to run a hundred miles a week but he could manage only eighty, probably because he ran too fast in training. He said he had also developed some illness before he could do his pre-Games anaerobic training.

'This was probably a blessing in disguise because he might well have overdone the anaerobic training, as the Americans tend to do, which would have taken the edge off him and upset the training balance.'

In this way, Arthur's influence spread through the States, and his methods generated satisfying results. In 1962 he received the first of many invitations to America, where he held week-long seminars in numerous locations, including Red Hook, New York and in the mountains of Colorado, where he influenced a marathoner, Ron Daws, who later ran for the United States in the 1968 Mexico Olympics. Bowerman ceased coaching at Oregon in 1972, which now had such a good name that all the top runners went there, and Dellinger picked up the reins. Some time later, though, Bowerman reported to Arthur that he was worried Dellinger was using too much anaerobic work.

'Dellinger, I suppose, was after quick results, but it's history now that the Oregon runners stopped doing so well once Bowerman left,' Arthur comments.

'When I lectured in Des Moines, one of my audience was a coach from Boston, Bill Squires, who I heard speak years later in 1968 at the Peach Tree Road Race, where two young women I had trained, Heather Carmichael and Karen Petley, finished first and third. Bill didn't know I was in the audience when he said that he had adopted my methods after hearing me in Des Moines. At the time, he was successfully training several marathon runners, including the great Bill Rogers.

'Heather Carmichael won the Peach Tree in record time but I hadn't expected Karen to do so well. She was there because my original choice, Glenys Quick, had been injured. Paul Ballinger, who won all the long-distance races in New Zealand and clocked a 2:10 marathon in Japan, was also in my team. I had been training Paul since he was 15 – he still holds the record for the tough Rotorua marathon, which he set many years ago now. The team and I travelled all over the States in a hired car and I even won a few races myself in my age group.

'We were standing at the finish line of the Peach Tree, which had 23,000 runners, and I was watching a television screen when Heather came in first. The announcer didn't know who the hell she was and was floundering around trying to find a name for her. Then Karen joined me and I asked her where she had finished, because I hadn't seen her come in. She said she didn't know. They began calling the results, starting from the tenth place-getter, and I could see Karen's face getting longer and longer. They then said Karen was third and her excitement was marvellous to watch. I imagine mine was, too. The placing gave her invitations to run in other places in America.

'The top runners in the race had all stayed in hotels the night before but we spent the night in a camp and got up at 4 o'clock in the morning to get to the start line in time.

'Heather won a scholarship to Penn State University after that and was third in the American cross-country championship that year. Sadly, she slipped down some stairs and hurt her back, so we never saw the best of her. She is now married and working as a dietician in Auckland hospitals.

'When I was in Red Hook, I influenced a high school coach, Al Devereaux, who had brought his cross-country team along to hear me. Al took his team on to win several state cross-country championships and trained himself to win the national Masters cross-country title.

'In following years, I took several week-long seminars in Dallas, Texas, and the coach most involved was Dr Robert Vaughn, who trained a number of US track champions, including Francie Larrieu. Among other coaches who turned to my system was C. Mark Wetmore, of the University of Colorado in Boulder. In 2001, his runners were individual winners in the US cross-country and also the team champions, a feat never before accomplished by any coach. Another, Harold Smith, at South Point High School, is improving his team steadily.

'Pat Clohessy, who now lives in Chapel Hill, Brisbane, used to write to me about a 14-year-old, Rob de Castella, who he began training my way when he returned to Australia from the States. Pat was excited at the way "Deek" was improving and predicted he would leave his mark later on. He was correct; "Deek" became one of the world's great marathoners. Later on, Clohessy and de Castella took over as the heads of the Australian Institute of Sport and from then on the institute began to improve its standards because they applied my conditioning principles to several sports.'

The Lydiard system seems to have spread everywhere. Larry Eder, the editor of *American Track and Field*, on a trip to Spain recently, found that the Spaniards were using Arthur's methods extensively. Spain's neighbour, Portugal, took on those methods and produced a sequence of good runners, including the Los Angeles Olympic marathon champion, Carlos Lopez, and a string of outstanding women.

Arthur says he often wondered whether he was wasting his time talking to people on these tours, not knowing if they would carry through what he recommended. Yet the examples presented here show that those who had the patience and understanding to carry the programme through in its entirety and didn't screw up by trying shortcuts did get results. The shortcutters did a lot to discredit Arthur in some quarters by insisting they were following his principles when, in truth, they were abandoning the essential core of his system, patience.

Arthur convinced Rothmans to put up £1000 a year to sponsor an international coach to New Zealand, the idea being that domestic athletes and coaches would be able to improve themselves by listening to the overseas experts. Bill Bowerman was one of those who came over on the scheme. By then, he was deeply into training his athletes by Arthur's methods and his team of mile specialists held the 4 x 1-mile world record, beating the time Lydiard's motley crew set in Dublin.

When Arthur suggested to the NZAAA that Bowerman and his top Oregon track team should be brought to New Zealand for a summer tour, 'the bureaucrats told me that was not a good idea because it was the holiday period in New Zealand and no one would turn up. I told them to take the tour to the holiday centres where the people had gone. So we packed them in at Waimate and Nelson, major holiday spots in the South Island, and in Rotorua, in the North Island's Bay of Plenty, and pulled in another thirty thousand crowd in Auckland. We had no trouble getting the crowds, but the athletics people were not happy with me because I had had to tell them what to do. It's a wonder they didn't charge me to go in the gate at these meetings, but they probably hadn't thought of it.'

The Oregon team visit had an unexpected side effect, which

was to make Arthur Lydiard even more of a household name elsewhere in the world. They arrived in December 1961, just as the Auckland Joggers Club was being established. What interested Arthur when he met Bowerman again was that he was 52 inches (132 centimetres) around the waist. Arthur discovered this statistic when he accompanied Bowerman to buy a pair of slacks soon after his arrival.

'I took him up to Cornwall Park to meet the joggers and he was persuaded to go for a jog with the club's slow pack. They rapidly disappeared ahead of him, except for Andy Stedman, who kept stopping and waiting for him and encouraging him to keep on. Andy was 74 and had had three coronary attacks but Bowerman was no match for him. It gave him the bloody shock of his life and he was nearly in tears when I got back to the starting point from my run.

'I asked him what was wrong and he said, "I'm an athletics coach and that old guy's had three coronary attacks and he had to wait for me. From now on, I'm into training." He was in New Zealand for about a month and he got stuck into daily jogging so well that at the end of the tour he was able to fold over six inches [15 centimetres] of his new trousers. Down in Arrowtown, deep in the South Island, he ran 20 miles [32 kilometres] with me. It was a mark of his determination and of the value of a sensible approach that he went from no miles to twenty in four weeks.'

It was typical of the sport's administration generally in those days that, although the invitation to Bill to come to New Zealand was sent to America months ahead of the visit, the Amateur Athletic Union sat on it instead of sending it on to him. When Bill rang Arthur to ask where the invite was, Arthur checked and found this out. Bill got smartly on to the Governor of Oregon and had the invitation in his hands the same day. This time, it wasn't the New Zealand administration messing up, it was the Americans. 'We just couldn't win,' Arthur recalls.

It is intriguing to speculate what direction history might have taken if Bill Bowerman had not known the Governor of Oregon, because after his New Zealand induction as a jogger, Bowerman went home and started the jogging movement in America. When

Arthur went there in 1963, Bowerman already had several thousand people up and running. 'I arrived to give a talk at the Oregon track and 3000 people were jogging around waiting to hear me.'

Some years later, Bill published his own book on jogging and the book's introduction, by James M. Shea, of Eugene, Oregon, had this to say, with a certain degree of poetic licence and American imagery:

> As with most good ideas, jogging began in many places. It has some of the flavour of scientific findings that are announced simultaneously by different discoverers. No one knows who was the first jogger. Maybe it was one of the Greeks. They were fond of physical exercise, particularly running.
>
> In New Zealand, thanks to the work of Arthur Lydiard, the New Zealand Olympic coach, jogging is almost a way of life. Lydiard developed his version of jogging for some of his runners who were about to retire from competition and who were unwilling to give up the high level of fitness built through training.

This wasn't strictly correct, although it made a good story. The real story was a better one: Arthur's first joggers were a group of men who had had heart attacks but placed their faith in his theory, for which he had backing from some sports medicine experts, that gentle running to exercise the heart, which is a muscle like any other in the body, could only be beneficial. It was. Some of those originals went on to run remarkable distances without any strain and just got fitter.

Shea went on: 'Lydiard came up with the idea of combining conditioning with the stimulus of companionship by slow steady cross-country running done in loosely organised groups or "jogging" clubs. The active citizenry took to it in a big way. Whole communities, from toddlers to grandma, jog on weekends and holidays.'

Interestingly, Bowerman chose for one of the pictures in his book a shot of the man who finally brought him to realise his level of unfitness – Andy Stedman, running on the Auckland waterfront with another amazing New Zealand jogger, Reg Dawson. Reg began jogging as a totally overweight traffic cop – it was once suggested that seeing Reg directing traffic gave roading engineers the idea of circular roundabouts to smooth traffic flow – and ended up running distances of 50 miles or more in a vastly slimmed down and superfit body. Loose flesh flopped around as he ran, but inside there was a great heart. Many of his runs were staged to raise money for charities and Reg, who has since died, pulled in thousands of dollars over the years.

While Bowerman was in New Zealand, Arthur also taught him about the design and manufacture of running shoes and he went back to Oregon and became affiliated with Tiger, a company that was very supportive of Arthur and his runners, who ran in Tiger shoes.

'Some mix-up occurred, however, and Bowerman began making shoes himself and developed the waffle sole, which was picked up by Nike and gained them a big slice of the market. What got them into the shoe business in the first place was a court case over the Tiger mix-up, but it would also be fair to say that Nike's origins are rooted in New Zealand.

'Sadly, Bowerman's experimentation with running shoes seriously affected his health. He was working in a confined basement area beneath his home and the concentrated fumes from the acetones he was using upset his nervous system. He lived until he was 88, but during his final years he was a shadow of his former big self.

'Overall, I found working and talking with American coaches a rewarding, if sometimes frustrating, experience. Most of them had open minds, wanted to understand different viewpoints and were keen to learn anything that might help them become better coaches. Their thirst for knowledge was similar to that of the East Germans. They felt they had special problems, such as their college student athletes' long hours of work and study and the need to reach peak performance three times a year for the three racing seasons of cross-country, indoor track and outdoor track, but I have never found a country where similar problems did not exist.

'The simple answer is the same all over the world, too: try even harder. And the evidence has been produced by all those nations that did try harder and whose athletes did break through the mental barrier of training over long mileages. Today, distance running, for stamina and endurance and as a basis on which to build other skills, is the core of training regimes for a wide range of sporting activities.

'The Americans soon learnt that well-conditioned athletes could maintain top form for months on end as long as they balanced their programmes of hard racing with training programmes which allowed for recovery. The coaches' main fault was a failure to explain to athletes why they were required to do certain exercises. An athlete who doesn't understand why he is doing something, or being asked to do it, is unlikely to work with the required willingness. I have been out with Americans on training runs and seen them take shortcuts back home because they didn't appreciate the physiological and mechanical aims and importance of their workout. Runners in other countries began much the same way but soon learnt that successful training is intelligent training and intelligent training is knowing not only the *what* and *how* of an exercise but also, perhaps most importantly, the *why*.

'Another major trouble in America was a misunderstanding of the value and purpose of anaerobic training, which they used excessively in both volume and intensity, even in high schools. Another was the lack of organised clubs to cater for young runners when they left college. A lot of talent was lost that way, because so many promising athletes went back to live in areas where there were no clubs and no likelihood of there being any. The United States had huge depth in middle-distance running between 1962 and 1965. They had many milers under 3:57 and a big number under four minutes but the depth lessened after that and I put it down mostly to excessive anaerobic training as the coaches drifted back to the old German interval system. I guess the objective was faster, more immediate results than are possible when the training is better balanced.

'The potential of the modern-day American middle- and distance-runners is huge, as they have proved before, but it is not being properly tapped. Potential Olympic distance and middle-distance champions are everywhere in all countries and would emerge if coaches would concentrate more on aerobic conditioning and not burn their young runners out with excessive anaerobic training to try to gain quick results and points for their institutions.'

Arthur, who continues to help many American high school coaches and regularly advises them by phone or e-mail when they strike problems, cannot remember exactly how many times he has been to the United States but he has been there most years during the past four decades. His first visit to the States was also his longest. It was originally intended to be three months' duration, but was quickly extended to eight months because of the success of his lectures. An interesting development during his visits was that, when he lectured at universities, football coaches would come along to see how they could incorporate his methods into their programmes.

'One coach in California told me he was having a lot of trouble with hamstring injuries, so I got him to erect a ramp up to a landing on a college building, cover it with coconut matting and use that for the hill springing exercise the athletes use to achieve muscle balance and strengthening.

'I also got a ballet teacher in to teach them techniques for ankle flexibility. These big guys doing ballet exercises might have looked grotesque, but it worked – the team had no more hamstring pulls or leg muscle troubles. Today, footballers spend long times out of the game with those types of leg injuries because they are not carrying out the proper strengthening and muscle balancing exercises. If the muscles around tendons weaken, they fail to support the tendons and tears result. The muscles have to be both flexible and strong. There is also a lack of appreciation of the need to have opposing muscles properly balanced. Building the quads, the front thigh muscles, is dangerous if the hamstrings are not equally conditioned. Actually, the hams should be the stronger.

'One fault of football training is that these days players seem to be surrounded by all kinds of "experts" but they don't seem to fully understand what they should be doing. For instance, a lot of players still suffer from cramp. I think the problem is that a lot of the experts haven't done the training themselves and don't get their gym work properly balanced for the needs of footballers. Sure, they have to be strong, but they also have to be balanced.

'I helped the American Greg Lousey to the pentathlon silver medal at the Los Angeles Olympics. He was getting on by then, but he moved up to running 100 miles a week and was superfit. At a seminar in the States, someone asked Mark Allen, the great ironman triathlete, what weights he was lifting. He said, "I don't lift weights. I get on my bike at the bottom of a hill, put it into the highest gear I can manage and put pressure on myself that way. I get a balanced resistance on my muscles which weights won't and can't give me." Allen never had muscular trouble and he was the world's best for a number of years.

As an interesting corollary, Peter Snell, now an exercise physiologist with the medical school at the University of Texas in Dallas, made the point in a 2002 interview that his 800 metres world record, set in 1962, would have placed him second in the World Championships in Edmonton 40 years later. His opinion, independently in line with Arthur's, when he was asked what distance runners were doing today that is better than four decades ago, was: 'Nothing at all.' With the best university scholarships, the best facilities and the best exercise physiologists in the world, runners' times were no better.

Snell said he could not believe that Arthur's ideas were now considered outdated and passé, given that nothing had been developed in 40 years to disprove, either in theory or practice, the simple core of the Lydiard system – that slow training makes you faster. But, when American distance runners were shut out of medals at Edmonton and the Sydney Olympics, because they ran out of gas and were often buried in the last lap, the track and field experts brought in a former hurdler to teach them sprint techniques.

What they needed, of course, was a fresh injection of Arthur Lydiard.

Between 1961 and 1965, Arthur's affairs seemed at last to be running smoothly. Jogging was about to explode as a recreational and fitness essential, Arthur was establishing what he hoped would be fruitful contacts with other coaches and, for the moment, he was being looked after by Rothmans for what he was, a natural moulder of athletic talent. Then the very coaches he was trying to help turned round and bit the hand that fed them.

13

'cancel it,' the coaches said

THE NEW ZEALAND Coaches Association had been based in Auckland but in the mid 1960s it moved to Wellington, the heartland of we-know-best, head-in-the-sand officialdom. Soon afterwards, the association announced that it didn't need the £1000 Rothmans was putting up for an overseas coach each year – 'Cancel the damn thing,' they said.

As well as Bowerman, Arthur had brought out Jim Bush, the American sprint coach; an English expert on mechanics; and the Russian coach, Khorobkov, and his team, and suddenly, none of their expertise was wanted. 'Maybe the powers-that-be were anti-smokers, I don't know,' Arthur says, 'though Rothmans kept well out of the limelight. They just helped to make things happen and, for New Zealand athletics, it was free money for valuable international experience. For example, the Russians who came out in 1963 with Khorobkov were all Olympic champions. They must have had something to teach us and one of the great benefits of these coaching tours was that we took them to the smaller centres.'

Arthur and his runners were putting themselves about, too. One remarkable day, Snell, Halberg, Bill Baillie, sprinter Doreen Porter, hurdler Avis McIntosh and some other athletes went north to the little settlement of Puhoi, famous for its rich history and its historic pub, and turned on races on a rough grass track marked out on their reserve. The entire population of Puhoi was there, along with many people from Auckland. No records were broken but the meeting was a huge sporting and social success.

Another time, Arthur and his troupe went to the tiny North Island township of Galatea, between the vast emptiness of the Urewera mountains, revered by local Maori tribes for their spiritual significance, and the huge sprawl of the Kaingaroa State Forest, then one of the world's largest pine forests. The Galatea club launched on that 1960s visit is still going today; Arthur went back there recently to present the prizes at their annual end-of-season function.

'Among the athletes at that first Galatea meeting was a young girl who had earlier won the club's 400 metres. When I was asked what I thought of her, I said she looked like an 800-metre runner. Later, in Munich, where I was attending the Olympic Games as the Danish coach, I was walking through the tunnel with one of my runners, when a young woman said, "Hello, Mr Lydiard". It was the same girl and she was running for England in the Olympic 800-metres final.'

That Galatea incident is significant, because it verifies Arthur's contention that, if you fit the athlete to the correct event, you can find Olympic-class athletes anywhere.

'It is,' he comments, 'one of the remarkable facets of New Zealanders and our way of life that a champion runner can come out of a place as small and remote as Galatea, which only just gets on to some maps of New Zealand. There are champions everywhere. Every street's got them. All we need to do is train them properly. The rest of the world now does, but we don't any longer.'

It has often been said that New Zealand suffers from the tall poppy syndrome and there are plenty of instances in many sports which suggest it is true. For some reason, there is immediate resentment when someone steps out of the shadows of mediocrity and achieves success by doing something different. When Snell, Halberg and company began running the rest of the world off their middle- and long-distance feet, a significant New Zealand reaction was that Arthur had struck it lucky by cornering a bunch of super-runners. But they weren't; they were mostly ordinary youngsters who lived around Arthur's neck of the Auckland woods, began training with him and produced the results that proved his system worked. Luck had nothing to do with it – dedication and belief had everything to do with it. But could you convince the knockers? Not a chance.

Arthur puts another amusing spin on it. 'When we ran the 4 x 1-mile relay record in Dublin, the beaten English team offered the excuse that they were just a county team. Halberg retorted that the New Zealanders were just a suburban team. However, the "experts" decided my system was a flash in the pan. I would burn the boys out in no time at all and then what would I do? Even the fact that most of the rest of the world's coaches and athletes are now training my way doesn't seem to persuade the New Zealand athletic fraternity that the Lydiard system is still the only way to go.

'It is my opinion that modern runners are soft. They want, and expect, to have everything done for them and they have no taste for the hard work that successful conditioning demands. They are satisfied with the shortcuts despite all the evidence that they don't work.'

As well as entertaining and encouraging people in New Zealand's smaller towns, the organised flow of coaches and their teams through the country had another benefit. Runners tend to be a close-knit and hospitable species, anywhere in the world, and allowing men and women of different nations to socialise brought down the same kind of barriers that are still claimed to be lowered every four years at the Olympics. The extra advantage of the Rothmans domestic tours was that the visitors had a chance to see, experience and understand how other people lived.

The Russians, who toured New Zealand at a time when their homeland was regarded with some suspicion, probably had a harder time than most. Arthur broke the ice by taking their coach, Khorobkov, and Vladimir Kutz, the team manager, to Wellington to see *The Sound of Music*, which they had heard about but never seen. Later, in Christchurch, he took them to a big party at the home of Daphne Jamison, who was a Canterbury athletics official for many years. 'The noise was astounding,' he remembers. 'The walls were practically going in and out – until Khorobkov walked in and said something in Russian. Everything stopped, silence descended and I decided it was best to get him out of there and let everyone carry on enjoying themselves.'

However, when the tour moved to Auckland, Arthur arranged for his athletes and their wives and girlfriends and the Russians to go to a nightclub and persuaded one of the young women in the office where he was working to go as Khorobkov's partner. 'He danced with her all night, and I know he was a very happy man. It was probably the first time in his life when he was somewhere where no one knew him or watched him. He let his hair down completely. I hadn't even told other people at the party who he was. By way of appreciation, when I later went to Russia, they arranged a beautiful blonde for me as my interpreter. It was a nice reciprocal gesture, but I didn't take the offer up.

During this period of comparative calm, in 1964, Arthur had turned his hand and mind to training Doreen Porter and Avis McIntosh, conditioning them with distance running during the winter to prepare them for the Tokyo Olympic Games. Avis relished the work, but the statuesque Doreen, who reigned over New Zealand sprinting for five years and also won a number of beauty contests, was somewhat reluctant. She had a tendency to complain loudly about how awful she felt. Both women went to Tokyo short of fast work because of an exceptionally bad Auckland winter. With no all-weather track to train on, they used the roads, parks and a trotting track for all their training and, when they stepped out for their heats in Tokyo, were running competitively on a track for the first time in more than three months.

Despite this disadvantage, Avis missed qualifying for her hurdles final by a mere five centimetres; she had unluckily drawn the inside lane on the cinder track and it was waterlogged after heavy rain. Doreen established herself as a world-class runner by running fifth in the 200 metres semi-finals and later performed well on indoor tracks in the United States.

Arthur recalls: 'When I was asked by Bud Winter, the US coach, what I thought I was doing training sprinters, I explained that I was merely conditioning them to do more slow training to go faster. They were doing hill springing and bounding and taking hour-long runs, which were all foreign to most sprinters in those days, and it worked because they gained the endurance to train longer and harder to run better than they ever had. They were breaking New Zealand records in training.

'There is no reason why New Zealand cannot produce good sprinters; it's only a matter of conditioning them properly so they have the endurance to handle the actual sprint training and racing. When Bud Winter saw how well and how quickly it had worked with Avis and Doreen, he went back home to San José University and started his sprinters running around the hills for an hour with his distance runners, much as Bill Bowerman had done. Typically, the sprinters weren't too happy until he made a game of it, with the distance runners in red singlets chasing the sprinters in blue singlets and trying to tag them. He also mixed a lot of fast, relaxed running in with his sprint drills.

'Bud helped me with the techniques of sprint training, I helped him with the conditioning phase and he won all the sprint gold medals at the Mexican Olympics. Bud, I believe, was the greatest sprint coach the world has ever seen. He died some years ago but he is still ranked as the best.

'He told me in Tokyo that Mexico would host the next Olympics. Since everyone was expecting Paris or some other city to win, I asked how he knew and he said the Mexicans were fêting the African nations' delegates in fine style and they would block-vote Mexico in. Back in New Zealand, I remarked to the media that Mexico would be the next Olympic Games host country and I was laughed at. But we all know where the Games went.'

14

the stable-mates

THE DEEDS AND the associated publicity which surrounded Arthur's Olympic medal-winning, record-breaking trio of Halberg, Snell and Magee have always tended to eclipse or at least obscure the talents of many other superb runners he moulded out of the raw material of his own neighbourhood.

Bill Baillie was perhaps the outstanding character in the stable – and still is. Arthur remembers: 'I was on the Auckland centre committee when Bill was running quite a bit and he used to get himself into all sorts of problems. The officials those days were very efficient and officious and if you didn't do things exactly right you got into trouble.

'A lot of runners went down to Tauranga every year for a big track meet. Bill went one year and apparently they slept on palliasses on the floor in a school hall. Bill had been out somewhere and he got back to the hall after midnight and found all the others asleep. So, being Bill, he got a hose and hosed them all out.

'He ran away when they chased him and decided to jump off the edge of the waterfront on to the beach to give them the slip. But there was no bloody beach there and Bill, still wearing his best suit, wound up in the sea. When this incident came up before the centre, they were going to crucify him, but I was able to talk them out of it. But it was typical Bill Baillie. He'd do silly things just for fun; there was no malice in the man at all.'

In another incident at the Tokyo Olympics, Bill led a bunch of athletes in a bowing demonstration in front of the Emperor. Again, it was all fun, but it caused a lot of upset because it was thought that he and his mates were being rude.

In those days, you had to be picked by your centre to compete in the national championships. Bill was the New Zealand 880 yards champion at the time he had to do his compulsory military training. He was a young man who put on weight very quickly, and he gained seven kilograms on army food. When he came out of the army, he had very little time to get ready for the Auckland champs and could finish only fourth or fifth in the half-mile because he just wasn't fit. So he wasn't selected for the Auckland team. However, as defending champion, he was entitled to enter anyway, so he ran in the nationals in Lynndale colours and was cheered loudly by the crowd because they didn't like the way the team had been chosen and Bill always had a lot of fans. He won the title again but, this time, not for Auckland.

One story which underscored Bill's belief in himself goes back to the daunting Lydiard weekend endurance course, the Waiatarua. John Davies, with a best time of 4:15 for the mile, had recently begun running the circuit. One particular day, he was struggling to stay near the lead pack of Lydiard runners, but as they reached Titirangi and headed downhill on the way home he caught up with Bill. He smartly tucked himself in behind Bill without saying a word. Bill soon became aware of the youngster on his heels, looked back over his shoulder and said, 'Boy, you're going to set a PB today.' That remark also showed Bill's ability to needle young runners and so inspire them to do better. Arthur was not above using him for that purpose.

'Bill won Auckland and New Zealand titles all the way through, from 880 yards to six miles because we used to sit down at a table each year and decide which events we would win and who would win them. Baillie said one year he wanted the mile, so the other guys all stayed out and let him win it. He never won the marathon because, although he was a good marathon runner, he was not a great one. I think his best time was 2:21.

'Bill was a very good, solid runner but he was hunch-backed because he had lifted weights as a youngster and this had given him a curvature of the spine. When he ran, he was always too tight. He couldn't relax, which is the key to good distance running. His best distance was 3 miles/5000 metres, but he never stuck to one distance long enough to make it his own.'

Nevertheless, he set world records for both one hour (running 12 miles, 960 yards, 7 inches) and 20 kilometres (59:28.6) in 1963 – wiping Emil Zatopek's times through a combination of pure guts and the pace-making cooperation of Magee, Puckett, Neville Scott, Jeff Julian and some Japanese runners then training in New Zealand. It was Puckett who made the greatest contribution.

'In the Tokyo Olympics,' Arthur remembers, 'I gave Bill and Murray a trial about ten days before their 5000-metre event and Halberg won by about a hundred metres. But he then got Tokyo asthma and couldn't run well. Baillie wasn't as fit as he could have been because he'd taken his wife on a trip to America instead of concentrating on his preparation and he was short on condition. But he got out there and ran fifth behind Bob Schul. Bill was annoyed because New Zealand wasn't doing very well at the Games and he tried his very hardest to make up for it. We never saw the best of him at the Olympics.'

Bill is still very fit today, but he does all his anaerobic running in the water because he's concerned about getting injured. He has worked his body hard all his life and he's very sensible about protecting it. He loves his running and has become a deadly competitor in masters' and age-group ironman triathlons all around the world.

'The great thing about my boys was that they helped each other. Halberg and Magee were a good example. They were never sure who could beat the other over 5000 metres and they fought some great races. But they always worked together.

'Bill Rodgers, the father of the fine middle-distance runner, Kerry, was another I trained. He won the national 6-mile title running in bare feet and broke the national record in the process. He went up to Queensland with Halberg and Baillie to get away from the bad New Zealand weather leading up to the 1964 Olympics, but he didn't gain selection for New Zealand. Instead, he got a job in the Olympic Village, sweeping up leaves and watching guys training who couldn't run as fast as he could. We never saw the best of Bill Rodgers. He had great potential and improved so rapidly in one year that, given the encouragement, he could have been another great New Zealand Olympian.

'It was bad selection. The main trouble with too many

selectors is that they go on current times. They can't foster potential because they can't see it. They don't understand. Instead of spending money on athletes who have been around for a few years, they should spend it on the potentially good ones. It's wrong to waste it on those who have already established themselves.

'Roy Williams was a classic example of poor selection. He was the 1966 Commonwealth Games champion and the eighth best decathlete in the world and they didn't pick him for the Olympics. What do you have to do? Get on the right side of the officials? Others get selected who never show their full potential because, in trying to qualify too close to the event, they leave their best on the track; and there are those who, once they're selected, seem to think they don't have to do much else. Being chosen is the limit of their imagination or their ambition. It's also a mistake to require athletes whose times already qualify them for selection, to do extra "proving" trials when they are in the middle of build-up work or it is too close to the event.

'Jeff Julian and some of the others were very tenacious runners. They aspired to be great and they did very well. Julian won the pre-Olympic marathon before Tokyo, but he blew it by tearing around Tokyo selling whisky. He'd been to Japan before and he decided he could make a nice profit by taking whisky with him and selling it to the Japanese. On this occasion, as on many others, he lacked the application needed to perform well.

'Ray Puckett was a classic example of someone who we saw run as well as he could and reached his limit. His best marathon time was 2:14. Ray had the mettle to run himself right out and he often did.

'John Davies in 1965 beat Schul and Ron Clarke over 3000 metres and would have been a very fine 5000-metre runner. He was another we never saw the best of, but he was possibly unlucky to have been around at the same time as Snell – and then he got injured. I was in Mexico at the time and I'm not sure what happened. I think it was a cycling accident. He wasn't quite as fast as Snell at the shorter distances so, although he got third in the Tokyo 1500 metres, he couldn't truly foot it with the world's best milers.'

15

the rising sun

SNELL AND HALBERG were invited to run in indoor meets in Japan in 1962 and Arthur went with them and was asked to stay on to help the Japanese with their distance training programmes. His interpreter for his subsequent lecture tour through the country was Professor Takanaka, who spoke very good English. He and Arthur have been friends ever since.

'The Japanese were great hosts and generous with gifts – and after a while I got used to sitting with my legs crossed and not getting cramp. Murray, who was never very supple, had to sit sideways with his legs out straight.'

That wasn't the worst thing that happened to Murray. Part of the early hospitality before the boys raced was a visit to a bath-house, where, before the attendant could stop him, Halberg put his foot into the bath, not realising the water was boiling hot. His foot came up in a mass of blisters and when he pulled his running shoe on the next day, the blisters bulged over the sides. It must have been total agony, but Murray had known severe pain before and he showed what a tough little guy he was by winning his race. Snell, without blisters, also won.

'I went out one day to teach the Japanese my system of hill training,' Arthur recalls. 'We went out into the countryside with a bunch of their runners and we were all standing round, with no dressing room or any other privacy. I had no alternative but to strip off and get into my running gear on the roadway in front of all these interested people. But it was a beautiful setting for our training. All the hills were terraced and covered with fruit trees. I sent the runners off up one of the hills, yelling at them to keep going and not to stop. When they came down, I said, "Okay, now do it again." Their jaws dropped. They didn't think I could be so hard on them. But they did it.

'In our last week in Japan, we went to an island, Oshima, off the coast at Atima. It was a beautiful island with an active volcano in its centre and we ran the 20 miles round its coastline for training. The island had no electricity, so the residents kept charcoal fires going all night under covers and took the covers off and stirred the fires back into life first thing in the morning, brewing a pot of green tea on top. While we were running round the coast, I spotted a track leading in towards the middle of the island. We were told it was used by students who had failed their exams and went in there to kill themselves in the crater's molten lava. Well, that's what they told us.

'On our last night, we had a question and answer session, during which one stern-faced athlete asked, "Coach, I am a married man – what about sex, satisfying my wife?" I said, "Well, let's put it this way. Don't use it for your warm-up." Professor Takanaka had to ask me twice what I said and it was the only time I got a laugh out of these guys. They took everything we did or said very seriously.

'The professor also caused me some embarrassment at a function when I told him I wanted to relieve myself. He called a girl over and she took me to the urinal and stood beside me, holding a hot towel, while I urinated. The habits and customs of some countries take a lot of getting used to.

'I was given life membership of the Japanese Racing Club and went to a meeting in Osaka while I was there. I was sitting next to one of Japan's princes, which helped to make it an interesting day, although he didn't tip me any winners. The people around me were drinking their way steadily through big quart bottles of saki. They had a very different system of betting, in which you split the race fields in three and back up to six horses on a line. It didn't work for me.'

Arthur had to return to New Zealand through Australia, where Customs officers went through his bags and found some pearl necklaces, which had been given to him as gifts. He hadn't mentioned them, but explained that they were gifts and he was taking them home to his wife.

'Customs said I would have to pay duty on them and I said I had no intention of doing that. I said I didn't know the value of the pearls, because I hadn't bought them. The Customs guy retorted, "We'll soon find the value of them." They held my plane up while we argued about it. In the end, I said, "Look, you do what you want, but I only came to your bloody country because I had to, not because I wanted to." After that, we went on through with no more problems.'

One outcome of Arthur's Japan visit was a meeting with the great coach Kiyoshi Nakamura, who subsequently decided to bring his team to New Zealand to train. This worried Arthur. He was concerned that bringing Japanese down here to train might upset the men who had been prisoners of war not so many years earlier. When he got back to New Zealand, he contacted one of his pioneer joggers, Nate Jaffe, who had also been one of the first New Zealanders to be captured by the Japanese and had come home after the war looking like a skeleton. Nate said bringing the Japanese to New Zealand would be no problem. It was his experience that they were far from being all bad. Some of the Japanese soldiers guarding the prison camp had shared their rations with him at the risk of being caught and shot. Nate was right and Japan sent teams of runners to New Zealand for years after that initial visit. Nakamura used to take them down to the wilds of the south-western South Island for long periods and they frequently competed with New Zealanders.

'The Japanese are still using my training system. I got a message recently from a runner who had been training with a little Japanese girl, predicting she would finish first or second in the marathon at the Sydney Olympics. She missed a medal, but apparently ran very well, so the effect on the Japanese has been a long-lasting one.'

By 1963, athletes from various parts of the world had climbed on to the Lydiard winning wagon, among them American miler Tom O'Hara, a tough runner from Chicago, who won the US championship in 1963 and made the team for the 1964 Tokyo Olympics. Two weeks before the championship, Arthur put him on the track with John Davies and Peter Snell for a trial over three-quarters of a mile. Snell was first, O'Hara second and Davies third, about 10 metres back, but Arthur considered then that all three would give a good account of themselves in Tokyo.

Unfortunately, O'Hara developed Tokyo asthma, the same ailment that afflicted Murray Halberg. Both suffered from violent headaches. They were not alone: many other athletes were affected.

'Halberg ran far below his capabilities in the 5000 metres because he was sick and O'Hara couldn't start in the 1500 metres, which made it pretty sure that Davies would get the bronze medal behind Snell, because we had them both in that race. Snell was favoured to win after his terrific win in the 800 metres and worked his way to the final comfortably. Davies nearly missed qualifying by leaving his sprint too late in the semi. He took off with about 300 metres to go but so did several others and he was left four wide on the bend. He was able to scramble desperately into the final by finishing fourth.

'I considered it important psychologically to discuss the final with the boys two days before it was run and I then cautioned them not to talk about it again – as if they needed to remind themselves how to run the race. I assured them they would do well anyway and it was better to play cards or go to the movies during those next two days than dwell on the running of the race.

'In planning how the race should be run, I suggested to John that he should take the lead at the start of the third lap so that he was in a better position to sprint at the finish. I knew the Frenchman Michel Bernard would lead early on as I had observed that that was the way most French runners ran their races. So it transpired. Bernard set the early pace. John took over with two laps to go and was able to maintain this placing until the last 200 metres, when Peter took the lead with a withering sprint. Davies slipped to fourth, but he was able to get past one of the runners again and finish third behind the Czech, Josef Odlozil.

'Before this race, John was under the impression that he could sprint well, but this was not so. Tokyo proved it to him.

Peter had run six races in seven days, yet he took the 1500 metres gold medal easily by about 40 metres. He said afterwards, "It was like a training run." He was not bragging, just stating a fact. He had dominated the 800 metres in much the same way. He'd made a lot of progress from earlier in the year, when he'd been drifting away.

'There was an occasion when Keith Scott, a wonderful stalwart of the Owairaka club, was giving Peter a massage and Peter said drowsily in the middle of it, "You know, Keith, Lydiard's getting too much of my glory." So when he asked me if I could set out a schedule for him, I told him to write his own schedule and I would have a look at it. He did that, I had a look at it and said, "Peter, you train on that and I doubt very much whether you'll make the [Tokyo Olympic] finals." I told him to use John Davies' schedules, which is one reason why he ran the 1500 metres as well as the 800. As it eventuated, it worked out very well.'

During the closing ceremony at the Tokyo Olympics, the Czechoslovakian managers asked Arthur to visit their country and lecture there. He agreed and went there as part of a tour of Europe in 1965. He spent a week visiting their facilities and talking to their coaches about training and other topics.

'They took me to their main stadium, where one of the coaches became very tearful as he told me about the people who had been shot there by the Germans during the war. One of his neighbours' entire family, including a 15-year-old girl, had been killed. They were all shot in the back of the head.

'The following week, I was a guest at the Spartakiad, a very big gymnastic meeting held in a large sports ground that measured about two hundred metres long by a hundred and fifty metres wide. Between seven and ten thousand athletes from all over the country were there for the two-day event. They provided a grand display which I enjoyed immensely.

'Bill Baillie and John Davies joined me as they were to compete in some meetings, then Bill and I were to go on to Belgrade. I remember, when I arrived in Czechoslovakia, being asked how much money I had in total. I thought little of this and filled in the form truthfully. Bill and I were staying in Brno, in the south, and were to fly to Belgrade but, for some reason, plans were altered and we were put on a train which was going to take twelve or more hours to reach Belgrade. I don't think they told the Belgrade people of the change in travel and that we were going to arrive by train.

'About three miles into Hungary, the train stopped and the police came through, checking our possessions and our money. This was to ensure we had not given any money to people trying to escape from the Communist countries. Since we had not expected to go by train, we did not have any Hungarian currency, so the man running the cafeteria on the train would not sell us anything. I guess he was too scared of the police.

'When we finally made Belgrade about ten o'clock at night, I went up and down the railway station asking for anyone who spoke English and eventually found someone who phoned the athletics people and they came and rescued us. The train journey had been interesting, although it was certainly not the best or most desirable way to travel, because you could see at an uncomfortably close range how the Communists controlled the people.'

Arthur returned to New Zealand with an enhanced and expanding international reputation. Despite this, however, sports management and most coaches continued to ignore New Zealand's most inspiring and successful coach. It meant that the country's magical era of track running was about to end.

Part Two: The Nomad

16
mañana land

ARTHUR TOOK UP a coaching contract with the track and field association in Mexico because 'I wasn't very settled in New Zealand and it offered the chance to do what I then most liked doing, training athletes. It was a challenge, too, and I approached it with considerable excitement. After the success I had had with my small group of New Zealand runners, none of whom was a superman, what could I do with a whole nation to work with? There is no country in the world that does not have the potential to succeed and Mexico had the added incentive of being the 1968 Olympic host.'

He arrived in Mexico City early one morning and that afternoon had his first experience of running at altitude – he was 3355 metres above sea level and out with the Mexican athletes for the first time. Fortunately for Arthur, he had very well-developed cardiovascular efficiency as a result of the huge running mileages he had accumulated, mainly in the midday heat in New Zealand.

'I found I could run better than they could, even though they were born up there,' he recalls with a slight air of astonishment. 'I had a dry throat because of the rarefied air, but that didn't affect my ability to run well. So one thing I was able to learn very quickly about altitude training is that, if you have cardiovascular efficiency, you can handle it. That has to come first or altitude training is a waste of time.'

The classy New Zealand miler, Dave Sirl, joined Arthur in Mexico for a time and was assessed by physiologists to see how he was affected by the altitude. 'They took him to their laboratory, did all the tests, then shot him into a plane and flew him straight down to Vera Cruz, took him to another laboratory and tested him again to see what had happened. They found that, very quickly, he lost red cells. He came back up to the high altitude, was tested again and it was found that, with the same speed, red cells were released again.

'New Zealand athletes who have used high altitude training have never done very well. Our walker at the Sydney Olympics had that experience and so did our triathletes. Our world-ranked Hamish Carter should have learnt that altitude conditioning was no good when he performed very poorly in Sydney. In contrast, Mike Ryan, who had never trained at altitude, only at sea level, came third in the Olympic marathon in Mexico and the Australian Ralph Doubell, who had also never done any high-altitude training, won the 800 metres.

'However, the belief in high-altitude training's benefits remains strong; the trouble is the correct method of using it isn't usually followed. Quite simply, the moment you get off a plane at a high altitude, your steady state, that fine point of balance between aerobic and anaerobic effort, becomes lower. What was previously high aerobic training becomes low anaerobic effort, and it is well established that you cannot do a lot of training anaerobically. High-altitude training can only work if you race immediately after you come down to a lower level. Another side-effect of this training is that, in contrast to the dry mouth and throat experienced at height, about three days after you come back to sea level you develop heavy mucous secretions and good sleep becomes difficult.'

It didn't take Arthur long to decide that the Mexican athletes had high potential – and not much longer to realise that he wasn't going to get the cooperation, politically, that he needed.

'When I wanted anything for my training programme, the man I had to see was General Jose de J. Clarke, who was in sole charge of Olympic preparations, and it was soon evident that we had different objectives,' Arthur says, with a strong touch of anger. 'The first frustration was the Mexican notion of time. I like to get things done, I don't have time to waste and the Mexican way took some adjusting to. Quite early, I made a three o'clock appointment for a meeting with General Clarke. I was there at three. He turned up at five. An American coach told me I should always arrive two hours after any time set by the general. I did that for my next meeting, trying to play him at his own game, and I still beat him by ten minutes.

'I didn't take kindly to his lateness or to the curt manner he adopted in his dealings, as if we were all privates in his army. And it always proved a waste of time. The American coaches had warned me from the beginning that I should just go with the flow and accept the situation, but the general had established through the media that he had brought the best coaches in the world to prepare the Mexican Olympic team and that the responsibility for success or failure was ours.

'The issue of running shoes was a classic example of his behaviour. The runners I was training didn't have any decent running shoes. Some of them ran with the soles of their footwear flapping around. It wasn't good enough for two-hour runs on hot roads.

'We knew General Clarke was getting money to buy shoes for them so, with my interpreter, Jose Contrares, who had been a room-mate of Jim Ryun at the University of Kansas, I drove twelve hours north-west from Mexico City to the Canada Shoe Factory in Guadalajara and told the manager what I wanted and how I wanted them made. He said, "Arthur, take some sample shoes back and show the general and tell him you can get all the shoes you want for nothing. I'll do everything I can to help you."

'We stayed a few days in Guadalajara, at the shoe company's expense, while the sample shoes were made. They were excellent but, when I showed the shoes to the general and told him of the offer, he threw them across the room and said, "We don't need any free shoes." Like a lot of other Games funds, any shoe money, I am sure, was going into his pocket and he didn't want anyone to know we could get shoes for nothing.

'I told the pentathlon coach about my shoe trouble and he laughed. "Arthur," he said, "you've got nothing to complain about. I don't have any guns to shoot with and I don't have any horses to ride and I haven't got a pool to swim in – nothing at all. You don't really have a problem."'

Dave Sirl trained with Lydiard's Mexicans and Arthur remembers one day when they ran into a small village – Arthur was following in his car – and stopped at a shop selling pulque, which he describes as 'a very nice drink made from fermented cactus juice'.

'The pulque was brewed in large earthenware jars and, to drink it, you just pushed the flies and muck off the top and dipped a cup in,' he says. 'I liked it. David was thirsty so I told him to have some of this pulque and he downed it as if it was just water. It didn't do him any harm, but he was rather startled by the effect it had on him. When you distil pulque, of course, it becomes tequila.'

From the start, Arthur had to outfox the cunning of his young runners. When he went out running with them first, he went ahead to show them the pace and style he was looking for, but, when he looked back, he found himself alone. The Mexicans were all relaxing on the team bus, watching Arthur do the running. One after another, they'd developed blisters, or sore heels, or muscle problems and had pulled out, leaving Arthur to run alone through the arid cactus country. 'After that, I always locked the bus door and told them they'd get no food or drink until they finished the run. A few put the ultimatum to the test and it was fascinating to watch the limps and hobbles vanish as it dawned on them that I meant what I said.

'But, once the rules were laid down and accepted, they proved to be good lads and, running through the villages, I always relented when they asked if they could have a drink of pulque. Because it was alcoholic, it wasn't permitted in the Games Village but it actually gave them vitamins and minerals they would never have got otherwise. They lived on corn and chicken and mice and stuff like that, so pulque was a diet supplement that, in moderation, was good for them.

'Tradition says that an Indian girl discovered how to make pulque and, when Montezuma found out how good it was, he married her. It was a good dowry.'

Arthur found the Mexicans were friendly, fun-loving and hospitable and, on one occasion, at Toluca, a town about 3000 metres above sea-level, which produced many good Mexican runners, he was a guest at a remarkably noisy party.

'Guys were coming in through the windows to join us and we athletes were looked after like rangatiras [princes]. But on the way home, the guys in my car suddenly fell very silent. I asked them what the matter was, because they were usually noisy and always chattering. One said quietly, "Arthur, you are on the wrong side of the motorway."'

Like the worthy General, some of the other coaches in Mexico were not exactly cooperative. Arthur was given the middle-distance runners to train and an American coach was given the sprinters. But Arthur soon found that the American was training one of his 800-metre boys to beat the distance runners. 'I noted the methods he was using, which were wrong, and when we all went to a Vera Cruz track meeting, I told one of my boys, Federico Vera, to go all out from the 300-metre mark and keep going. He did and gained a long lead which he had the stamina to hold the rest of the way. The American's runner was left struggling in his wake.

'I went to the American and said, "The day you can out-coach me is the day I give up coaching." I had no more bother with him.'

Arthur is not a picky eater, apart from a total hatred for fish, but he found he had to be ultra-cautious about what he ate in Mexico. The main problem was the risk of ingesting amoeba, which were a constant in much of the vegetable foods and could cause anaemia. He still thinks today that an amoebic infection might have contributed to Mike Ryan's form decline after he came back from Mexico.

'For instance, you never eat lettuce there because you cannot wash the amoebas off. We always had to wash bananas under the tap to get the amoebas off the skins to avoid infection. I never ate the skin of tomatoes. The centres were all right, but the skins were dangerous.

'It was an oddity, but a Mexican doctor, who became a good friend, told me that, in Mexico City, it was safe to drink tap water because it came from an artesian well underneath what was once a lake in the middle of the city. But he said the bottled water should be avoided. The water in the villages was always unsafe. Although Mexico City now has a vast population, the artesian well still operates safely.'

Bandits, like amoeba, tended to be everywhere in Mexico in those days and Arthur was never allowed to drive his Games' car out of Mexico City at night because of the danger they presented. It was not uncommon for bandit gangs to place logs across roads to stop the buses going down to Acapulco so they could rob the passengers. And Arthur soon learnt never to put his shoes on in the morning without shaking them first. Otherwise there was a chance your foot might be sharing the space with a scorpion. All in all, life in Mexico was an education.

'Norman Read, after the 1966 Commonwealth Games in Jamaica, came to stay with me for a couple of weeks so I introduced him to the Mexican walking team's coach. It was to Norman's credit that, from then on, the Mexicans produced some very good walkers. The boys I trained were good athletes and they would do anything for me. When the Mexican Olympic committee asked me, after I had been there a few months, who I thought would be the best athlete at the Games, I said it would be Alfredo Penaloza, a funny little guy known as Cheevo, which is Spanish for goat. They thought it was a great joke, but he got eighth in the marathon and ran third in the Boston marathon in 1969. The other Mexican star was Juan Martinez, who came fourth in the 5000 metres and fifth in the 10,000; a third runner set a new Mexican 800-metres record.

Arthur recalls ruefully: 'The Mexicans should have become very successful runners over the middle and long distances but this is a potential that can be developed only through a systematic three-year training programme. I could not get the officials to appreciate this and it was something I was not destined to carry through. There were other problems, too, that I could do nothing about. Many of the lads were in the army and most were Catholic, a faith that encouraged them to marry young and beget an endless stream of children. They had often fathered five or six by the time they were 22 years old.

'To make their army life bearable, they had to pay some of their wages regularly into a fund established by the officers –

for the officers. If they didn't pay, they found themselves on latrine duties, weekend exercises or other disciplinary punishment until they toed the line. So they existed with financial problems, which made it virtually impossible for any of them to get anywhere on their own, especially in athletics. I couldn't help them much because I had problems of my own and I didn't have the time.'

While Arthur had some success producing vastly improved runners, he did experience one notable failure. 'We were told that there were Indians living in the mountains who could run a hundred kilometres without stopping. These, I decided, were the guys to train to win the marathon for Mexico. We managed to arrange a trial marathon for them and brought them down from the mountains to see how they went.

'Unfortunately, the local officials knew nothing about organising marathons. When they were told that feeding stations were required, they happily went ahead and organised a complete banquet for each station. The Indians were accustomed to living simply and, when they reached the first feeding station and saw all the wonderful food spread out for them, that is where they stopped.'

Arthur was joined in Mexico by Jean and their daughter, Fay, and one day he took them to stay with a wealthy Mexican in Cuanavarque, a beautiful place where many American film stars had homes. The large house where they were guests was surrounded by a big wall. The owner explained it was to keep the thieves out, but he also had another deterrent – he pointed to his gardener and said he had already killed two guys. That was why he was there as a gardener – thieves, even if they could manage to scale the wall, would be too scared to come in. He had proved he was a good shot and was not to be messed with.

Arthur remembers a trip he made to a village about 160 kilometres north of Acapulco, on the Pacific coast, with some locals who had become friends. Their cars were laden with guns and they said they were going to shoot jaguars.

'But I was told that was one thing you didn't do. The Indians were quite likely to kill you if you went into their jungle and even the army was too scared to go in there. The village itself was a beautiful little place and I was admiring a donkey, which was elaborately decorated with a colourful saddle and bridle, when an American guy walked up and asked me if I liked it. He said he was the donkey's owner and an ex-US marine who was living in Mexico like a king. In Texas, he had lived like a bum on his war pension, but he didn't need much to enjoy his new life, he said. He was on his own and when he wanted a woman he just went into the village.'

Arthur joined some men sitting under the palm trees on the beach, drinking from coconuts. He found out they added Bacardi rum to the coconut milk and sucked it through a straw. He was also warned that there were murderers wandering around the village and, although it looked beautiful, it was a wild place. 'So we went fishing,' he says.

'It was a fascinating place. We were there for Mexico's national day and sat outside in the plaza that night, drinking a fairly large quantity of beer and watching the dancing. Three soldiers came along with guns, put their flag up, fired their rifles and went off again. The remarkable thing was how clean all the peasants' clothes were. They lived in adobe huts with dirt floors and how they did it I don't know, but their clothing was always spotless.'

On one occasion, one of Arthur's athletes went missing from the camp. Arthur was told his baby had died, so because he was the only one with a car, he went to the funeral, which was held on the other side of Mexico City.

'They had a tiny coffin, which they carried down the road. It began raining as a car came racing past, with the driver sounding his horn. I saw that he was a Catholic priest and asked my interpreter why he wasn't helping the family. He said that priests didn't recognise babies until they were six months old. The baby hadn't lived long enough to qualify.

'At the cemetery, they pulled a slab of marble back from a grave site. There were already three little coffins in there and they put the latest one on top. It made me realise that life is cheap in Mexico.'

Arthur stuck out eight frustrating months of his three-year

contract and then had another meeting with General Clarke, at which he managed to bluff the general into agreeing that the contract should be declared null and void.

'I then made plans for a quick exit from the country. I knew that, because of my reputation, my early departure from the scene would cause the general some embarrassment. I also knew that an Italian cycling coach, who had earlier caused red faces by becoming involved with the girlfriend of an Olympic committee member, had been dealt with drastically for stepping out of line. He was bundled out of bed in the middle of the night with a pistol at his head, forced to sign a statement breaking his contract, and was then dumped on the next plane out.

'I quietly booked a flight to Canada instead of New Zealand and was gone before the officials were aware of it. It was depressing to leave behind a group of young men who could not have become more dedicated to my programme. It was a pity because they were good athletes, but I couldn't handle the officialdom and the corruption. Some of the lads wept when they farewelled me at the airport. They didn't have much money but they gave me a lovely woollen jacket, which must have taken most of what they did have.

'I know they could have done more wonderful things for Mexico in 1968 if only we could have got the official cooperation we needed. It was galling to know that money that had been allocated to them would never reach them.'

Arthur can claim to have done something for the Mexicans because, when he arrived in Canada, he frankly told the media what was happening in Mexico. Everything was behind schedule for 1968; the rowing course was still a swamp, another venue supported nothing but weeds. The media took up the story with gusto and, three weeks later, General Clarke was deposed as Mexico's Olympic chief and a new man installed in his place. 'He was the architect who designed the beautiful Mexico City University and he turned round what would otherwise have been a shambles.'

And, in a sense, Arthur also had the last say. 'I was coaching in Finland when someone asked me if I had heard that General Clarke had died and if I had any comment about that. From memory, my answer was, "That, in my opinion, is the best thing he has done for sport".'

Arthur had been banking his Mexican pay in America and sending funds back to New Zealand, but when he reached Canada he couldn't find his bankbook. He reported this to the bank and they discovered that the Mexicans had got hold of it and were trying to work out how to get the money out of the account.

'The bank sorted that out quickly, but it demonstrated how you had to watch yourself with the Mexicans.'

So Arthur abandoned the height and heat of Mexico and, unexpectedly, found himself knee-deep in snow.

17

non-flying Finns

WHEN THE FINNISH Athletics Federation (SUL) learnt Arthur had left Mexico, they called him and asked him to go to work for them. He agreed and arrived in Finland in mid-March of 1967. He knew the Finns had been, were or could be again good runners – as he says, you can find them anywhere – so his first task was to find out why they weren't succeeding, given their illustrious history as a distance-running nation.

'One reason was immediately obvious,' he says. 'They'd gone soft, lost their toughness. In the winter-time, the athletes were no longer getting out skiing and running as they once did. They either retired indoors to sit in front of television watching the ice hockey or grabbed some of the money the Finnish administration was spraying round and went off to chase the sun in the Canary Islands, the Caribbean or somewhere else where the weather was good. The intention was that they continue training, but mainly they concentrated on acquiring good tans.

'Most of the administrators were business executives who thought the solution to the lack of good athletes was to throw money at them. An affluent society was emerging in Finland and the young men and women had vanished into it. Older runners I talked to, such as Viljo Heino, one of the world's best post-Second World War 10,000-metre runners and a respected coach, spoke sadly of the softness and saw it as a bad omen for a small country, with the Soviet Union on one border, Sweden on another and no military alliances to provide protection. A lot of money was being spent on promoting sport, but it was not being spent effectively and Finland was losing its backbone.'

A prime example of this malaise was the best Finnish distance runner at the time, Juoko Kuha. Arthur remembers: 'He was a talented young man who, when I met him, didn't really want to have anything to do with me. He was a big star but, although he had been running around 8:29 for the steeplechase, he was far from being among the best in the world. Nevertheless, the Finns were treating him as the great runner they had been seeking to lead a revival. His picture was on magazine covers, his name was all through the media and he was acting as if he was already the great Olympic champion. It was largely wishful thinking.

'When winter came to Finland, they sent Kuha to places like Majorca or the Canary Islands or Brazil to train. So he was enjoying glorious training holidays and then, when he came home, he did not run as seriously for his country as he did for himself. He was a victim, though a willing one, of the lavish state sponsorship that exists in countries where there is a belief that liberal spending is the answer to sporting achievement.

'Kuha was so highly regarded that the management of the timber mill where he worked rigged up floodlights and hurdles so he could train at night. He did go on to break the world steeplechase record. He disagreed with my training system because I disagreed with the federation sending its top runners away for the winter. They had a good time, but when they came back, they didn't train. Instead, they chose to race because of the brown envelope system of paying amateurs. One of them, Mikko Ala-leppilampi, ran seven 5000-metre races in ten days. Then, when he was required to run for Finland against Italy, he couldn't lift his bloody legs. But he'd made a nice amount of under-the-table money.'

Arthur set out to prove his point in his customary effective way, found a young prison guard in a town in central Finland and trained him to beat Kuha in the Finnish steeplechase championship.

Arthur discovered there were running tracks everywhere in Finland. Tampere, where he was based, had twelve. One was an all-weather surface and the others were all cinder tracks. The contrast between the Finnish facilities and what New Zealand had was startling but the athletes' approach to making the best use of the tracks was much the same. They came out on to the tracks in the summer and immediately started doing repetitions. It was all anaerobic training, with no aerobic base at all, so it was easy for Arthur to see why they weren't succeeding.

'I had to get them out marathon training, but all the government money for athletics had been spoken for so I went private. I asked which brewery was the biggest in Finland. They told me it was Malas Jourma, in Lahti, and put me in touch with the manager, who fortunately could speak English. I talked him into sponsoring a 100-kilometre ten-man team race from Hämeeninna to Lahti. I knew some club athletes were distance training and my aim was to get them all out to compete for team places. The brewery supplied the transport to get the teams between the relay points and it was great free advertising for them. Their name was spread on their brewery vehicles across the whole 100 kilometres.

'The race was a huge success and, coupled with the fact that I went distance running, too, motivated the athletes to start conditioning the way I wanted them to.

'If Rome in 1960 was the first high point of my career, Munich in 1972, although I didn't know it then, was destined to become another. Most of the intervening years were dominated by my athletes setting national and world records as they totally commanded middle- and distance-running. This was a period when we were assured of winning all the races we chose to win, because we alone were employing the best training system. It is gratifying to think now that this system is being used all over the world in a wide range of sports – but galling to know that the only country which still treats it with a mixture of suspicion, disdain and jealousy is New Zealand.

'It is an interesting, if unfortunate, fact that wherever you find success you find critics who try to detract from it or totally discredit the causes. When the Finns re-emerged as world-leading runners, they were accused of replacing their athletes' blood with higher-oxygenated blood. This accusation came after Munich and was renewed when Lasse Viren repeated his 5000 and 10,000-metre gold medal double in Montreal four years later. It was absurd, but allegations like these are accepted because they are what a lot of people want to hear in order to explain away what they are reluctant to try to understand or believe.

'If the Finns had taken blood from runners like Lasse Viren and Pekka Vasala and put it into some other athletes, there might have been something in this theory but the reality was that they were just better runners than anyone else. Viren was already the Finnish under-18 age-group champion when I first met him. He came to the training centre at Viremaki with his coach and mentor. His systematic training was what made him perhaps the finest distance runner the world has seen. He has four gold medals to prove it. But he already had the potential to be that good when I met him.

'He still sends me a card every Christmas and gives me the credit for his great successes, but I never trained him. I coached his coach to do that.'

The blood doping theory, which had a short and merry life, was that 400ml of an athlete's blood was taken from him and stored under controlled conditions for a maximum of six weeks. Just before competition, the athlete was infused with his own stored blood. By this time his body would have manufactured replacement red blood cells, so the infused blood increased the concentration of erythrocytes and hence improved the athlete's oxygen-carrying capacity.

Arthur says: 'One argument supposedly supporting Viren's blood doping practice was that, between the Olympics, his efforts were comparatively poor. But the fact was that, after Munich, he suffered a leg injury serious enough to need an operation. He tried to continue training without the operation, but was finally forced to have it. Then he purposely took his time over recovering and building up again. He approached Montreal exactly as he approached Munich — he knew how to prepare himself for the big competitions that mattered.

'The blood doping insinuations were an insult to the two great Finnish coaches, Kaari Sinkkonen and Pentti Karvonen, who were responsible to a large extent for these athletes becoming Olympic champions.'

Arthur's first long run in Finland is etched in his memory. It was in Kuortin, on a 32-kilometre course round a frozen lake.

'I was driven round it first so that I could see what it involved. It was 28 degrees below Celsius and all I had was a thin Mexican tracksuit, so they fitted me out with a hat that covered my ears, a muffler to wrap round my face, newspaper to protect my penis so that it didn't get frozen, thick socks and gloves. But I was still so bloody cold, I ran fast and was the first in. The newspapers promptly suggested that Finland should get me to represent them. In those days, of course, I could run 1.51 for 20 miles [32 kilometres]. But if I had known the ice on the lake was about two feet thick and cars could drive over it, I would have cut across the lake instead of going right round.

'The cold was a new and unpleasant experience after the heat of Mexico, although I soon adjusted to it and startled everyone by sometimes turning out in shorts and a light top in order to demonstrate that the fit body can withstand extremes of temperature. It was part of my psychology to rid the Finns of their softness that I went to that extreme, but I had a level of fitness that made the cold no problem for me.

'So my initiation into Finnish running was a freezing contrast to Mexico, although the coldest place in which I ran was right on the Russian border at a town called Imatra. It was 35 degrees below and I ran for two and a half hours. My mouth muffler was covered with a lump of ice from the moisture of my breath. It is so cold and the temperature falls so fast in Finland that you can't make snowballs and snowmen unless you're very quick about it. It's a dry snow.

'There was a large water tower in Imatra and I was told that, when Hitler flew in there during the war, his plane just missed it. A shame, because it could have finished him off and history would have been very different.'

Arthur soon discovered another oddity of Finland's cold: if you leave your car standing too long at minus 35° Celsius, the tyres freeze where they touch the ground, so, when you drive off, you have an uncomfortably bumpy ride until they thaw out. He learnt that at Imatra when he got back in his car, drove off and couldn't understand at first what kind of disaster had happened.

Arthur, coming to grips with the athletes' attitudes to training, had an early experience similar to the Mexican ploy of the runners retreating to the comfort of the bus and leaving him to train on alone.

'I met Viljo Heino at a place called Kahula, on the coast east of Helsinki, where he was coaching. He told me, "Arthur, these guys aren't training properly," and he gave me twenty of his runners to take on a 25-kilometre out and back course. I ran out with two of them who could speak English, leading the rest, but, when we turned at the halfway point, there were no other runners behind us. They'd all gone back home long before and, by the time we three got back, they'd had their sauna and coffee and were dressed ready to go home.

'I gave the media a statement about this incident, saying it was no wonder the Finns couldn't win any medals. I said they had no *sisu*, which is the Finnish for pluck or plain old guts. It's a strong word. Tell a Finn he's got no *sisu* and he's likely to pull a knife on you. They don't like it.

'But, from then on, the guys came out and always ran with me. They never funked it again. I should mention that the girls always ran as I required them to; it was just the men who were unwilling. But, once I'd got them going on regular distance runs through the forests, I found myself in a race every day. Now they all wanted to show me how fast they could run and I had to work hard to stay with them so that I didn't get lost. I was getting bloody tired because, unlike in a city, where you can always get a taxi back if you run out of steam, in the Finnish forest you just had to keep running. After a while, my legs were jumping round like violin bows every night and spoiling my sleep, so I went to an exercise doctor.

'"Arthur," he said, "you're getting cramps. You need calcium for your nervous system. Every muscle contraction requires calcium ions." He gave me Calcium Sandoz, a form of calcium gluconate, which I'd never seen before, and it fixed the problem almost immediately. I've been a fan of it ever since and have used it on many of my runners.

'I was also feeling unwell, lethargic. The doctor said the trouble was that I was trying to keep to the New Zealand diet of meat, vegetables and fruit. The vegetables I was eating came from Spain and Italy and were so old by the time they reached my plate that they'd lost much of their food value. In Finland, people ate a lot of the berries that grew wild in the forests, preserving them and eating them during the winter with every meal. This gave them a good supply of vitamins and minerals.

'The physio said I should be taking vitamin and mineral tablets to correct this. I'd been opposed to them ever since I attended a lecture in Champagne, Illinois, where a diet expert told us that pills were all right for young people under five and old people. "Otherwise," he said, "all you're going to do is enrich your urine."'

Arthur had been an outspoken critic of American track and field athletes' habit of taking a plethora of vitamins and diet supplements. He saw many of them carrying bags of multi-coloured pills with them at meetings, and used to wonder what colour their urine might be. He felt that the food we ate was packed with everything we need for optimum health.

'Now, on the physio's advice, I began taking them and I came right. I satisfied myself that vitamin and mineral pills *do* count so the Illinois expert, although he sounded convincing, didn't know what he was talking about.'

Today, Arthur believes that the extensive use of fertilisers, intensive production methods and the growth in popularity of packaged foods has meant that a lot of our food has lost its goodness and controlled supplementation with vitamins is a sensible way to compensate for this.

'The Finns ate a lot of fish, which I don't like. I don't mind catching fish, but I hate the smell of it and, in Finland, I wasn't too sure at times about the water the fish came from. I still remembered a banquet I had gone to when I took my athletes to Finland in 1961. There were thirteen main dishes – twelve were fish and the other was reindeer meat, which tasted like raw bacon. I didn't have much to eat that night – until I went down the road after the banquet and had a hamburger.'

While Arthur had quickly discovered that the Finns weren't training properly, it was a bit longer before he realised one of the reasons why. They were listening to the exercise physiologists at a major university at Jyvaskyla, in central Finland, who were preaching the gospel according to Per Olaf Åstrand, the Swedish exercise physiologist. Arthur had read Åstrand's book and disagreed with its theories. However, the Finns were hypnotised by the fancy diplomas hanging on the experts' walls, lapped it up and were deeply into using anaerobic training for conditioning, which, in the book of the real expert on conditioning, you must never do.

But the athletes didn't like one thing the experts were doing, which was taking them for weekend laboratory tests. The Finns are home-loving people and home is where they like to spend their weekends. Arthur had to find a way around the problem of convincing everyone that his layman's knowledge was superior to the physiologists'.

'I went to the Athletics Federation, SUL, and asked them if they were happy with what was going on. They were not – it was costing them a lot of money and the athletes were getting worse instead of better. When I was asked if I could do anything, I told them to get Professor Dr Schuster, the head of physical education in East Germany, on the phone for me.

'"You'll never get an East German here," they said.

'I said, "Well, let me try."

'It was Friday afternoon in Helsinki when I talked to Dr Schuster and told him how all these guys with diplomas were upsetting my programme. I knew I was right and they were wrong, but I was only a layman and I needed someone who also had diplomas to convince them of that.

'Dr Schuster asked me who I wanted and I named Dr Reiss, who had visited New Zealand under the Rothmans scheme with Jurgen May, the man who had just run the world's fastest mile on grass [3:53] and had also won all the mile races in Europe that year. Dr Reiss was an exceptionally good coach and understood my methods because the East Germans were the first people to analyse my training. After his coach died, Jurgen got a copy of *Run to the Top*, switched from the interval training methods he had been using and trained according to my programme with the guidance of Dr Reiss. May was East Germany's first world record-breaker.

'Dr Schuster asked me when I wanted Dr Reiss.

'I said, "As soon as possible."

'He replied, "Would Monday morning do?"'

Arthur explains that the closeness of his connection with the East Germans came about in 1967 when he was invited to visit the Leipzig Sports Medicine Institute to discuss his training theories and practice with them. 'I jumped at the chance and spent two days discussing training with East German coaches and physiologists. I was impressed by the open-minded approach to training and exercise physiology of all I met. Many of the best East Germans in the field were involved in improving athletic standards as well as the health of the whole nation. I could see that, with their approach, they were going to succeed and become a country to be reckoned with in any sports they chose.

'I later predicted that East Germany would become one of the world's great sporting nations and, within a matter of years, they were. Their medal haul at the Montreal Olympics exceeded even the United States' total, a remarkable achievement considering the huge population difference – 200 million Americans against 18 million East Germans. Only the vast Soviet Union bettered East Germany.

'The East Germans were equally interested in what I had done in New Zealand so I presented Professor Dr Schuster with a copy of *Run For Your Life*. Soon after, they set up what they called the 'Run For Your Life' national health programme and, within six months, had doubled the membership of sporting clubs through the country. They assembled some of their best doctors, physiologists, coaches, sportsmen and administrators and mounted a television campaign designed to encourage people to look after their own physical welfare. It worked.

'I found on my lecture tour that the East German facilities at that time were the foremost in the world and so was their progressive attitude towards improving their sporting achievements.

'Peter Snell went with me on one of my visits to East Germany and when we arrived at the Brandenburg Gate and were taken through the Berlin Wall to get our visas we were shocked to see a middle-aged man crying his eyes out.

Apparently he had been on his way through the wall to West Germany, but the East German guards had used a hand-truck with a mirror on it to check underneath his car and they had found something he was not permitted to take out of the country. He was obviously in trouble. On the way west at the end of our trip, we were horrified to see the security fencing and armed guards with dogs patrolling the border near Nuremberg.

'Later on, in Australia, I met the East German marathoner, Waldemar Cierpinski, who became only the second man after Abebe Bikila to win consecutive Olympic gold medals [Montreal in 1976 in 2:09:55 and Moscow in 1980 in 2:11:03]. He told me his old coach in East Germany had trained him using my schedules. The East Germans had made an interesting discovery when using my training methods to condition their swimmers: if they allowed them to stop their exercise for more than fifteen seconds the swimmers would lose a degree of muscular endurance development.'

After the 1976 Olympics, Arthur was dismayed by comments in the media suggesting the East Germans were developing a class of Amazons, who were taking drugs and so on. He wondered at the intelligence and ethics of people who said and wrote 'such trash' without knowing what they were talking about. 'The East Germans excelled because they were more scientific and meticulous than others in what they were doing,' Arthur says. 'Certainly, some evidence of the use of drugs emerged, but the incidents were hardly more prevalent than they were in some of those countries which produced the most vocal critics.'

When evidence emerged recently about state-sponsored drug use among East German athletes, Arthur was quick to point out that his comments applied only to middle and distance runners. Other athletes may well have taken drugs or been encouraged to do so, but middle and distance runners could derive no benefit from them.

'But, to get back to my Finnish troubles, Dr Reiss arrived and we toured Finland with Eira, the interpreter who would later become my second wife, and we straightened everyone out. Then we got on with the five-year programme I wanted to implement. In five years, the Finns were the best in the world again. I travelled all over Finland and Lapland, visiting little villages to find their coaches and the athletes they were training, getting all the information I could about them and setting out their training programmes. The coaches learnt from me by using my schedules to train their runners. In effect, I was now only coaching the coaches, because I realised this was the most efficient way to achieve results.

'I soon had eight hundred people on my programmes throughout the country. One comment in the newspaper was that, if young athletes were made to do all I wanted, their school work would suffer. Three young guys who subsequently won their junior championships were also duxes of their schools, which, to me, was the perfectly logical outcome of their running. The endurance training's beneficial effect on their oxygen uptake improved their central nervous systems so they were in a tireless state mentally as well as physically. I knew that would happen because girls I trained in New Zealand to become champion runners were also smart girls who became duxes of their schools.'

But life was far from easy. The Finnish press didn't understand what he was doing and many of the Finns were still not very cooperative. So once a month he sat down with the president and secretary of the Federation and explained exactly what he was doing. They were happy with what was going on and understood that champions cannot be made overnight, but the media and many others didn't appreciate that until many years later, when it was too late.

'So I was under duress for much of the time and I needed all the support I could get. A constant problem in gaining the acceptance of my training system is that people are always in a hurry. If they don't get immediate results, they think it doesn't work, even though I've told them plainly enough exactly how it does work. They don't realise you can't change the cardiovascular system rapidly. It's a progressive development.

'Juoko Kuha was one of those who thought he knew better than I did and I had always thought Juha Vaatainen took his side but, years later, Juha confessed that he had gone to one of my lectures, in Oulu, where he lived. He was too big-headed to come into the lecture room, but he and and another athlete sat outside behind a partition and listened to me. Then he changed his training to my system and, although he had been an 800-metre runner, he won the European 10,000 metres title, covering the last 400 metres in 53 seconds.'

Saunas are a way of life in Finland and Arthur found that the farther north he went, the hotter they got. For visitors, they made them really hot. Because he'd spent a lot of his life running marathons and training in the hottest part of the day, he was used to the heat. Finland's saunas were no problem for him, even at 57°C. The surprised Finns gave him a certificate for surviving it. Most visitors didn't.

'When the New Zealand journalist Norm Harris came over from London and stayed with me he wanted a sauna, so I took him to the one upstairs in the building where I had my apartment. I stoked it up but, when I threw water on the heated rocks, Norm was out of there like a rocket. I've never seen anyone move so fast.

'Incidentally, like the saunas, which get hotter as you move north, the local beer, *olut*, also changes. It gets worse. I found the beer down south was excellent. Up north, it tasted like swamp water.'

Norm had gone across to interview Paavo Nurmi but he couldn't get to see him personally. Arthur says Nurmi was like God in Finland and about as approachable. 'Often, when I was out running with my boys, a car would cruise up alongside us and keep pace for a while. I finally asked who was watching us. "Oh, that's Nurmi," I was told − and that's as close as I got to meeting him, too. The Finns tend to be a reserved people and Nurmi was a perfect example. About the only way to get to see him is to visit one of the two statues erected in his honour − one at Turku and the other at the stadium in Helsinki.

'Nurmi was getting old when I was there [he was 69] but apparently he could still run pretty well. I was told that, when he was asked to train some young runners, he took them into the forest and, when he came back, declared, "They're no good." He'd run out with them and left them all behind.'

One of the young Finnish runners who impressed Arthur greatly was Pekka Vasala, a 1500-metre runner, but the Finns didn't choose him for the Mexico Olympic team. They told Arthur he wasn't good enough. Arthur agreed but said, 'What about next time? Give him the experience now.'

So they added him to the team for Mexico. He ran dead last in the 1500 but, four years later, he won the gold medal at Munich. 'Experience of the kind he underwent in Mexico is important, because many young runners can be so overawed by finding themselves among the best athletes in the world at an Olympic Games that they lose confidence and don't run to their capabilities. We have to see the potential and add the experience to it.

'I also told the Finnish authorities that their athletes should only get money through their coaches, who could determine whether they were worth it. They agreed and began doing everything correctly. Pay for results but don't always expect results for pay.

'I believe New Zealand is making a mistake in setting up so many sports centres, just because Australia seems to have done well with its Institute of Sport. The centres mean nothing; it's the teachers who count and a good teacher who knows what he or she is doing doesn't need the facililties.

'Vierumaki, in Finland, has the most modern sports centre you can think of. A 400-metre indoor track, Olympic-sized pools and beautiful outdoor facilities where you can run for twenty miles through the bush. But the standard of Finnish running has gone down. The reason for this is that they have gone off the programmes I set when I was there. Last year, they had the head coach of Kenya up there and I knew he would fail, because anyone can train a Kenyan. They run all the bloody time from early childhood and have a high oxygen uptake level, so all you have to do is give them speedwork and they succeed. Unlike the Kenyans, the Finns don't run to and from school and attain and maintain their cardiovascular efficiency while they are young.

'Now they are not doing the necessary work to reach the level of endurance they need. After my two years there, I used to go back from time to time to check that they were staying with my programmes, but now they've drifted off it. There were no Finnish middle- or distance-runners at the last Olympics. It's not because they don't have the runners any more. They have other Virens and Vasalas, just as New Zealand has other Snells and Halbergs. They are simply not being trained properly.'

18

parting shots

ARTHUR LYDIARD IS not noted for pulling his punches when he is dealing with athletes and coaches. Excuses for failing to do something are not often accepted. Just do it, is his attitude. But he really hits straight from the shoulder when he is dissatisfied or disappointed. A spade is a spade. This trait is perhaps nowhere better illustrated than in these excerpts from his 31 March 1969, wind-up report to the SUL, the Finnish Athletics Federation, in the late 1960s. This report has not been published before.

My work here was primarily to find out the various problems associated with the running sport and to endeavour to lay a solid foundation for the future development of the athletic potential. I stated when I first arrived that only through cooperation would it be possible to succeed and that the 1968 Olympics were too close to my arrival here to allow my work to be effective for those competitions.

Since I have been here, I have found many problems which are all instrumental in keeping the standard of the sport low and only through careful thought, understanding, applied logic and patience will these be overcome. It calls for sincerity by all sections of the Finnish sports fraternity. Sincerity that is sadly lacking generally.

When I outlined my plans, I wasn't guessing and any coaches and athletes who carry out my programme will eventually be successful. Of this I am sure.

When I arrived here, I came at the wrong time of the year,

In Denmark, Arthur checks a trial time with Loa Olafson, who he predicted would become European 3000-metres champion after running a time of 8:31, but who then broke an ankle in a cycling accident. Later, training in New Zealand, she damaged her feet by training in the wrong shoes.

Arthur with the great double Olympic gold medallist Waldemar Cierpinski at a marathon in Finland.

Arthur with his second wife, Eira, whose tragic early death was the low point of his life.

The great Japanese coach Kiyoshi Nakamura.
Maier Media

Arthur's Japanese squad run along the scrub-lined track encircling the active volcano on Oshima Island.

Running to the top... enticed back to coaching youngsters in the early 70s, Arthur paces a group of college girls up the steep side of One Tree Hill in Auckland, one of his preferred sites for the rigorous hill-training section of his schedules.

Lydiard often held training camps around the farmland and beaches of north Taranaki, near Tongaporutu. Here, Arthur washes his shoes and cools his legs after a cross-country run.
Tim Chamberlain

Arthur takes colleagues for a jog in Chicago. Third from left, and just ahead of Arthur (right) is the city mayor Michael Bilandic.

Arthur and friends, marathon training in South Africa – to the top of Table Mountain.
Cape Town Argus

i.e., when the conditioning period was over. It was necessary to try to pressure the runners and get them into some sort of shape which would allow for reasonable results. However, I didn't know how soft these runners were and that they weren't capable of working as hard as a boy in many other countries. This put things off on the wrong foot and the Finnish press then took the opportunity to destroy any further work that I attempted.

I was sadly mistaken when I thought that I was to be amongst a sporting fraternity who would be cooperative and keen to see Finland's prestige once again respected. Instead, I found runners who considered themselves God's greatest gift to Finland, runners who couldn't and had never beaten one great international runner from another country, runners whose ambition wasn't to win gold medals but to win brown envelopes, who cared little for their flag, Finnish colours, or prestige, nationally or personally. Selfish, soft individuals who blamed everything and everybody for their poor showings, particularly when Finland needed them most. People who completely lack sincerity and appreciation and expect everything to be made easy for them.

Amongst the coaches, there are also the individuals (too many) who are guessing, people who lack logic and experience, who have selfish interests and are missing the potential of many of the country's promising athletes. These coaches are invariably having their charges carry out schedules that are unbalanced and ruinous to their later prospects and development.

In administration, the same insincerity is prevalent, with the usual 'boot-lickers and back-stabbers', whose main goal is social standing rather than effective work and talk that could affect their possibilities of climbing the social and administrative ladder. I have noted some who use their positions to further undermine the sport by continually offering the so-called leading runners 'brown envelopes' for competing in their local meets, even though some of these races could and often do detrimentally affect the performances of these runners in important competitions for Finland. There are many who don't seem to understand that their work as track and field administrators is to foster the sport in their district by providing all-year competition, training and incentive. In some districts, clubs are only clubs in name and hardly ever hold a club track competition or arrange cross-country races.

Then there is the press. The sporting press of Finland. From my observations, many of these individuals don't know the meaning of the word sport and, for that matter, don't want to. It seems a shame that many of these people could do so much good for the youth of Finland but prefer to take the opposite view, endeavouring to destroy the work others are trying to do to assist young people as well as their country.

These particular sports writers show a complete lack of ability to write factually, interestingly and constructively, mainly through their lack of knowledge of the subject, their hastily arrived at conclusions and erroneous information, which they apparently fail to verify; but above all their wish to resort to sensationalism, possibly through the orders of their employers.

Types of people I have mentioned in these categories are undoubtedly holding the sport back and are responsible for the present poor standards. I have repeatedly tried to appeal to the logic of the Finnish people but have met with little success. Most don't know and don't want to know. They just want to continue on as before and change nothing. There appears to be little wish to change the present order and plan ahead, so as to systematically develop the country's potential athletically.

Basically, the problem in the sport here is lack of control, of athletes [and] clubs. If an athlete doesn't get his way with one association, he goes to another. Clubs openly contravene the amateur code. This, in turn, has led to a form of semi-professionalism, with athletes going on SUL- or club-financed training vacations, resembling Cooks tours, to various parts of the world during winter months. On their return to Finland, their concentration is then upon making as much money as possible at the various club meetings throughout the country.

International meets mean little to these athletes, as there isn't any money to be made in them.

The whole concept of these athletes has been wrongly developed and only a strong man with strong men to support him can change this unfortunate trend. However, any man who would try to change things for the better would undoubtedly be sacrificed by the 'boot-lickers'.

For the athletes' part, most of them don't want a change to this trend, as at present they have everything going their way. Paid and subsidised trips to warm countries during winter months. Sometimes to a different country each year. Return to Finland for racing for money with paid training camps. A press who lauds them as 'great and wonderful' people and even if they get licked (as they most often do) they get called 'heroes in defeat'. They can't lose and they know it.

For SUL to invest money in athletes and then let them do as they like just borders on the ridiculous. Athletes who are given every possible assistance, such as Finland's, are invariably soft and will let you down when the going gets tough and you need them most. My experiences have proved this time and again.

The top international runners today are the men brought up and trained the hard way. They are not pampered and petted as these particular Finns want to be.

The worst feature of all this is the effect the SUL's appeasement policy is having upon the up-and-coming youngsters who, at present, are proving the best Finland has ever had. These young people also need incentive, but of the right type. Their only ambitions should not be for the material gains but they should be psychologically developed to take pride in their flag, their country and its sporting prestige. This is clearly lacking in your present-day top group.

There can be only one of two reasons why the general running standard is so low. Either the athletes are basically not good enough or the wrong approach is being made. I know that the former is wrong and that the potential of the runners is as great here as in any country. If Finland is again to produce great runners, it will only be through hard,

systematic training over a number of years. Training designed
to develop potential, not to get quick results. I can fully
appreciate the feelings of many Finns who love the sport and
long for days, such as in pre-war years, when the blue Finnish
singlet was feared on the track.

Today, in Finland, there are numerous groups of young
men training harder than Finns have ever trained before,
under the guidance of competent coaches. Top results will
surely come by at least 1972 if these young men are not
psychologically ruined like the present group of so-called élite.

It is in the hands of administrators to see that the hard
work of these athletes and coaches coming up isn't fruitless
and that a more sensible policy is implemented than at present.

Arthur laid out his ideas of how the SUL should and could
wake its ideas up and ended: 'In many ways, I will be sorry to
leave your lovely country, cold as it is. However, I don't believe
I could have stood another track season watching those soft,
insincere, so-called running champions of yours, knowing all the
time that if they had a little of the right spirit and sincerity they
could be great instead of looking like clowns.'

As mentioned earlier, Arthur does not mince words. And it
is significant that his prediction that Finland would again be a
leading running nation in 1972 was exactly on target.

On his way home from Finland in 1969 Arthur spent a month
lecturing in Germany and then bought a car in Denmark to bring
home to New Zealand. He shipped it to England and spoke to the
New Zealand consulate in London about his intentions.

'I discovered that between deciding to buy the car as a
cheap way to get wheels in New Zealand and actually buying
it, the laws had changed and the duties New Zealand was now
imposing were going to cost me just about everything I had
planned to save. The guy at the consulate thought this was a
terrific joke. He laughed at me, which completely pissed me off
because the car was on a ship which was already heading for
New Zealand. So I rang my lawyer in Auckland and told him
what was happening and that, when the car arrived in

Auckland, he was to send it on to Australia, where I would pick it up and use it. I said if it was going to cost me money, I would rather spend it there than let the New Zealand government have it.

'An apartment was arranged for me in Sydney. I flew Jean over – our marriage was just holding together, although her dislike of spending time alone and abroad was making it very difficult for us. We spent nine months there. Ken Stewart, who was later the coach of the Australian Olympic team, told the Minister for the Interior in Canberra that I was in the country and the minister and one of the New South Wales sports ministers, Ken and I toured the Northern Territory to estimate the potential of the Aborigines as athletes. We went into parts of the country where very few Australians have been.

'Our tour took us to Darwin, Groote Eylandt, Bathurst Island, Bamyili (out through Katherine), the Daly River, Maningrida, Yuendumu and Alice Springs. We found the Aborigines were very bouncy people, very good at jumping, but they never had proper food. At age twelve, the kids could run very well, but by the time they were nineteen they couldn't. It was simply a matter of nutrition. They needed a bloody big steak or two.

'When the boys reached maturity, they were circumcised and thrown out of their families to live on their own. They very rapidly learnt the skills of self-survival. One of the Aborigine teachers demonstrated this for us. He called a lad over and told him to show me what things he could eat from the trail we were on. He showed me eighteen different things, including ants and God knows what. I wouldn't have found a thing, nor would I have eaten any of it. Plenty of protein, I suppose, but not much else for growing boys.

'The teacher asked the lad where he was sleeping that night. "Over there," he said and pointed under a tree.

'When he was telling me about the corroborees at which the boys were circumcised, the teacher said, "We use modern methods now, of course, We use razor blades – or a bit of sharp glass." No wonder they jumped around and made a lot of noise.

'I think a lot of good came out of that tour. The Aborigines are excellent at games such as basketball and have become good footballers at the highest level. I wasn't there long enough to go on a follow-up trip, but others have gone since – it's important to keep the encouragement going.

'About a third of the people up in Maningrida, one of the places we went to, had either leprosy or TB and it annoys me when I hear blanket statements that Australians don't look after them because, when I was there, a great many young Australians, with their families, were up there helping them. They were doing what they could, but there are always going to be problems when Aborigines are uprooted from their traditional way of life. Perhaps the worst was their introduction to alcohol. They couldn't handle it.

'We found beautiful white beaches up at Torres Strait but you couldn't walk on them in bare feet because of the hookworms and you couldn't swim in the inviting blue water, either, because in the summertime the sea was full of sea wasps, which have long tentacles hanging in the water. A sting from them and you have about ten minutes to live.

'We went to Yuendumu, about 650 kilometres north-west of Alice Springs, and were watching a sports meeting when a number of the old men of the tribe came along and put a wooden effigy of a kangaroo out in the middle of the field. A young boy came up to me, put his arm through mine and said, "Mr Lydiard, I'd move if I were you."

'I asked him why.

'He said, "The old men are going to throw boomerangs at the kangaroo."

'"That's all right," I said, "it's out in the middle of the field."

'"Yeah," he replied, "but they can't see the bloody thing."'

19

tragedy

WHEN HE LIVED in foreign countries, Arthur always tried to pick up as much of the language as he could. It wasn't always successful.

'I found it important to learn the right words to help me control the runners and to go shopping for the foods I preferred. These seemed to be the two most important requirements. They say you should learn a word a day, but my memory wasn't as good as it had been and getting my tongue round the correct words was difficult.'

He found the complicated language of Finland a particular challenge. 'The phonetics are okay, but the nouns are confusing. Even with place names, the endings change. You can get a noun which can be spelt eighteen different ways. They also pronounce each word and each letter in each word very distinctly. The first day I was there, I wanted to buy some bread. I told my interpreter I wanted to find a baker's shop, but I used the usual slack New Zealand pronunciation, which tends to end a word with an 'a' sound rather than an 'er' sound. The interpreter said I should say bak*er* not bak*a*.

'When I wanted to shop at the local store for my usual foods, including eggs, I was told the word for eggs is *muna* and the word for six is *kuusi*; so I asked for *kuusi muna* and wondered why the shop girl giggled. I couldn't understand what she was on about. I told my interpreter and he asked me exactly what I had said. I said, "I asked for *kusi muna*." No, no, he said and explained that there were two u's in *kuusi muna*, not one, as I had said, and both had to be pronounced separately.

'"So what's the difference?" I asked.

'"*Kuusi muna*," he said, "is six eggs. *Kusi muna* is a leaking penis."

'No wonder she giggled. From then on, I bought five eggs. It was a lot safer.'

However, Arthur learnt enough Finnish to enable him to get along with the athletes without too many communication problems. He found it was best to run with them at the tempos he wanted them to maintain and doing that also meant he could watch their development and their running styles and correct any faults as they occurred. For much of the time, however, Arthur was accompanied by an interpreter, one of whom, Eira, was to become a vital part of his life. Sadly, as one of his athletes once remarked with deep and sincere sadness, 'She lit up his life like a brilliant rocket – and you know what happens to rockets.'

The interpreter was a lovely young woman, who gave him wonderful support and encouragement for his coaching programme and eventually became his second wife. Eira was a teacher of teachers at the magnificent sports centre in Vierumaki, about 190 kilometres north-east of Helsinki, which Arthur visited several times. Eira had spent four years at university in Helsinki, spoke seven languages and was the Finnish gymnastics champion.

'Our mutual attraction was immediate. Unfortunately, she had developed asthma in her early thirties, as a result of standing round too long training girls in the cold. She might have been well wrapped up, but that doesn't make any difference when you are breathing in temperatures of minus 30 degrees Celsius. By this time, I had realised that my life with Jean and my family was more or less shattered. Jean had come to Finland and Mexico with me, but could not stand the isolation. We had a beautiful apartment in Finland, but she couldn't speak the language and I was constantly away in various parts of the country, for days or weeks on end. Eventually, she returned to New Zealand and our marriage broke down.

'The worst day of my life was when I walked out of the family home for the last time. Ever since, I have felt remorse. I have never been happy about the circumstances which forced us apart – my need to go overseas to secure a good living for my family and Jean's inability to tolerate the solitary life that she was forced to live. Her death in 2002 hurt me deeply.

'Eira came to New Zealand and we were together for twelve years, but she then developed cancer of the ovaries, apparently caused by using a copper IUD. She knew she was going to die but she kept mentally above it. She got a lot of support from her Lutheran minister. He would come around and talk to her and help us through what was a terrible time. I came to realise that the Lutherans were very nice guys; very genuine. Eira was a very brave girl as she died, but I believe the Lutherans did a lot to help her through it. So I still go to the Lutheran Church from time to time. I lost several kilos in weight just watching Eira go down. We even sent her to Mexico in the hope of a cure but, like everything else we tried, that didn't work. You do what you can but it is unbelievably distressing to watch someone dying of cancer. Especially someone as young and full of life as Eira, who was only 45 when, finally, she died.

'She never told anyone she had cancer; she always kept it to herself. Apart from my loss, the tragedy was that she had so much to offer young people. She loved teenagers and was loved by everyone at the schools where she taught in New Zealand. She took a position at Epsom Girls' Grammar School when she arrived in New Zealand and, because she was a gymnast and had competed at the Olympics as the Finnish gymnastic champion, she was busy helping the girls to improve their gymnastics. Then she asked me if I would come to the school to help the girls with their running. I said I'd just come back from Europe after being away for several years and didn't again want to get involved with going to the track several days a week.

'But Eira reminded me that I always said there were champions everywhere and more or less twisted my arm until, finally, I went along one day, met the six girls she had singled out and asked them to run 880 yards on the school's grass track. Heather Carmichael was home first in 2:56, which a dozen girls in any school could do, but I trained her and later she won the New Zealand secondary schools national cross-country and 1500 metres track titles.

'This was possibly the worst thing that could have happened as far as my time was concerned because the nearby private girls' schools, Diocesan and St Cuthberts, asked me if I would help their runners, too. Thanks to Eira's persuasion, I finished up with about twenty young women runners under my wing. But they were lovely people and it was a pleasure to work with them. Twice a week, I ran with them for an hour and a half and I ran further with some of them at the weekends. This lasted for several years, during which the girls won most of the national secondary schools' track and cross-country championships for their schools.

'The youngest was only twelve when she started with me, but she went on to be the cross-country title-holder. The fourth best girl in my group was Christine McMikken, who won the national schools 1500-metre track title and later tried to get into Otago University as a PE student. Although she was a well-educated young woman and a very good athlete, she couldn't gain entry. Visibly upset, she came to see me, because her parents were then living in Malaysia. I asked her if she would consider going to a university in the United States if I could arrange it for her. She agreed and I got a place for her at the University of Stillwater, in Oklahoma, where I knew the coach. Unfortunately, he moved to another university after a few months and I wasn't enthusiastic about the coach who replaced him.

'However, I was in the States the following year and Christine phoned me to say she was very happy – she had run third in the Big Eight, the competition between the neighbouring states. My response to that was that I was disappointed, because I considered she was good enough to have come first. The next year, Christine won the national cross-country title and went on to represent New Zealand in the world cross-country championship. She ran seventh, a very good performance.

'One of my group of girls later ran a 2:29 marathon and another ran 2:31 to win the Fukuoka in Japan. The long running they had done through their school years had paid off. Many of these young women went on to academic professions, otherwise I'm sure they would have left more of their mark in the record books.

'So I had Eira to thank for that rewarding period of my life and her early death was a shattering demonstration of what often happens when life seems to be close to perfection. I have never fully recovered from losing her.'

Eira and Arthur had bought a two-and-a-half acre property at Kerikeri and had taken out a hundred orange trees and put in all the services ready to start building. Then Eira became ill. Arthur had the money to put a house on the property but he didn't do it because of this sudden, tragic downturn in his life. He sold the land, which, he now says, was probably a mistake because it had great potential to increase its value, but, emotionally, it was too difficult for him to go there without Eira.

Instead, they built a house at Beachlands, where Arthur still lives. Eira planned the design and the decoration and furnishing of the house down to the last detail and it was almost ready for them to move in when she died.

But before this sad event in his life, the former shoemaker was back in the footwear business. Only, this time, it wasn't for his livelihood but for the prospect of establishing a useful sideline to his seesawing coaching career.

20

shoe business

WITH SOME RELUCTANCE and considerable disappointment, Arthur left Finland. He then spent a month in Germany working for the German Athletics Federation and, as part of a lecture in one town in the Rhine area, he talked about running shoes.

'The Germans were contending that if you ran a hundred miles a week you would get injured. My response was that they didn't have the right shoes. They said they had the best shoes in the world. No, I said, you have the prettiest shoes in the world, not the best ones.

'The adidas shoes used to bite me in the tendon at the back of the heel. So I asked if anyone in the audience ran big mileages and three men put their hands up. I said, "Come out and let me see your feet." I knew what I was going to see – toenails off, sticking plaster all round their feet. Then I showed them my feet with not a mark on them. I had run a hundred miles that week in training camps and my feet didn't have a mark on them and were as soft as a baby's feet. I said that was because I ran in good shoes, not pretty shoes.

'The shoes I was running in were made in Finland yet, when I went up there, I found the athletes couldn't run the mileages I needed them to. They were all wearing adidas. I wrote to adidas explaining that I wanted these athletes to run big mileages and their shoes weren't right. Adidas sent me a whole lot of shoes but, when I checked them, I could see they weren't much better.

'I went to Karhu, a major manufacturer of sports gear, who had already given me good support, and told them what my problem was and they had some shoes made for me the way I wanted them, with a soft sole so that they didn't slip on the ice.

'Anyway, after my lecture in Germany, a man called Eugene Brutting, who was sitting at the back of the hall, approached me and said he had a company, EB, which specialised in making women's fashion shoes. He asked me to go to Nuremberg with him to meet the manager of his shoe company and talk about running shoes. We spent two weeks in Nuremberg, making a last and beginning the manufacture of running shoes. We tested them on runners on 15-mile runs through local forests while we adjusted the initial mould until we got it just right.

'I set up a market for them in America and had guys lined up who were prepared to import them and arrange for them to be distributed through universities, where they could expect high sales. But the Germans didn't meet the deadline – they are not as efficient as you might think – the university coaches got sick of waiting for the shoes and the whole deal fell through. EB made outstanding running shoes, but they just couldn't market them.

'Back in New Zealand, I took the EB last to Bridgens, where I used to be foreman, with the proposal that the EB shoes should be made there under licence. I left the last with the company, where my brother Wally and his son were working, Wally as a clicker and his son as a cutter. Wally and I had got along well when we were young and we were still reasonably close.

'The next thing we knew, my last had been developed and the EB running shoe was being produced with the Lydiard name. Wally established his own factory, Lydiard Shoes, and, quite frankly, traded on my name and reputation. He even ran an advertisement for his company which featured a picture of me and implied that the shoes were mine, although I had nothing to do with the factory. That was soon stopped.

'Eira was very upset by this. She was in Queen Street one day and saw "Arthur Lydiard" shoes on display in a shop window. She went in and made the manager remove them. Things between Wally and me were never the same again after that. It wasn't the right thing to do, but I didn't make a big deal of it at the time and I'm not going to now. If they had said to me, "Arthur, can we use your name and can you help to market the shoes?" I would have done it, but they went the wrong way about it, behind my back. The last they used was essentially mine – they had just made it a little bit wider to suit New Zealand feet.

'Even now I get calls from people asking what happened to my shoe factory, but Lydiard Shoes, which has gone into receivership since Wally died, never had anything to do with me. At the time, I was still trying to help the Germans to market their shoe and get it established in America, but the trouble with them was that they didn't keep up with the evolution of materials and continued making their shoes with pigskin leather. It was a very good shoe and people have approached me in the States with EBs they have had for years. The leather tended to get a bit stiff with age and sweat – which meant they were inclined to cause blisters – but these people had maintained them well. The last time I was over there, a guy showed me his old pair of EBs. The uppers were just about falling to pieces but he was still running in them because they were such wonderful shoes that he just kept on resoling them. He loved them.

'At that time, adidas had moved on to use kangaroo skin, which was very thin but also very strong. It's thin because their food supply is meagre; well-fed New Zealand animals, by contrast, have thick skins but the texture is not as good. The tanners split the New Zealand skins to get the thin leather, but this weakens the fibres.

'The EB shoes should have grabbed the market in the States because they were so good. I later had some involvement with Converse, too. They were specialists in basketball shoes, but they wanted to get into the running market. Using the same last, I got them to make all the fittings from A through to double E and people really appreciated that and loved them. They could get a fitting that was exactly right for their feet. But Converse took them off the market.

'Greg Lousey, who I helped to win a silver medal in the modern pentathlon, ran a hundred miles a week. He was a big guy and the Converse shoes worked so well for him that when he heard they were going off the market, he said to his wife,

"Clear out that cupboard for me", and he went out and bought a hundred pairs of them.

'Later, I went to the States as a guest of Brooks Shoes and they told me they didn't make their "running shoes" for people to run in, they were for people to walk in. Go anywhere these days and everybody is wearing so-called running shoes for everyday wear. They don't run in them. You can't anyway, because they are so stiff in the sole. Some manufacturers are starting to make more flexible shoes these days, but they're still largely a fashion item. Like gumboots, good for mowing the lawns in.

'The great thing about the EB was that you could buy a pair and run twenty miles straight off without making a mark on your feet. I wish I had a few pairs left now.'

So Arthur never got involved in the running shoe market in New Zealand. It is not a big enough market to make it worthwhile, because of the set-up costs, but he says it would be simple enough to make a last off the battered pair of EBs he still owns.

Arthur's dabble in the shoe market also introduced him to the thrills of European fast driving, in light of which his own reputation for being a fast driver in his younger days paled into a shadow. Still, he did move the wheels beneath him with much the same energy he poured into his running and coaching, but he recalls that he met his match in EB Shoes' Eugene Brutting. He invited Arthur to travel from Nuremberg to Zurich with him and Arthur, the keen tourist and sightseer, was happy to accept.

'He turned up in the biggest Mercedes Benz you can get. Before we started, he said, "Arthur, we won't be going down the autobahn because the traffic's too heavy. We'll take the back roads. Now, if anything happens, say, we have an accident, you'll find some tablets in the glove compartment. Just give me one." Obviously, he had a heart condition of some kind.

'We took off out of Nuremberg and we were doing 240 kilometres an hour on these back roads. They were good roads and the car was flying. He still had studs in his tyres for winter driving and they were flying out and pinging on the mudguards. Even when he slowed down, he was still doing 160 km/h. But the change was so marked I thought he'd stopped.

'We raced through Austria to Zurich and he stopped there and sold a couple of hundred thousand dollars' worth of women's shoes, some of the best fashion shoes in the world. We got a bit pissed together that night in the lovely mountain chalet where we stayed and he told me seriously that he hadn't had a very good year. "I only made 12 million marks," he said.

'We drove back to Germany more slowly because, I think, he didn't want to shake up the beautiful Swiss wine he'd filled the Mercedes' boot with. All I can say is that he was a very good driver, but most of the way I had my seat belt on and I was hanging on to my seat with both hands.'

Brutting gave Arthur a second-hand Renault to drive back to Finland. He was on his way back through Germany, it was getting dark and the car conked out.

'I pushed it off the autobahn and ran back about five kilometres to a shop and was lucky to find a couple of guys who could speak English. They told me there was a mechanic in the village who could fix Renaults and he turned up, towed the car away and fixed it for me. It cost me 300 marks. I finally got to Denmark, where I was going to stop over, about 4 o'clock in the morning but, as soon as I arrived, my hosts came down and we all had schnapps, despite the hour. The Danes are certainly very hospitable people.'

Having survived the bitterness of Finland's winter and its hostile press and the drama of German driving, Arthur was now drawn back to the heat and sunshine of South America.

21

Venezuela vision

ARTHUR WENT TO Venezuela twice, once in 1971 and again in 1974, courtesy of the Venezualan Athletic Federation. The country – with its profuse variety of flora and fauna and its sunny warmth – fascinated him. Beside the verandah of the apartment he had in Caracas stood a huge mango tree which was always full of colourful – and noisy – birds. His initial impression of the locals, however, wasn't so favourable. He arrived in Caracas in the middle of a riot. Armed police were rounding up rebellious students and shoving them into vans. The university was closed and for eight to ten months their education had been at a standstill – and, as Arthur quickly realised, they needed education to give them any chance of escaping the poverty cycle which was at the heart of their protest.

But he subsequently discovered a less rebellious side to their nature. 'The Venezuelans loved to run and they had excellent athletes.' And inevitably linked with that: 'The coaches were none too eager about me being there. They obviously took exception to me trying to help them. They seemed to think they already knew it all. It's a frame of mind I have come to expect and accept over the years.' Not that constant repetition made it any better. There have been many times when Arthur's tolerance of unbelievers has been stretched so far that a lesser man might have given up.

'My athletes were quartered close to a lovely park, Parque del Este, which again was full of flowering trees and gaudily coloured birds. I decided it would make a fine training ground, not just because it is one of the world's most beautiful parks, but because Caracas had few areas satisfactory for long-distance running and this was the most suitable. The first time I sent my runners out to train there, I told them to do an hour's fartlek and meet us at the bus outside the park gates.

'What I didn't know was that by law in Caracas men were required to wear a jacket in the business area of the city, and the park was in the business area. Anyone who ran about in shorts was likely to be jeered at – or worse. When the hour had passed and only three of the twenty runners I sent out were back at the bus, I asked Lloyd Murad, the American sprint coach, who was with me, if he had given them the correct directions. He assured me he had, so we set off to look for them.

'We finally found them, locked in a police compound and guarded by Alsatian dogs. Their offence was running in the park in shorts. I wondered then how I was ever going to train these young guys. It took several phone calls to the secretary of the president of Venezuela to secure their release and, later, permission to train in the park in shorts.'

By contrast, Arthur found, the Venezuelan women, although they dressed very well, were often scantily clad in public. They were also aggressive, taking a 'get out of my way' approach in the streets.

'I liked the country and the people and, on the first of my two visits there, apart from the reserve of the coaches, I got cooperation from the officials.

'My runners were full of life. I took ten athletes and two coaches to San Cristobal, in the Andes, and got up one morning to discover they had all vanished. Around mid-morning, they came drifting back to the motel. "Where have you been?" I asked. "Did you get up a bit early?"

'"Oh, no," was the answer, "we've been over to Cucuta."

Cucuta was about 20 kilometres away, just over the border in Colombia. So what was so interesting about Cucuta that they had to stay there all night?

"Ah…" they said with a huge grin, "the girls over there are very beautiful and cheap, so we spent the night there."'

Arthur says the boys went over the Colombian border to see

the girls more than once, but they also came back with 2-kilogram tins of Australian butter, which pleased him enough to forgive them, because the Venezuelan butter wasn't too good. 'I often thought: Why isn't New Zealand selling butter here? Mind you, that was in 1974 and I would hope things have changed since.'

That first night trip over the border can't have done Arthur's boys much harm because they ran pretty well in their road race that day – but for a time he thought he'd had lost his whole team. 'I hadn't learnt yet that in these countries brothels are more or less legal and the men go to them quite a lot. In fact, at the weekends in San Cristobal, I didn't see many men about at all. They were away over the border.

'In another Andes town, Meridas, a bit over 2000 metres above sea level, we ran for several kilometres through deep ravines on a road which twisted high up on the steep mountainside. We came to one particularly sharp bend with a sheer drop off the outside edge. It was unfenced and there were thirty or forty little crosses with flowers on them on the road edge. I asked what had happened. Had a bus gone over?

'"No," I was laughingly told, "the men leave town and go down the road to the brothel area, drink and carry on, then they come back and drive clean over the cliff." In Venezuela, life, like the brothel girls, was cheap. The mass of crosses looked pathetic, but I had to see the funny side of it.'

Arthur found that, while obtaining the facilities and the time to develop the potential of his athletes was difficult, getting the Venezuelans to run was easy. In the little town of Tucapita, near the mouth of the Orinoco River, he took half a dozen runners out one morning, heading along a road that speared straight into the thick jungle. 'We ran for nearly forty-five minutes in the hot sun and by the time we got back our numbers had increased to about thirty,' he recalls. 'Girls and boys of all ages, in bare feet, sandals or shoes, had joined our run for the sheer fun of it. Kids would often accompany athletes for miles in marathon races. There was wonderful material there, if I could only have found a way to organise the administrators to harness it.

'I spent four months working with two young runners,

Henrico, who was 15, and Hernandez, who was 16, schooling them for the 1500 metres. They were a skinny couple who looked as if they had never eaten a square meal, but they possessed the fantastic qualities I sensed in scores of Venezuelans. At the end of the four months, Henrico ran 4:01 and Hernandez 3:57 for the distance. Another 16-year-old was running 400 metres in 45 to 46 seconds. The possibilities were vast and the kids worked hard, but the coaching was so counter-productive that I knew they would never develop to their world-class potential.

'There was plenty of money available but it was channelled in the wrong directions and I couldn't get what I needed to finish my programme. Venezuela was a wealthy country, but the politicians were handling the spending for sport and looking after their own political interests rather than the best interests of the country's youth. It was like Mexico all over again.

'Some of the racing was enough to turn a coach's hair grey, if it wasn't already. I recall one marathon race I put my boys into. They were nicely out in front as the race carried on into the dark of night. But, after the race, when the third place-getter was announced, I heard my runners muttering among themselves. I asked them what the trouble was and they told me they had passed this very talented runner early in the race and couldn't understand how he got up to finish third without passing them back. We concluded that, in the cover of darkness, the runner's coach had picked him up and driven him back to the front of the field.

'Another marathon, held in Caracas, featured two very good runners from San Cristobal, which is over 2000 metres up in the Andes. They didn't know the race route but, by the halfway mark, they were out in front and well clear of the rest of the field. I was cruising back and forth on a motorbike watching the race, but mainly following the progress of another runner. Then, on my next run up to the front to see how my leaders were doing, the San Cristobal pair were no longer in front. The local coach's pair were.

'I found out that he'd taken advantage of the visitors' lack of course knowledge and had turned them down the wrong route to let his boys get in front. This was the kind of problem I was up against and there was little I could do about it except admire the cunning and ingenuity they put into their race planning.

'Venezuela is full of snakes too. I was training with the marines in a suburb in Caracas, running through tall grass rather like small bamboo, when the front runners stopped dead. I asked them why they'd stopped and they said there was a traga-vernadas in the trail. Traga-vernadas turned out to be a type of boa constrictor about four metres long, yellow, orange and white in colour. Their hunting technique apparently is to lie on a trail and, when an animal comes along, hiss out a gas which puts the intended victim into a coma. Then the snake crushes and swallows the victim. The marines killed this one, but I later saw many more snakes and never had any problems with them.

'I was asked in Tucapita if I would like to go hunting for jaguars. I asked where we would find them and was told they were where we had been running that morning. It might have been an interesting experience, but I did not accept the offer.

'Usually, when I went to places I was not familiar with, I would ask first if there was anything I had to look for, to be sure I didn't get into any trouble. But I didn't when I was in Tucapita and often went walking at night along the river beach. I learnt later that the numerous large tributaries of the Orinoco – big enough to be rivers in their own right – were home to caymans, a nasty type of alligator, and snakes as well as the fish the villagers caught for food.

'Occasionally, natives arrived in dugout canoes with wares to sell. They were interesting-looking people because they all sported a pudding bowl hairstyle. Among the things they sold were birds in small cages plaited from some sort of grass or vine. They even had the big-beaked toucans in these small cages. Tucapita was fascinating, and I was happy there among nice and friendly people. Because of the heat and humidity, none of the homes had windows, but the village's fine gymnasium did. It was fitted with the best weight-training equipment, all of which was going rusty. I guess they didn't know how to use it.'

It was typical of the difficulties Arthur experienced in South

America that, although the Federation president was a pleasant man and very helpful, there never seemed to be enough money to go round. They were paid monthly and every month Lloyd Murad would ask Arthur to lend him hundreds of bolivars so that he could help to feed some of his runners, because they were not getting enough to eat. He would always pay Arthur back next pay day but, inevitably, a week later, would ask to borrow more money. In the end, Arthur said, "Whose money is it, Lloyd, because you have it for three weeks and I have it for only one?" Arthur says he really didn't mind, because Lloyd looked after his athletes well.

Before Arthur returned to New Zealand, he suggested to Lloyd that, since he was always giving his money to the athletes, it might be a good idea for him to come to New Zealand and take up a teaching position, for which he was well qualified and for which he would be well paid. He told him he'd lend him the money to get started and he could pay it back out of his teacher's salary.

'Lloyd agreed so I went to the headmaster at Papatoetoe High School to see if I could get him a job there. He sent me on to Edgewater College, whose head offered Lloyd a position. He came out to New Zealand with his young wife and settled in, later moving to Auckland Boys Grammar, where he had considerable success training their soccer team and sprinters. Lloyd had been trained by the great American coach, Bud Winter, who had trained most of the track gold medallists at the Mexico Olympics. He'd run the 100 metres in 10.2 and had competed at Olympic level. He is now in San José in the United States. I think he found New Zealand a bit slow.'

On Arthur's second visit to Venezuela, he was supposed to train a team for the South American track championships in Peru. However, a revolution put Peru out of contention and it was too late to switch to the back-up country, Colombia – they always had an emergency country in South America in case of political upheaval – so he came back to New Zealand, leaving behind some very fit young men pondering what might have happened.

'On this visit, I took a bus trip to Maracaibo at night-time and was fascinated by the continual flashes of lightning over the distant jungle. It was a phenomenon they called *catadumbo* and it flashed every few seconds 24 hours a day. The cause was never explained to me, but I learnt that ships used this *catadumbo* for navigation in the Caribbean. Watching it was a spectacular way to pass the time on a night trip.

'Maracaibo is in the north of Venezuela, about ten degrees off the equator and with jungles to the south and east. It was so hot and humid that I would shower, walk down the road for a few minutes and be wet through again.

'I was in the hotel when three Australians arrived. They had driven a car from Panama through Colombia and had been robbed by bandits. The woman told me they had lost a lot of their gear but when I asked if she had been molested, she said, with typical Australian humour, "No, unfortunately, because they were good-looking guys."'

Despite the Australian tourists' experience, Arthur found the city of Caracas and the country around Merida and Tucapita quite safe to travel through. 'It may have changed since I was there but it is the people who make the country, and the Venezuelans in my experience were helpful and friendly. I rate it the most interesting country I have been in, and there are few that I have not visited over the years. The food was excellent. They don't eat tortillas like the Mexicans, but favour *arepas*, which are small buns like a bread roll. They pull the middle out and pack the cavity with a variety of fillings. And the tropical fruits were delicious. I'd never seen many of them before because globalisation wasn't the force in the 1970s that it is today.

'Looking back though, I don't think South America was the place for me. The athletes were very good, but the coaches held the athletes back and, as far as I was concerned, the officials held the coaches back. They wanted immediate success, but it takes at least three years on a well-balanced programme to get top results. I have experienced this impatient desire for quick results all around the world – but no one has yet found a way of getting them – simply because there is none.

'The United States was the same under the old American

Athletic Union [AAU]. The universities were producing the athletes but the AAU were in control and going on the trips.'

So, like Mexico, Venezuela's athletic prospects foundered on the rocks of officialdom's indifference and Arthur moved on again. And on and on. The world was his oyster, but getting the pearls out was never easy. A classic example was Turkey.

22

far and wide

IN TURKEY, A major glassworks, Sise-Cam, was keen to sponsor the country's athletics programme. They had millions of dollars waiting to be released, but were not impressed with what they had seen, so they asked Arthur to help. 'The glassworks company called me because they wanted some results before they put more money into the athletes. I decided I'd go over for nothing; I didn't want any money, I just wanted to see the results come through. I stayed there three months and worked with some very good athletes, the kind you can find all over the world. They were very enthusiastic and could do all the endurance training, the hill training, everything. They were mostly very poor and the glassworks was looking after them well, paying them a retainer to train.

'I talked to the Athletics Federation in Ankara and quickly realised they were a pack of no-hopers who didn't understand about training and weren't too interested in learning. They thought you just suddenly got a champion. I began working closely with two very good marathon-running boys and arranged for them to fly to America when I went over there for a week-long seminar. Then when we were in the States I got a call from Turkey saying they were wanted back to run in the Balkans marathon. They went back and I asked the Turks to send them on to Denmark, where I was going next. They never came.

'The glassworks sponsors were very good people, but for me it was just a waste of time. They had everything they needed for training, the money was plentiful, the conditions were good, but the administration was useless. They could not understand that it takes several years to develop Olympic champions. Everything else was set up for the Turks to succeed – the only missing ingredient was that understanding. If they had kept to my programme over two or three years, I am sure they would have produced some of the world's best athletes. The potential was all there and it was a tragedy that it was never allowed to develop.'

In 1970-71, Arthur spent nine months in Denmark helping the Danes to prepare for the Olympics in Munich the following year. He warned them when he arrived they should not expect miracles and that if they got anyone into a final they should consider it a victory. Despite the short lead time, he achieved that victory for them.

'Their top runner was Tom Hansen and we got him into the 1500 metres final and another reached the semi-finals, which was pretty good in nine months. Tom was tired by the time he reached the final because he was not conditioned enough. He'd had nothing like the build-up my athletes got in New Zealand in the 1950s and early 1960s.

'I took the Danish team to Munich and just missed striking an unusual treble. I was to be the official coach for New Zealand in Tokyo in 1964 and the Finns had wanted me as coach for their team to Mexico in 1968. I declined, advising them to appoint one of their own coaches to give him experience. It was a good idea and it helped them four years later when they got to Munich but it would have been a feather in my cap to have been the Olympic coach for three different countries.

'The Danes were very happy with the results we achieved. They had never had any success in international track and field meets but we set them up well for Munich and they beat both Northern Ireland and Holland for the first time at an international track meet.

'I have maintained contact with the Danes over the years. I helped to prepare their team for the world cross-country championships in New Zealand in 1988 and, the same year, their runner Allan Zachariessen won the Wang men's marathon in Auckland and Kersti Jacobsen won the women's section. It was further proof, if proof is still needed, that champions can be found and moulded everywhere you care to look.'

By 1972, Arthur was back in New Zealand again and, with the help of Auckland Amateur Athletics Association secretary Graham Davy, he was given a job with Winstone Ltd, a company that was a major player in the construction industry. This position enabled him to assist coaches and athletes throughout the country.

'One of the coaches was Wayne Smith, of Napier, who coached a Colenso College girl, Dianne Zorn, who later won the secondary schools 800-metre championship and was a record-holder for some time. When I talked to her college assembly one day, I saw her sitting in the front row, drew attention to her and predicted she would be an Olympic rep one day.

'That girl, who later became Dianne Rodger, proved me right with a remarkable running career which took her to two Olympic Games, in 1980 and 1984, and several records. It was a demonstration of her ability and determination that, the first time she raced 3000 metres, twice the distance she was used to, she was only half a second behind the fine Australian, Angela Cook, and ahead of Anne Audain and Heather Matthews, two world-class New Zealand internationals. Since it was also the first time the distance had been raced in New Zealand, it gave her the national resident record. She did the same when she first raced and won over 5000 metres.

'I was still working with John Davies and John Robinson, who were then with the Tokoroa Club. It was a strong club, which also produced Lorraine Moller and Mike Ryan. Their four names still rank highly in New Zealand athletics.

'The coaches I supplied with schedules were very good at following them. They were easy schedules to read, in the sense that the various segments and activities were carefully but simply explained. But there were still occasions when the schedules didn't work. A classic example occurred in 1974, when Dick Tayler got ankylosing spondylitis and lost about three weeks' training at a critical time before the Commonwealth Games in Christchurch. His coach, Alistair McMurran, who was very good, got a bit mixed up and didn't know know what to do to get him back on course. He called me and I took over Dick's training. As part of it, I took him down to a college track one day, in Te Kuiti, I think it was.

'The kids asked me what Dick was going to do and I said, "I don't know. He's just going to run repetitions around the track."

'They asked, "How many times is he going to do it?"

'I said, "I don't know."

'"What times is he going to do?"

'"I don't know. It doesn't matter. How far round is the track anyway?'

'They must have thought then that the coach didn't know what he was doing. So, when Tayler finished, they asked him how many laps he did.

'He said, "I don't know. I never counted them."

'They asked, "What times did you do?"

'"I never timed them," Dick said.

'I explained to the youngsters that the details they were seeking were not important. What was important was that he did it until he hit the wall. That would tell him and me that he had done enough. They couldn't understand. Maybe, when Dick romped away with the 10,000-metres title and Commonwealth Games record in Christchurch, it might have dawned on them.

'I was with Dick and his girlfriend in Hokitika a long time after that 10,000 metres win and someone asked him why he threw his arms up in the air and lay down on the track when he reached the finish line. TV never tires of replaying the film of his antics.

'Dick said, "They'd just told me the bars were still open."

'Dick was – and still is – that kind of guy.'

In 1979 Arthur was invited to South Africa by South African Breweries. He'd been there previously, in 1964, with Peter Snell, on a tour arranged by Rothmans. Arthur gave talks and Snell competed in some races but didn't run well because he hadn't done the necessary training.

Arthur remembers, 'For some reason I could never understand, we had a New Zealand manager with us. He had never been away before so we virtually had to manage him. The New Zealand Amateur Athletics Association had a habit in those days of appointing managers who couldn't manage. I got up one morning in Cape Town, went downstairs and found our public relations man with one of his eyes closed up. He said he and our manager had got into an argument in the bar the night before and the manager had hung one on him. Peter and I were totally embarrassed, because the South Africans were looking after us so well.

'During the tour, I was invited to go to a distance-running conference in Duisburg in Germany, so I flew up there for a couple of days and then went back to South Africa. I met Woldemar Gerschler and Herbert Reindell for the first time on this flying trip. They were the experts on anaerobic repetitions. Dr Ernst von Aachen, who believed in my type of training, was also there. He was the man who really got women's marathon running going. The meeting was also a starting point for world-wide interest in our training methods.

'On my second visit I was really impressed with the South African athletes and I could see the potential in them. Unfortunately, at this time, the South African Amateur Athletics Union was suspended and its runners couldn't compete against other countries. Several marathon runners had tried to get into the Boston marathon early in 1979 and were barred and criticised for not having permission from the SAAAU to be there. But I told them to get out and run; to show their colours around the world and not be afraid of criticism.

'I also caused a bit of a stir by stating that top athletes should be paid under the table to take part in races to keep them going financially. It was common knowledge that this is exactly what was happening all over the world and officialdom was closing its eyes. I told them that Sebastian Coe, then at his miling peak, could make £50,000 a year and still remain an amateur.

'I also had a crack at the stupidity of South Africa's best runners taking up scholarships to American universities, pointing out that Henry Rono, of Kenya, had smashed six world records before he went to the United States. The Americans had then run the guts out of him and he had done nothing since. Then, as now, many American universities destroy good athletes. The competition among coaches is so fierce that they'll do almost anything to get to the top of the heap. It's all to do with attracting funding. Consequently, universities make fantastic offers to attract athletes to their campuses and then expect them to run their hearts out. In those earlier days, training facilities were poor, the education they offered was equally poor and many a fine runner was ground into the dust just to earn pixie points for his coach and his university.

'I also got involved in the controversy over Professor Christian Barnard's criticism of jogging. He claimed it would put people at risk of heart trouble. I knew that millions of joggers all around the world had treated his adverse remarks as a joke and it had by then been proved that jogging strengthened the heart and added enjoyable years to the lives of many people. I was quoted as saying I would rather keep my own heart healthy by jogging than have someone else's heart transplanted into me.

'I was also drawn into the controversy over pre-competition sex, because Gerrie Coetzee and John Tate were preparing for a world heavyweight boxing title fight in Pretoria. The bout was four weeks away and Tate had already sworn off sex and Coetzee planned to leave his wife for several weeks. The view I expressed was that it was a load of rubbish, which earned me the newspaper headline "Bedroom romps help, says top track coach". I had told the the media I knew athletes who found that having sex the day before competing relaxed them so that they slept better.'

During that same 1979 trip, Arthur ran in the 50 kilometre Stock Exchange race from Pretoria to Johannesburg in a starting line-up of more than 2000 runners. Many of the competitors had little running experience, yet most finished. This amazed him, but he reckons it was because they'd seen people complete the Comrades Marathon, and never had any doubt that they could manage the shorter distance themselves.

'The top Bantu runner in South Africa at that time was on holiday when I was there and, although I was there for a month, he never came to my seminars. He was being paid to train, but going to a training session in his holiday time apparently didn't rate as part of his programme.

'The South African custom was to provide both soft drinks and beer at lunchtime and it was interesting to me that the whites went for the beer and the blacks always went for the soft drinks. But they were all nice people and a pleasure to be with.

Our wives were given a nice time and I assume the New Zealand manager had a nice time, too. I don't know; I didn't see too much of him.'

'The South Africans had such a good heritage of distance running that it was no trouble to get them to do the conditioning training I prescribed; but they were screwing up the speed work and, by not doing it properly, they couldn't reach their potential.

'When I was in Bloemfontein, I took a seminar at which, unbeknown to me, there was a coach who was training a young woman who was later to become very prominent in distance running. Her name was Zola Budd. When she became prominent and went to England, it was suggested to the coach that he must be exceptionally good to turn such a slight young woman into a champion – he had the grace to say that he only trained her to my schedules.'

When he was in his mid-60s, Arthur carved a cross-country coaching trail right across Canada from Vancouver to Nova Scotia, talking to and running with athletes and coaches for several weeks. He then flew down to Texas, to take part in activities centred around the 1982 Dallas marathon, but found that he was also expected to run in it. Although he had partied in Dallas the night before and had had only two hours' sleep because he'd intended only to watch the race, he was fit from his Canadian tour and, typically, rose to the challenge. He surprised himself as much as anyone else by winning his age group by a good margin, but confessed that he had to walk the last three miles.

Two years earlier, Arthur had run what he thought would be his last marathon, in Hamilton, New Zealand and, again, the last three miles undid him. 'It was 26 years since I had last actually raced a marathon and I was on a 2:40 finish,' he recalls, 'but three miles from the end, my legs seized up. I finished in 2:58:58 and I lost 130 places over that last stretch.' The fact that so many runners streamed past him rather ironically highlighted how much marathon racing had grown over the previous two decades. Where once there was a handful of competitors scattered over miles of the course, today's major races feature an endless procession of athletes.

One of Arthur's greatest satisfactions while working for Winstones was setting up walks in the Waitakeres, the hills in which he used to do a lot of his own training and where he took his athletes. People were normally reluctant to go in there because they were afraid of getting lost, but hundreds turned up to Arthur's Sunday walkabouts and he effectively opened up the ranges to a lot of people, popularising bush tracks all over the forest. Winstones operated a shuttle service, using their company vehicles to get people to and from the starting points of the various walks that Arthur had mapped out. He was given great support and co-operation by the Auckland parks organisation and the park rangers. As well as encouraging the general public to take more exercise, Arthur was also sought out by athletes in other fields.

'While I was with Winstones, the kayaker Ian Ferguson asked me what I thought was wrong with his training, because he wasn't improving. I looked over his programme and saw it was all mixed up, there was no balance. I straightened it out and he went on to win the world championship. Then we refined the programme for all our canoeists – I think we had eight in the whole of New Zealand at the time – and they went to Los Angeles and won four Olympic gold medals. They might have known more about paddling than I did, but I knew more about making them paddle better.

'Unfortunately, once again they drifted back to anaerobic training and by the next Olympics they didn't have one competitor taking part. It was another occasion where we could have gone on from Ferguson and got even better, because we have good canoeists in this country, and they only need to follow a balanced programme to become world leaders.'

Internationally, the demand for Lydiard's know-how continued. His reputation had already reached the Far East through his involvement with Japan; now a booming new economy sent out a call. As usual, Arthur responded.

23

Far East expeditions

'IN 1983 NIKE arranged for me to go up to speak to the South Koreans and I took a lot of them through the philosophy of my training. They were doing far too much anaerobic work. As a result of my visit, they decided they would send a group to New Zealand. The following year about twelve runners under their head coach, Mr Choi, and another coach came down to New Zealand and we accommodated them at Auckland's Totara Park, in South Auckland. I remember taking them shopping. The coach paid for it all from a brown paper bag stuffed with several thousands of dollars in American and New Zealand notes, which he carried everywhere and kept somewhere in his bedroom at night. They looked after themselves, cooking their own meals and so on, while we settled them into training to our programme.

'It caused some amusement. The two Korean coaches would get out on the road and urge the runners, "Faster, faster" while I was out there telling them, "Slower, slower". Interestingly, they all entered a marathon in Hamilton later on and the two guys who were always last in training finished first and second. After that, the rest of them and their coaches began to understand more about training according to my system. The marathon had been a good demonstration of how well the method works.

'Subsequently, I sent Jack Ralston to Korea to help them. Jack had used my schedules to train for middle-distance events, so he was well grounded in my methods and was later to become the coach of several leading international short- and long-distance triathletes. But Mr Choi had come fourth in an Olympic marathon and therefore thought he knew better than Jack, who hadn't been an Olympian. Okay, I said, we'll send Barry Magee over. His third in an Olympic marathon ranked him over Mr Choi. Barry delivered exactly the same message as Jack, but this time they listened to it. Barry brought a team of them back to New Zealand and looked after them. One of them went on to win the Olympic marathon in Barcelona and one of the girls later won the world marathon championship. They learnt fast.

'I subsequently sent one of the boys to Korea whenever they needed help – I didn't enjoy going there because I didn't like the food. They served up far too much fishy stuff for me and I don't eat fish. I let the others go through the agony. Both Barry Magee and Jack did good jobs up there, but they faced the occasional difficulty because some of the people they were dealing with thought they knew better.

'By this time, however, about the only country not using our training methods was New Zealand. But that's not surprising once you understand New Zealanders. They have a strange outlook – the moment you succeed, they are anti you; they don't want to find out how you succeeded and get up there with you. They want to keep on doing it their own way, even if it's been shown not to work.'

In 1982, Arthur was one of four coaches invited to take the first seminar for the Olympic Committee in China, at Nanning, located in the south-west of the country, about 160 kilometres north of Vietnam. The other coaches were an Indian, an East German and a Canadian.

He recalls: 'China was a good experience for me, except for the food. I just don't like their food. I was out one morning and saw an animal like a possum lying on the footpath, with a piece of fur and flesh cut out of it. Later, at dinner, when some black-looking meat was put in front of us, I asked one of the English-speaking Chinese what it was.

'"Bamboo cat," he said.

'I said, "That animal I saw on the pavement this morning...?"

'He nodded. "That's it."

'The other coaches got stuck into it. I don't think they knew what they were eating, but I did and I didn't touch it. Anything that moves in China, they eat.

'After our seminars, I was offered a week's all-expenses-paid tour round China and, much as I was tempted, I said I had to go home. It might have been a chance to see the Great Wall and other sights, but I just could not stomach the food. I can see the Great Wall on television without ruining my digestion.

'But the Chinese were very nice people. One of my knees was giving me trouble at the time. Mr Wu, my interpreter, suggested acupuncture so I had some treatment by the official Chinese method. It did not do me any good. My knee was such a mess anyway and even acupuncture can't repair bone-on-bone damage. Mr Wu and the acupuncturist chattered away in Chinese and I asked what they were talking about.

'Mr Wu asked me if we had acupuncturists in New Zealand. I said we did and they laughed. Mr Wu said the guy treating me just commented, "There are acupuncturists – and there are acupuncturists."

'The Chinese coaches I talked to at the seminar were all pretty old. I thought they looked as if they might be past it, but they took in what I told them. Several years later one of them, Junren Ma, made headlines with a team of girls who broke all the world records. They were all genuine runners to whom Ma had given big training mileages after listening to my theories.

'A New Zealander who was coaching some girls in Hong Kong sent one of them up to work with Ma and discovered that they ran twenty miles every day. When Ma came into prominence, a reporter from England rang me up and asked if I thought he was using drugs to get such results. I said I didn't think so; it was the big mileages they were doing. The reporter said Ma had told him the training he was doing was a cross between Lydiard's and Cerutty's. He'd struck a compromise between our two methods and he was conditioning his athletes well.

'There was a lot of hilarious talk about him feeding his girls on caterpillar juice. It was actually the juice extracted from the roots of a tree with a Chinese name that sounded like caterpillar. I was reminded of Lasse Viren's thoughtful response when reporters asked him how he ran so well. He said he drank reindeer milk. He told me he felt he had to say something to give the reporter a quote – it's the training that makes the difference, of course, but he realised that's not headline stuff, so he fed them something they could get excited about.

'Before I left New Zealand to visit them, the Chinese Olympic Committee had sent me a green tracksuit. I learnt about it only when I was phoned by Customs asking me to call and collect it – and they wanted to charge me for it. I told them what to do with the bloody thing. I never got it and I don't know what happened to it. I couldn't see why it should cost me money to go to help the Chinese. I suppose if I had been an official Olympic coach, it wouldn't have cost me anything. So I was the only one of the coaches there who didn't have an official tracksuit. I felt that it was an honour to represent New Zealand at this seminar.'

Though Arthur continually came up against barriers of jealousy, scepticism, inedible food and awkward administrations, one area of his expertise was accepted and diligently pursued by millions of people. That wisdom was the concept of jogging. It began more than four decades ago and it continues today all over the globe. It is perhaps the single factor that elevates Arthur beyond the realm of the successful coach to the role of the people's guru.

24

the birth and life of jogging

LIKE MANY GOOD things, jogging began in a small way and I don't think anyone who was involved in the early days thought that it would eventually sweep the world.

After Arthur returned to New Zealand from the Rome Olympics, he was invited by the Tamaki Lions Club in eastern Auckland to talk to them about how New Zealand had suddenly produced these Olympic champions. In the course of his talk, Arthur explained how he trained his athletes to the point where they could run and run and run, virtually tirelessly, yet still finish very fast. The secret was that he had developed their cardiovascular systems and so enhanced their cardiac efficiency.

'At the end of my talk, three men came to me and explained they were retired businessmen and had coronary problems. One said, "In the light of what you have just told us, slow running could help us but the medical people have told us not to do anything of an energetic nature." I said, "Well, put it this way – if you sit around and don't use your body intelligently, it's going to deteriorate on you, so anything you do to prevent that deterioration, as long as it's carefully controlled, is going to help you."

'Which was enough to get them into jogging. First, I advised them to get the green light from a cardiologist, as I wasn't sure that the average family doctor knew enough about exercising. Then they went down to the Auckland waterfront, walked from one telegraph pole to the next, jogged to the one after that, walked to the next, jogged to the next – until they had covered a mile. It took quite a long time at first but, gradually, they got fitter and fitter until they were running the whole distance – and still getting faster and faster until they were running seven-minute miles, which is a fair pace – eight and a half miles an hour.

'Some of these men went down to Christchurch and met business associates, whose first question was, "What have you been doing? You look so thin, are you sick or something?"

' "No," they said, "we're fitter than we've ever been."

'So, the next thing, I was in Christchurch talking to groups down there. The police and others got involved in a sudden push for a jogging movement and I guess that's when the snowball began rolling.'

A year or two later, Arthur sat on a plane next to Colin Kay, a former fine athlete, an athletics administrator and later mayor of Auckland. Arthur knew Colin from earlier days and he could see that he was somewhat overweight; not obese, but obviously out of condition. So he talked to him about exercising and told him what he'd been doing with his joggers, although that term hadn't come into vogue then. He also suggested that Colin needed some exercise to reduce his expanded waistline.

Colin, being the organiser he is, gathered together some of his business associates, many of whom had had coronaries. He enlisted the help of a cardiologist, Dr Noel Roydhouse, and they all met Arthur and some of his leading athletes at Colin's home one Sunday morning. Arthur talked about the practice of easy running, using his athletes to prove his point. Dr Roydhouse gave his views on the medical implications and, that morning, the group started running. Jogging was properly born.

Arthur: 'I remember telling these guys, "First thing, whatever you do, don't get competitive." They looked at each other's pot bellies and laughed, but I knew the competitive aspect had to be watched. I knew that, if they stayed within their limitations, they couldn't hurt themselves; if they started racing each other, they could. They had all had medical checks before they started, so that was no problem.

'I told them I didn't care if they smoked or drank, but they should get out and exercise because if they did not use their bodies sensibly, they would deteriorate. I assured them, whatever their bad habits were, they could lower their pulse rates and develop their cardiovascular systems to take the pressure off their hearts and coronary arteries with surprisingly little effort. And they'd probably give up smoking and reduce their drinking in the process.

'I got a lot more help from another cardiologist, Jack Sinclair, who had been the New Zealand mile champion in his younger days, and his advice helped ensure we never had any problems. Our first easy run was about three miles from near Meadowbank down to the waterfront, where some of the group had a swim before we jogged back home again. None of them had run that far before. Actually, it was very slow because some walked as much as they jogged and I enforced my rule that they should go at the pace of the slowest and never try to go at the pace of the fastest.

'Later on, when jogging was permanently established, the idea that the fastest should run at the pace of the slowest was galling to the more competitive joggers, and club runs were eventually split into fast, medium and slow packs – and eventually into walking groups as well – so that everyone could work within their own limits more acceptably.

'The word "jogging" was adopted because it somehow fitted in with the easy running concept of what we were doing. In those days, before seven-day shopping became the norm, many of us worked on Saturday mornings and shopped late on Fridays. So I had made Friday an easy day for my runners and marked my schedules with a half-hour jog that day. Eventually my Sunday group became the Auckland Joggers Club and jogging became an international cult.'

The first joggers were a motley bunch. Some wore ordinary shirts. None had singlets. Some didn't have shorts. And they mostly ran in tennis shoes, invariably made of canvas with soft soles. But, since they were not running fast, they didn't bang their joints around too much. Initially, some could barely manage a quarter of a mile before they had to stop to catch their breath, but very few quit and the overall rate of improvement was astonishing. Theoretically, that Sunday jog was all that was involved and there were some who were satisfied with that, but a great many became every-day joggers who progressed to being every-day runners.

The jogging phenomenon was a snowball which just kept getting bigger and its momentum faster. Only two years after that inaugural meeting one of the foundation joggers, Win Nelmes, aged 49, ran a marathon in 3:26 and was seventh on handicap in a field of about 100, most of them practising athletes. He missed qualifying as an Auckland marathon representative by only 11 minutes. He began jogging because he'd started to put on weight and Arthur's blunt message had turned his concern about his health into real fright.

In time, Cornwall Park became the recognised home of Auckland jogging. 'I don't know how they got the then One Tree Hill Borough Council interested, but they became established there and now have their own clubhouse in the park grounds,' Arthur says. 'It was chosen, I imagine, because it is central to the whole of Auckland and it's a beautiful place for running, with flat areas, not-too-difficult hills and nice varied circuits. I used it extensively when I was training athletes, cross-country races were once held over it and it is still thronged with exercise buffs.

'The movement grew mainly by word of mouth. It advertised itself; people could see their friends looking fitter and better and joined in. And we had newspaper journalists taking part, too. They had a good insight into what we were doing and could write sensibly about us, which increased public interest.

'It had its not-so-good moments, of course. Forty years ago, people didn't run on the roads in broad daylight. Even my athletes did all their road running at night to fit in with their work hours. So the pioneer joggers took some stick from people who didn't have any idea of what they were trying to achieve and regarded them as stupid old plodders. Now, you see men, women and children of all ages and sizes running and the people who jeer and catcall are in the minority. There have been instances of bottles and other objects as well as abuse being thrown at runners, but these are isolated incidents and the abusers are the ones who are stupid.'

In the early days of jogging, some very odd reactions

occurred. A friend of Arthur's went running after dark from the Naval Base at Devonport, on Auckland's North Shore. A police car came along, stopped and he was asked, 'What are you doing?'

He replied, 'I'm running for my health.'

'Oh, yes, we know all about that,' the cop said. And they slapped him in jail for the night. They knew people didn't run on the roads in those days just for their health.

It was by no means an isolated incident. Not long after I started working with Arthur on *Run to the Top*, I went out for a run early one morning from my home, then near Otahuhu. When I say early morning, it was actually about 2 a.m. I was working long hours in the PR and advertising racket, on top of trying to write the book, and Arthur's message had so enthused me that I'd given up smoking and was actually working on his marathon training schedule.

So I needed long runs and the only time I could fit them in was when normal people were asleep. So this warm night, I was coming home from a 12-miler along the Otahuhu Highway when a patrol car cruised alongside; a torch was shone on me and a voice said something like, 'What's *your* hurry?'

'I'm running home, just round the corner.'

'What are you running from?'

'I've been out for a run to Onehunga and back.'

Their disbelief was evident. I was still jogging, they were still cruising, the torch still had me covered.

'You're just running?' the cop in the passenger seat asked. His irony was heavier than the car he was sitting in. I was wearing a pair of running shoes and a pair of shorts, without pockets.

'Do I look like a burglar?' I asked.

'Why are you running this time of the morning?'

'I just finished work an hour or so ago... I needed a run.'

'What work?'

'I'm a writer. I'm writing a book... on running.'

One of them laughed and said, 'On your way then.'

But the car followed me for about half a mile before it veered away.

The spread of jogging was interesting. Arthur recalls: 'I

encouraged several All Blacks of the time to take up long running to improve their endurance and to keep them conditioned out of season. Kel Tremain, who became one of the great try-scoring forwards because he could run as hard at the finish of a game as when he started, got the whole Hawke's Bay team up and running and they beat all the odds by winning the Ranfurly Shield. Nev McEwen, of Wellington, was another All Black who used long running effectively.

'In Hamilton, jogging was started by a cardiac specialist at Waikato Hospital, who had himself had a heart attack. It became a very strong movement in Waikato. In Dunedin, Dr Norrie Jefferson, who was involved in both athletics and cardiology, got a group of eighty people together and gave them a three-month jogging and testing trial, which wasn't long enough and didn't convince other medical experts – but at least they did do something about it. I was fortunate that I met a lot of medical people who were cooperative and helpful. I really knew nothing then about the physiological and medical aspects of running and jogging but I learnt quickly through their interest and support.

'The Auckland Joggers' Club was responsible for starting the great annual Round the Bays run along the Auckland waterfront, which each year draws up to 80,000 people, who run or walk the course. That event encourages a lot of people to take up regular jogging to keep fit.

'Some of the results people achieved through jogging were amazing. Men who couldn't manage a quarter-mile when they started became competent half and full marathon runners. Women got into it and they also became great athletes in their forties and upwards. Jogging has made a great contribution to the huge masters' fields which compete in marathon races all over the world.

'Jogging took different forms in different countries. There was more hype in America, of course, and in Denmark, when I was living and training there, three cardiologists organised the first 100km run I'd ever seen. About sixty men and women took part and the most interesting thing was that, at the end of it, the men were all lying on the ground and the women were still standing up and talking. Women have more subcutaneous fat than men and can handle runs like this better.

'The Auckland club now has as many women as men and as many walkers as joggers. That's good. Some people are too big to run and pound their joints too severely by jogging and some are hindered by arthritic joints and so on. They would run lighter if they could run faster, but they can't and walking is a good alternative, as long as it's purposeful.'

Unfortunately, at the other end of the scale, is the dark side of running – the insidious use of performance-enhancing drugs and the growing battle to control it and catch the cheats.

25

doping

DRUG TAKING IN sport could be a coincidence – its spread has fairly closely followed the expansion of professionalism. And it's nothing new. Even in New Zealand over 50 years ago some professional cyclists competing in the annual race round Mt Taranaki were known to have collapsed and fallen from their machines because they had miscalculated the timing and quantity of their benzedrine intake. Nowadays, the drugs are more sophisticated, but the cheats have to work hard to keep ahead of the anti-drug experts. One regrettable but inevitable consequence is that athletes can be punished for taking fairly conventional remedies for minor complaints, such as coughs and colds, because they contain small elements of drugs that could help them perform better. America's Olympic sprint star Carl Lewis is a case in point. The brilliance of his career has been tarnished by drug-taking allegations – not the steroids that transformed Canada's Ben Johnson into a gold medallist, but a stimulant apparently present in a cold medication.

Arthur Lydiard deplores the fact that there are people who try to improve their performances by taking drugs. In his opinion, there is no need to resort to these unfair tactics. And he knows the dangers from his own personal experience of benzedrine.

'I read about benzedrine many years ago, when I was still a competitive runner, and talked to my family doctor about it. He suggested that, to be clear in my mind, I should experiment. I had no intention of using drugs to enhance my race performances but I had an inquiring mind, so I got a few benzedrine tablets, which the German stormtroopers had been credited with using during the war. I used to run an eighteen-mile course every Thursday evening in about an hour and fifty minutes in training, so I took one of the tablets and ran the course and I actually felt that I was running faster than I had ever run the course.

'But, when I finished, I found that my time was the same as before. I felt well but, that night, I could not sleep. I have always been a good sleeper. That was my experience with a drug and it satisfied my curiosity about taking stimulants. I was never seriously interested in using them, regarding them then as I do now – unnecessary, unwise and to be avoided. I can't see how drug-taking can improve most athletes. Steroids may make you big and strong for shot-putting and events such as that, but I cannot see any benefit for endurance athletes. Drugs are not only dangerous, they don't do much for your balls, either.

'The risks are huge – and I'm not talking just about the taking of drugs either, but about what can happen with testing procedures and officialdom's sometimes offhand and even negligent approach to a lot of drug policing. In New Zealand we saw one of our top swimmers, Trent Bray, get caught up in a drug controversy which came close to wrecking his career. Eventually there was a court ruling that said his urine samples were so badly mishandled that the test was unlawful. He's not the only one to suffer and we need to make sure proper systems are in place, otherwise the innocents will keep getting punished.'

Drug-taking and the determined, if not always perfect, pursuit of the takers, is the grim downside of professional sport, but Arthur also sees an upside to the end of the amateur era. He believes the payment of athletes was long overdue. It takes a lot of time and hard work to become a top athlete and they now draw big crowds in Europe and America and make a lot of money for the promoters. 'We never got any money in our early days and it's only fair that they should now be able to share in the profits if they are good enough,' he says without a trace of rancour.

But there is a tinge of scorn in his voice when he touches on the issue of some athletes' demands for upfront appearance money. He regards this as 'a little over the top' but adds that the whole sporting world is now so highly competitive there is some justification for it.

'The only trouble now is that it is very difficult for a country like New Zealand, with such a small population and a lack of interest in track and field because of its low standard, to find the money to pay the expenses of these top athletes and coaches to come here. Many of them demand large amounts of money before they will go anywhere and, although New Zealand has plenty of money which should be used to develop the sport, it isn't enough for appearance fees. John Davies and Dick Quax promoted some international meets, but I think the cost got beyond them in the finish.'

A notable lesson in the dangers of appearance money to New Zealand promoters was Tiger Woods' visit to play in the New Zealand Golf Open in 2002. He asked for and got some NZ$5 million before he agreed to come. Sadly, those behind the promotion faced extreme financial difficulties because the income from sponsorship arrangements and gate takings was nowhere nearly enough to meet Woods' fee, the running costs and the prize purse.

'Perhaps if we had athletes like Snell and Halberg and Walker here again we'd attract television coverage, which is necessary these days, but we just don't have them. We should, but we don't. It can happen again only if they train the athletes properly,' Arthur says.

'We had some golden days and it would be great if we could relive them but without the nonsense that went on with the administration. We had to fight officials to develop our champions. They were the opposite of cooperative. Every time we were invited to go overseas, they hung on to the invites and then let us go only if we took a manager with us. They were generally useless. It was 1964 before there was any change in the system.

'Athletes now go overseas without managers, but still not always with the assistance of Athletics New Zealand. They get private invitations – if you can run a 2:09 marathon, you can go anywhere you like. But we're not using people properly. There is plenty of money about now but it's not being used properly because the people in control of the money don't know what to do. They've never produced a champion in their lives and they never will. We are disorganised at the present time and the organised will always beat the disorganised.

'Sending our woman discus thrower, Beatrice Faumuina, off to Australia to train for the Sydney Olympics, and paying for her mother to go with her instead of a good coach was a waste of money. You can't buy gold medals that way. They spent about $50,000 on that and it was all for nothing. She has come back to form since, but that doesn't get the money back.

'Another downside is that so many of today's athletes want everything laid on for them, They've gone soft, they can get financial assistance far too easily and many won't respond unless they get it first. It doesn't work. Becoming a topline athlete demands hard work and dedication, not easy money. Sure, they should get paid, but only after they've produced something worth paying for.'

26

on coaching

AFTER THE ROME Olympics, when Arthur began working as a columnist for the *Auckland Star*'s *8 O'Clock* sports edition, he expressed the view that New Zealand athletic coaches were as good as, if not better than, coaches in most other countries, but he said they lacked confidence. 'If they had only realised how good they were, they could have produced many Olympic medallists,' he says.

'At the time, I pointed out that Jim Bellwood had proved the point when he coached Yvette Williams to her Olympic gold medal in Helsinki in 1952 and we had other fine coaches, such as Frank Sharpley, Arthur Eustace and Bish McWatt. Les Barker, who trained Gary Philpott, had as great a practical understanding of middle and distance running as any coach anywhere. Lawrie King, the first man I trained, was coaching a fine team of young runners; Joe McManemin was the finest sprint coach we have ever had and there were others who were making a great contribution. However, none of them had facilities like those that were provided for coaches overseas and, as amateurs, they couldn't always give enough time to bring their pupils along fully.'

But he did have one criticism, which might well be as valid today as it was then.

'A common difficulty was that they were not encouraging athletes to train for events for which they were best suited. This meant we threw away a lot of Olympic medals. At the time I cited Doug Harris, who was a potential Herb Elliott if ever I saw one. He was a sprint champion who could win cross-country races, but it was only when Ron Agate beat him as a sprinter that he turned to the events for which he was best equipped – middle-distance racing.

'As it happened, he progressed to the 800 metres in the London Olympics in 1948 and I believe he would have won had he not been spiked. But for that, he would have been the first man to break four minutes for the mile, because he was both fast and strong.

'I considered that two other runners, John Grierson and Herb Carter, were both capable of world-class performances but trained for the wrong events. Grierson won the national mile title in his first race over that distance but collapsed at the finish, and it was announced he would never run another mile race. He failed to qualify for the Helsinki Olympics as a 400-metre runner yet, with the right training and encouragement, could have qualified for the 1500 metres.

'I urged Carter, while he was the national sprint champion, to run the 800 metres. He did not have it in him as a sprinter to become an Olympian, but he could have been an Olympic 800-metre champion. Years later, he admitted that I had been right.'

Possibly, Arthur Lydiard has always had advantages over other coaches. He could work out with his runners, which enabled him to assess their strengths and weaknesses accurately, as they ran, and encourage them to get the all-important aerobic base. But he was also teaching them according to a training system that he had exhaustively tested on his own body until he knew it worked. And his charisma is legendary. Over the years, scores of people have experienced the same reaction on meeting Arthur: 'When Arthur stops talking to you about running or fitness, you just have the urge to get up straight away, go out and do what he tells you.' Arthur has the gift of instilling total trust in his philosophy because of his sincerity and the strength of his own convictions.

Looking back, he says now of his pioneering runners, 'They were all very sincere boys and they had great role models to start with in Murray Halberg and the other athletes I trained in the early years, such as the late Colin Lousich, who were all New Zealand champions at one time. They had no doubt in their minds that I could develop their potential and get them good results. They accepted and adopted the long view of their training because they kept improving.

'The endless injuries our national cricketers and footballers suffer from these days are almost always due to poor conditioning and/or the wrong kind of conditioning. Especially the cricketers. They should be working on their legs to make them strong, the way I've always done with my runners. Hill training strengthens the muscles and sinews so that ankles don't get damaged under pressure.

'Hamstring injuries are rife in modern sports, but they could be avoided if the athletes did hill training. It doesn't have to be fast, just enough to make the muscles feel they've been working. Balancing the muscles between the front of the thigh and the back is essential to ensure hamstring problems don't arise. Some athletes seem to be constantly getting over or suffering from injuries and are, as that old Auckland running coach Lex Barker used to say in his suave voice, "up and down like a whore's drawers at a piledrivers' picnic."

'You can understand to some extent why cricketers get hurt. They stand around all day in the field and, every now and again, are called on to suddenly sprint for the ball or turn quickly from virtually a standing start. They should devise some sort of exercise they can do while they are standing around, something to keep them moving and reduce the sudden strain on the muscles and tendons when they have to move quickly. I have long been a fan of ballet dancing exercises for athletes. I had a gridiron team doing them in Los Angeles, big guys doing ballet steps. It looked silly, but it was sensible. They didn't have any more leg trouble afterwards.

'The issue of coaches being associated with touring teams or Games teams has been a controversy for a long time. Usually, coaches were not included, possibly because they would take authority away from officials sharing free trips among themselves as a reward for their administrative efforts.

'But there has been change over the years. Some time after I had been coaching in Finland, I was talking with Mr Unilo, the president of the SUL (Finnish Athletics Federation). He mentioned that he had been talking after the Munich Games to the presidents of the Norwegian and Swedish teams, who had commented on the fact that the Finns had won three gold medals and a bronze and said how poorly their own teams had done, even though all three teams had about the same number of athletes. Mr Unilo replied that this could have been because the Norway and Sweden teams had several managers and one coach and Finland's team had one manager and several coaches. For years, New Zealand never sent coaches with its teams. I was actually the first, when I went to Tokyo in 1964.'

Despite his international reputation, when Arthur offered to help New Zealand coaches by correspondence some years later, only three took him up on the offer – Eric Rowe, who trained Peter Renner in Christchurch; Alistair McMurran, of Dunedin; and Wayne Smith, of Napier. Arthur set up programmes for them and much of the subsequent correspondence from Rowe mentioned how upset he was that other coaches in Christchurch were laughing at him for the training he was giving Renner. Arthur's response was typically blunt and confident: 'I assured him that he should let them laugh, because he would get the last one. He did, with Renner ranking sixth in the world in his best year. They would love to have a Peter Renner in Christchurch now.'

Renner was New Zealand's junior steeplechase champion when he was 17, broke 8:50 for the 3000-metre distance just after he turned 18, was second in the Pacific Conference Games at age 21 and, before he was 22, had run faster than 8:30. He was being groomed for the 1988 Olympics yet, four years earlier, in Los Angeles, came second in his heat in 8:23. It was then the fastest run of his life, yet he ran 5 seconds faster to take second in his semi-final and set a New Zealand record.

'He was being hailed as another sensational gold medallist, as Snell had been in Rome, but the rest of the finalist steeplechasers foxed him out of it,' says Arthur. 'Perhaps because of the speed he had shown so far, they moved off at a comparatively slower pace, forcing Renner, who didn't have the explosive finishing power of Snell, to take the desperate measure of going to the front and cracking off at world record speed. It was somewhat like the coup Halberg had delivered in Rome when he burst away with three laps to go, but Renner's bid didn't have the same wonderful ending. He led for eighty per cent of the race and then was swept up by most of the field and finished well out of the medals.

'That the gap between the winner and the also-ran in this level of competition is a fine one was demonstrated in Europe soon after, when Renner ran against five of those who ran him down in LA, including two of the medallists, and beat them all.'

Renner then became another victim of the New Zealand tenet that, if you wanted to achieve something, you did it under your own steam. Renner was a bushman and he had to work to support his young family; the opportunities to train properly and get out against top competition just weren't there. He was never given another chance to prove how good he could have been. And Arthur believes that, had he been helped to mature as a steeplechaser, none in the world could have touched him.

'It's obvious that the administrators still don't want to know about my system, and I'm sure it's because they haven't thought of it themselves. It's a strange sort of jealousy. Extremely petty, and I'm too old now to be bothered. It was interesting to read recently that New Zealand was bringing out a Brazilian to coach middle-distance running here. He's got an Olympic medal of some sort, but I don't know his background.

'New Zealand has many fine coaches who could bring New Zealand's running back to the international forefront if they were given the organised backing this country needs. We need a national coach to coordinate a programme. Someone like Barry Magee would be ideal. People like Brian Taylor in Christchurch, Alistair McMurran in Dunedin and Arch Jelley in Auckland could all do a wonderful job for us at a national level. So could Waikato coach Allan Middleton, a good coach who has kept in contact with me over the years, and trained Bruce Milne, who has been a successful coach in Christchurch for many years.'

Arthur hasn't entirely given coaching away. He operates a website, and he has several invites to travel abroad. And near his home at Beachlands he trains a small stable of promising youngsters.

'Since I moved to Beachlands, I have trained a lot of the young local kids. They came to me and asked if I'd coach them for the Auckland secondary schools sports and I was happy to help.

'One of them, Matthew Shirley, was the New Zealand junior mile champion. He won by fifty metres down in Wellington and then I got him a scholarship and he went to America. What I've done around here is just what I did many years ago when I lived in Owairaka. They weren't kids I picked. They picked me and they've thrived on running bigger mileages than they'd ever done before.'

One success that particularly pleased him is an American, Regina Jacobs. She was 37 and in the twilight of her running career when she read one of Arthur's books. The result: in 2001-02, she ran personal bests for 800 metres, 1500 metres and 5000 metres and wiped everyone away in US Olympic trial events. In only her second 5000 metre attempt, she broke the US record. If ever there was proof that anyone can do it, given the will to follow his guidance, she provided it.

Arthur simply took Jacobs back to the basics he has always preached, and proved they are as valid today as they were when Murray Halberg was a skinny youngster. The sad ending to this astonishing comeback is that Jacobs caught a virus, which prevented her from competing at the Olympics.

One of today's leading New Zealand coaches of triathletes and Korean coaching stand-in, Jack Ralston, is a product of the early Lydiard school and uses his adaptation of the Lydiard system for his athletes. He is comfortably satisfied with the results. Among the athletes he has handled are Cameron Brown and Hamish Carter, New Zealand long course and Olympic distance champions respectively – Carter has achieved the world number one ranking more than once and Brown has had podium finishes in Hawaii's gut-buster – and Terenzo Bozzone, who, at 17, was a double world junior champion. Jack fell under the Lydiard spell when he was just a teenager. His parents gave him a copy of *Run to the Top* for a Christmas present when he was only 10.

'Full of youthful aerobic ability, I went out and ran, or tried to run, twenty by 400s because that was in the book,' he recalls. He was an average runner also involved in other sports, but he began applying Arthur's schedules more sensibly 'and suddenly I was up among the top runners'.

In 1966, he attended a Lydiard lecture at school. He was older than the rest of the audience and Arthur noticed him and he was taken under the enveloping wings of Lydiard, Baillie, Halberg and others. He ran his first Waiatarua when he was 15 but his second soon after is the one that sticks in his memory because it was a startling demonstration of the tough Lydiard approach to training.

'Norm Harris and I ran into Titirangi where we stopped for a drink and saw Peter Snell walking. He said he was tired and was walking back to the start, which this day was at Bill Baillie's place. I was flat out all the way back to Bill's to tell them and found Arthur there. I said Peter was walking home and someone should go out in a car and pick him up.

'Arthur said, "How old are you?"

'"Fifteen," I said.

'"How did you get home?" Arthur asked.

'"I ran."

'Arthur said, "Then so can Snell. He's not injured."'

This was a period when Bill was looking after Peter and giving him a hard time to toughen him up, especially knowing he was not fond of long runs such as the Waiatarua.

When Ralston began coaching with the Calliope club, he gained immeasurable help from Arthur. 'Nothing was ever too much trouble. He always had the time, no matter when I called him.' Amongst Arthur's advice was the injunction to keep a diary record of his own training and that of all his athletes for use as a learning tool. The irony of this, of course, is that Arthur never kept any training records at all.

Ralston recalls, 'Arthur was working for Winstone then and he gave me his big company diary. I guess he had no intention of using it himself.'

Arthur regards Ralston as one of New Zealand's great coaches and has remained virtually at his side throughout his successful coaching career. Ralston has taken on board one of Arthur's great beliefs – that every athlete be treated the same, whether an Olympian or a mere club hack. 'I know when I was training with

Halberg, Snell and the others Arthur yelled at us all exactly the same – they were training for the Tokyo Games and I was never going to be a world star,' recalls Ralston.

In 1983, 'right out of the blue', Arthur called to ask Jack to go to Korea in his place because he could not face Korea's food again. Jack found his first trip to Korea interesting, because he came up against the country's stubborn, stoic older coaches. He was given a large group of junior runners to train instead of the seniors. 'They wouldn't let me near them.' He took the juniors on a 10-kilometre run and, although he was then 38 and had never been more than an average runner, the Koreans could not keep up with him.

But he used the Lydiard method on them and was rewarded with the Korean 800 and 1500-metres titles and the first three placings in the women's 3000 metres. 'The women,' he remembers, 'were treated like second-rate citizens. They had to get the food for the boys and do all the kitchen work.'

At the time of Ralston's visit the Koreans were using the Zatopek marathon training system, even though his old record of 2:21 had been brought down to under 2:10 by the American Alberto Salazar. Ralston went to great lengths to demonstrate how the improved conditioning system developed by Lydiard had overtaken the Zatopek method. They eventually got the message.

Another coach currently using Arthur's methods is C. Mark Wetmore, coach at the University of Colorado in Boulder, who in 2001 trained the individual winners and the winning teams at the American cross-country championships, a feat no other coach had achieved.

Arthur recalls, 'I first met Mark when I gave a talk at Barnsdale High School, in New Jersey, where he was teaching. I stayed with Mark and we ran fifteen miles on the roads together several times. On my second visit to Barnsdale, I ran in a half-marathon race with some of the pupils, who were now on a distance training programme and were already showing benefits from this. When I suggested to Mark that we should go out for our fifteen-miler, he told me he could no longer run because he had one leg longer than the other.

'Puzzled, I pointed out that he was OK last year and asked to see his running shoes. The sole of one shoe had been built up a lot more than the other to allow for the shorter leg. Even more puzzled, I asked to see the shoes he had run in the year before when he ran fifteen miles with me.

'He brought them out and I could see that they were evenly worn, so it was hardly likely that he had one leg longer or shorter than the other. I told him to put the old shoes on and we went out and ran the fifteen miles without any trouble. His legs were both the same length but, for some reason, his shoes were not the same height.'

Mark trained his high school to win the New Jersey State championship for twelve years in a row before moving on to Boulder. Late in 2001, he sent Arthur this letter:

Dear Coach Lydiard,
I have waited a long time to write this note of thanks. I wanted to be sure our accomplishments deserved an asterisk on your resumé.

In late November, our men's cross-country team finally won the NCAA championship. With that win, we have completed a championship sweep of all four available titles – men's team, men's individual (Adam Goucher '98), women's team ('00) and women's individual (Laura Wheeler '00). This sweep has never been done before.

Our mutual friend, [airline pilot] Larry Sullivan, introduced me to your work in the late 1970s. The immediate result was a high school team that won its State [New Jersey] championships 12 years in a row; and then all that we have done here at CU: 9 individual NCAA champions, 2 team titles, 3 Olympians, innumerable other smaller titles and records.

I have served only as the delivery boy of your remarkable message. For your insight, hard work, openness to young coaches and your incalculable influence on distance running, I sincerely thank you.

Even though Arthur has strong ties to the States, his influence is not limited to that country. Australians using his methods include David Power and Pat Clohessey, who was the coach of Rob de Castella. 'Pat used to write to me regularly when he returned from America, telling me about this lad he had begun training at fourteen years of age. Pat was excited about the way he was improving and predicted he would leave his mark later on. He was correct.'

Later on Clohessey and de Castella took over as the heads of the Institute of Sport in Australia and that is when the Institute's standards began to improve, because they used Lydiard's methods and applied them to several sports.

'Alastair McMurran once went to Morocco and found my methods being used there. They're also being used in mainland Europe.

'I trained an Aucklander, Tim Parcell, years ago to win the New Zealand mile championship. His wife later visited Portugal and, when she came back, phoned me to say that the Portuguese had asked if she could get in touch with me about my training methods. That began the era which saw the emergence of the LA Olympic marathon winner Carlos Lopez and the subsequent host of brilliant Portuguese women.

'Then the Spaniards picked up my programme. Larry Eder, editor of *American Track and Field*, told me about that development.'

Add to that list Finland, Germany, South Africa and South America, and you begin to appreciate the vast and enduring legacy of Arthur Lydiard. And it is not restricted to runners.

27

the Wright way to swim

THE ARTHUR LYDIARD-David Wright story began a long time ago, but it is a classic example of the doggedness with which Arthur has lived his life and pursued his passion. David has displayed the same persistence and passion in his pursuit of swimming. Curiously, he excited the same hostility and rejection from officialdom as Arthur but drove on, as Arthur did, to prove them wrong.

David's mother set everything in motion when she gave him *Run to the Top* for a Christmas present when he was 14 years of age. The family was living on a farm about 12 kilometres out of Wairoa, a rather remotely situated township on the east coast of New Zealand's North Island. He read it, was enthused and started running.

'His training ideas were a bolt from the blue for a fourteen-year-old. His methods were simple, straightforward, obvious and they worked,' Wright recalls. His first application of the system, however, showed he had a lot to learn. He divided the basic 100 miles-a-week marathon prescription by seven, went out and ran that 100 miles the first week and was so stiff and sore he gave it away until, older and wiser, he experimented with the programme for several years until he was able to comfortably run 100 miles a week for 10 consecutive weeks. Eventually, this led to success as a running coach, followed by success as a swimming trainer.

Wright's qualifications as a swim coach were achieved in much the same way as Lydiard's as a running mentor. He was a determined and successful swimmer first. He won his first swimming race, the 10 yards freestyle, and gained his 800 yards distance certificate when he was only four. Thirty years later, his Lydiard-system trained daughter Jane gained her certificate when she was only three.

In his 10 yards race, he was forbidden to dive start because none of the other swimmers could do it. He was, incidentally, the only competitor not wearing floaties. When he swam the 800 yards, the officials didn't think he would make the distance, so no one was appointed to count his lengths. They realised their error when he went on swimming long after the other, older swimmers had either finished or given up. Even then, his mother had to intervene before they would award him his certificate.

As Wright recalled, 'By the time I turned five, I had two swimming memories tinged with official trouble, an ominous sign of things to come.' In fact, Wright became the stormy petrel of swimming in much the same way Lydiard did in athletics and for much the same reasons – petty jealousies, resentment of his successes and his outspoken bluntness when he came up against the dead hand of the sport's bureaucrats.

Wright pursued his swimming career against the odds. His parents were both country schoolteachers and they worked at remote schools at Horopito, in the shadow of Mt Ruapehu, and then Te Reinga, which was 30 kilometres from the nearest shop, while David was a child. His swimming development occurred mainly in the Hapua River until, at age 13, he spent two weeks holiday in Auckland training with the Parnell Baths swim coach, Paul Kraus. 'It was a shock,' he recalls. 'The schedules might as well have been written in Chinese and all I could do was swim behind the Kraus squad and try to do what they did.'

Wright persevered and won six titles at his first college swim meet, setting two records. One of them, the 33^1/$_3$ yards breaststroke, stood for 27 years. On the side, he won his school's junior mile title and made the team that won a Hawke's Bay schools team cross-country championship.

In his mid teens he joined the Comet Swimming Club in Gisborne, a two-and-a-half hour train trip from Wairoa, travelling there every weekend. He went back in the winter to continue training – this involved swimming to and fro across the chilly Gisborne harbour. He won an Auckland breaststroke title, was second in the Kapiti Island ocean swim and the Taupo lake swim, won numerous other events as far up the ladder as the New South Wales championships. But he knew his limitations – he was not going to be an Olympian.

'Lack of real talent, combined with less than ideal training conditions, made that goal unattainable, but did it really matter?' he said. 'What did matter was that I worked as hard as I could and enjoyed it.' That's the dictum, reminiscent of Arthur, that he was later to impress on his swim pupils.

Wright then spent a year in Thorp, Wisconsin, on an American Field Service Scholarship, where he learnt an unforgettable lesson in gamesmanship. Swimming wasn't available at Thorp, so he joined the school's state champion gridiron team and discovered the Americans' fanatical desire to win.

'Cheerleaders, weekly school pep rallies, medical back-up, support staff and so on, even at high school level, with calisthenics conducted to the shouted chants of the players and spectators of "Beat Owen, beat Owen", or whatever the name of the opposing team might be,' he says. 'A pre-game pep talk was nothing short of a call to arms and a recital of the Lord's Prayer while the players encircled their coach and laid their hands on his.

'I loved it until one episode alerted me to the dangers of this kind of hype, mass hysteria created for the sole purpose of winning. The night in question, we were playing a team which had a very good offensive forward. As the kicker, I was told by my coach to go out to take a kick – I was to tell the other players to let this forward through, allow him to dive on the ball, at which point I was to kick him in the head.

'The terrible thing is not that I did it and had their player taken off the field, but that I did it without it even entering my mind that it was wrong or bad. I believe this was a direct consequence of the high-pressure hype, team chants, Nuremberg rally hysteria that was deliberately created around these games... it was blind obedience to orders.'

Back in New Zealand, he moved to Wellington to attend

Victoria University, and threw himself once more into swimming, covering 3000 kilometres in his first year, an enormous distance in those days. There he met future wife Alison and they went to England together while David furthered his education at the University of London. At the same time, he took on the role of Alison's running coach, using the knowledge he'd acquired over the years.

But he still had a lot to learn and Alison's progress was anything but forward until, on a visit to New Zealand, he contacted John Walker's coach, Arch Jelley, who taught him to understand the Lydiard schedules, how to balance the programme, how aerobic and anaerobic work dovetailed. Jelley coached Alison – and David – by correspondence and she developed into one of the finest women runners New Zealand has had – and one of its least recognised.

She represented the United Kingdom, New Zealand, Oceania and Scotland, and still holds the New Zealand 1000-metre record. She became New Zealand's all-time number three in 1979 at both 800 metres and 1500 metres, was UK indoor champion and New Zealand's number two at 3000 metres.

The understanding Wright gained from Jelley came in useful again back in New Zealand, when David began adapting the Lydiard way for swimming. But he needed still more help, so he rang Lydiard and began a weekly telephone communication which lasted nearly a decade. It often seemed that they made every mistake possible as they struggled to determine how a swimmer could achieve the same physiological objectives as a runner covering 100 to 150 miles a week.

He and Arthur had to make hundreds of separate decisions. In each case, the physiological result that Lydiard sought and the method of attaining it had to be translated to swimming. The equivalent of hill bounding, the validity of fartlek training, the comparison between 25 minutes of anaerobic swimming and 25 minutes of anaerobic running, the use of weights and stretching, Arthur's famed Waiatarua weekend run, what kind of swimming exercise equated to 120-metre running sprints, what variations were needed for sprint, middle distance and distance swimming – these were just some of the factors they struggled with.

The conversion was not easy and Wright says it would not have been possible without Arthur's patient and skilful guidance. Mistakes occurred and other coaches and administrators were quick to sneer and belittle the use of Lydiard's methods. But the principles were never wrong, only the application. Variations had to be tried and tested over as long as a whole six-month season and then were often rejected or refined, involving more months of experimentation.

Wright's principal guinea-pig was his teenaged daughter, Jane, and she flourished as a swimmer, capturing numerous national and Australian titles before she won a scholarship to the United States. Today, the Wright-Lydiard style of conditioning is being used by a growing number of international swimmers, including Ian Thorpe, Alexander Popov, Michael Klim and Amy van Dyken, and coaches Jonty Skinner and Gennadi Touretsky of the United States and Australia, respectively. They validate the David Wright system and the shrewdness of Lydiard as a conditioner of champions.

28

courses for horses

ARTHUR HAS ALWAYS been a diligent, if not necessarily successful, follower of horses and he became involved more closely when one of his good harriers, Merv Hellier, leased a horse called Bon Fils.

Arthur confesses: 'We thought it was sound, but we didn't know much about horses, except that they tended to lose when we backed them, and this one had scar tissue on its left front fetlock, which prevented it from striding out properly. But we took it to the Avondale racecourse and we gave it a hundred kilometres a week of steady trotting along. Merv did the riding.

'Clive Conway, who was then writing for the *Auckland Star* racing pages, watched us bring the horse back one day from its training session. It looked like it had just been hosed down, it was so wet with sweat, and he asked us what we were doing. We knew that other trainers were shaking their heads about us and reckoning we'd kill the bloody thing. We also knew that the horse was getting fitter.

'We explained to Clive that we were trying to give Bon Fils cardiovascular efficiency. Most racehorses are bred for speed and a lot of them get halfway down the finishing straight and then stop – especially if I've backed them. They might have the speed, but they lack the endurance. Clive took this theory in and then asked if we could give a horse he had, Gauntlet, the same training. Merv and I put him on the hundred-kilometres-a-week schedule and when the Easter Handicap, which was then the biggest mile race in New Zealand, came along, Gauntlet won it. Clive promptly took out a public trainer's licence and for three years was the leading horse trainer in New Zealand, exercising his charges to our system.'

Conway set up at Kariotahi, a long ironsand beach on the west coast of south Auckland, and he employed girls to work his horses, because he found the animals seemed to respond better to females. They took the horses for two-hour workouts right down the beach to the Waikato Heads and back, keeping their fetlocks in the cold sea to keep the heat out of them. Arthur told Conway hill training was also very important, so he started his horses on that and immediately found they developed more power and drive. New Zealand's leading trainer today, Ken Browne, does the same thing, but no one else did in those days, so Clive's horses began to give him good results.

Arthur says it's a characteristic of Ken Browne's horses that they're always last in the early stages of a race but then because they have the endurance they come through and finish well.

'Before one Great Northern race meeting in Auckland, someone came knocking on my door and introduced himself as David Meikle, who used to have a farm down by Te Kowhai in the Waikato. He said he'd brought two horses up for the meeting but the better of them, Sabre, had injured a fetlock getting into the horse float and wasn't going to start. The other, Royal Cipher, was entered in the first race, the Greenlane Steeples. He said he'd been training the horses to my system and thought Royal Cipher could win. He'd got my method from Keith Trow, a good Waikato runner who farmed next to him.

'He exercised the horses up a steep hill and down the gentle slope on the other side. He said that the first time he took his string up, "they bloody near crossed their legs and died." But now, he said, they went up over the hill with no trouble at all. I was at work that Saturday morning and I told the guys I worked with they had better back Royal Cipher. Huh, they responded, that bloody thing wouldn't have a chance. Royal Cipher won by 25 lengths and, over a period of time, David Meikle won all the big jumping events in New Zealand and thoroughly established that the system does work.

'Care is needed, of course, that the horses aren't taken up the hills too fast. The idea, the same as with humans, is to make the legs feel the workload but to avoid letting the exercise become

Arthur training in South Africa in 1979. This is how you run when you're only 62 years old. *Cape Town Argus*

Heather Thompson, whose talent combined with Arthur's training to send her to second place in the 3000 metres at the Commonwealth Games in Edmonton, Canada.

Arthur with some of his running pupils on one of the synthetic running tracks in the excellent stadiums specially built for black athletes in South Africa.

Great get-together. Arthur (third from left) tucked behind an aging collection of some of New Zealand's greatest middle-distance runners. From left, John Walker, Neville Scott, Arthur, John Davies, Mike Ryan, Bill Baillie, Ray Puckett (hidden), Barry Magee and Murray Halberg at a South Auckland reunion on the Manurewa track.

Lydiard-method training under coach Pat Clohessy led Australia's Rob de Castella to the tape first in the 1986 Boston marathon.
Sailer/McManus Photo

Peter Renner (centre) became one of the world's finest steeplechasers after he turned to Lydiard training. Here he is in action at a World Cup meet.

'Nobby' Hashizume with coaching legends Bill Bowerman and Arthur Lydiard.

anaerobic by climbing too fast. Steady hill climbing makes the legs stronger and stronger.'

Sadly, Bon Fils remained an unsound horse. Had things been different, Arthur and Merv knew they could have gone on with him and done well. They conditioned him so that he was fit enough but, as soon as he reached full gallop, the old fetlock injury unbalanced him and they were advised to stop training him. In one race in Rotorua, Bon Fils turned into the straight two lengths clear, but then just stopped. Arthur asked the jockey what happened and he said he'd just hit him with the whip and he stopped. Arthur said he'd never been hit before. 'The shock must have been too much,' Arthur said. 'You should just have whispered in his ear.'

'When our experiments were in their infancy,' Arthur recalls, 'one racing reporter ran an article dismissing the idea that my system would work. This was about the time Geoff Whyman, in the *Weekly News*, referred to my experience with the first horse I ever had a financial interest in and my development of what I called the Halberg Schedule of Horse Training. This brought a response from another racing writer, 'Galopin', of Waitara, who said he was all for my system and would try to prove it.'

'Galopin' wrote:

The first example is Rusto, who came up consistently each year for the Auckland Cup on what most thought was too short preparation but proved most efficient. His trainer, the late N. A. Martin, knew what he was doing, That horse walked up to 20 miles a day all through the winter. When it came to racing, Rusto needed only his wind cleaned up as he had the condition and a thorough ground preparation.

Next are the horses of Sid McGreal, of Waitara. Sid gives his team about six weeks of road work before they go to the track. If they are given much more time than that the boys are hard put retaining their seats – their mounts are so well. Now, here is where the importance of time comes into it. The McGreal team does approximately 10 or 12 miles of working and jogging a day, which takes about two hours... this, in my opinion, is the main reason why McGreal is so successful. His horses can have a strenuous racing season and yet they can line up each time looking as big and bright as ever.

Our horses could all be given the Lydiard type of preparation within reason. We would have better horses and the ones which would show the most improvement would be our sprinters. A sprinter who is worked off the lead soon becomes light-hearted and full of pep when the saddle is put on, which is the way it should be. Sid McGreal won 14 races with sprinters last season.

Today, many trainers use the Lydiard conditioning system to prepare their horses for the racing season. One of New Zealand's most successful mares is Sunline, who won more than NZ$10 million in stake money. Arthur has been informed by one trainer that Sunline has done more conditioning mileage than any other horse in the country, which does tend to underscore the benefits of the Lydiard way.

And the gospel may spread further yet. When Arthur was in San Francisco, he met a world authority on horse training, Tom Ivers, who has written a comprehensive book on horse training, called *The Fit Racehorse.* Apparently, he was lecturing trainers and owners in Australia when some guy in the audience stood up and said, 'Lydiard doesn't say that.' So he made it his business to see Arthur to find out what he did say. At the end of their exchange of views, Ivers gave Arthur a copy of his book, inscribed, 'It was an honor to shake your hand'.

29

the fan club

ARTHUR LYDIARD'S MAILBOX constantly receives letters from people all over the world who have taken his teachings to heart and benefited from them. For example, American Tom Gaudette wrote, with a poetic fervour, in June 2001:

Thank you for coaching three generations of runners all over the world. When you came to San Antonio in November, 1999, I said to you: 'We [USA runners] have already assimilated your training methods into our running culture.' Today, I say to you that we are asleep in front of our computers and televisions… dormant athletes.

I just completed two full cycles of your four-week hill bounding, ten-week time trials marathon preparation. This produced, at age 46, 2:43 in Chicago and 2:45 in Boston. These are easy courses, I know. The times are adequate enough. What is remarkable to me is that, other than a little stiffness, I was able to resume regular aerobic running two days after each race. At the end of Boston this April, I stood comfortably, calmly in a triage-like area past the finish line. I kept saying to myself, 'Lydiard's training did this. Lydiard's training did this.'

You know exactly why this is. I felt during the hills and time trials that I was being gently moulded. I did $2^1/2$ years of aerobic running before this. The bounding strengthened and developed skills in my middle-age legs which were dormant. The weekly rotation of middle distance repeats (for muscle viscosity, you wrote), two time trials and a regular striding session was like a college course in literature (my specialty). Your mind and hand formed me into a fitter and fitter runner. But you are gentle. I did each step carefully, aware that maybe the best runner's mind was at hand. At the race, I would say, 'Ah. The twentieth time trial'. I ran negative splits in both races.

'You have placed your knowledge and wisdom in print. In *Running to the Top* there is stated exactly how to correctly prepare for one's best marathon. Condition yourself to get into top condition. The promise is obvious, the steps are precise and your own craft. In the US, it seems that people simply do not have the time/patience to follow the schedule correctly.

In his 1990 book, *Flying Finns – the story of the great tradition of Finnish distance running*, Matti Hannus wrote:

Arthur Lydiard arrived in Finland on March 20, 1967 [as Finland's national distance coach], and he was not about to waste his time. At the Kuortane Sports Institute – on a freezing cold late winter morning – the cream of the Finnish running corps did not believe their eyes when the short and stocky New Zealander emerged from the door, wearing a pair of shorts! And he meant business: it was a 30k run around Kuortane Lake at such a speed that the road was burning! Embarrassing but true: Lydiard, almost 50 years old, returned from the jaunt among the leaders, in front of several internationals.

When someone summoned up enough courage to marvel at the 100-miles-a-week regimen Lydiard was recommending, he dryly commented: 'As a youngster, I chose myself, as an experiment, to run 250 miles a week. It was too much but it did not kill me. There is nothing better than experience.'

The book continued to describe the difficulties under which Lydiard had to work in Finland and the bitterness when, at his farewell, he recalled those problems.

'But there are those, too, who believe in my ideas and will go on,' he said. 'I wish the best of success for them.'

So, this weather-beaten and quick-spoken man shook the Finnish dust from his shoes. He was the last straw for our distance running and many years later we finally understood the full meaning of his stay. Thank you, Arthur – you did your job even better than we could appreciate at the time.

Pekka Vasala, 1500-metre gold medallist at the Munich Olympic Games, recalls: 'In 1950, Finnish runners began to be coached using interval-training methods. It was a big hit and for the next ten years my country trained virtually no other way. The method produced good results for a time, but then international successes became fewer and fewer.

'Arthur Lydiard changed all this during his time in Finland as chief running coach and gradually both new and long-time coaches began to include his conditioning and speed-training methods into their own programmes. After Finland's triumph at the Munich Games, even the press was ready to take back its criticism and give credit to Arthur.

'Although I didn't belong to the group trained by Arthur himself, I was able to enjoy the benefits of his teaching through my coach, Kari Sinkkonen. When Arthur left, I was only twenty years old but I'd already managed to become an Olympic representative. My 1500 metres time had improved by five seconds to 3:41.8 and qualified me for Mexico.

'Kari supported Arthur's methods fully – this was not always easy. For one thing, everyone there thinks they know something about running and most people think they know everything about it.

'I spent half a year in New Zealand and it was noticeable that the average man in that country has a habit of running daily just to keep himself in good shape. That's what Arthur brought to Finland – the enthusiasm for running, simply for fun and health.'

At the Munich Games, Arthur's star Finnish pupil, Lasse Viren, won the 5000 and 10,000 metre gold medals. In the 10,000, he fell over but got up and went on to win. He repeated the double four years later at Montreal.

New Zealand journalist Geoff Whyman, in a 1960 article

headlined 'Coach with the golden touch', was utterly positive. The Halberg-Snell double and Magee's marathon bronze, he said, were as gratifying to New Zealanders as they were surprising to everyone at the Games. 'Surprising, that is, to everyone in Rome with the certain-sure exception of one man: Arthur Lydiard.' Whyman recalled that, three years earlier, when Snell won the Auckland secondary schools 880 yards title, Lydiard forecast to his nearest neighbour: 'This boy will win the 800 metres Olympic title in 1960.'

Whyman continued:

> Nor was it idle chatter when he predicted that Halberg would become one of the world's greatest distance runners, for Arthur never chatters, never talks without thinking deeply and earnestly. There is one more prediction... but we must wait – perhaps another four years – to assess its accuracy. Lydiard has said of Snell that he will one day become the greatest 1500 metres runner of all time – and Herb Elliott is not excluded.
>
> The story has often been told of a mile event in which Lydiard had three runners. To Tom, the coach said, 'You have the speed to win this race if you can shake off Dick before the last 300 yards.' To Dick, he said, 'You have the stamina to win this race if you can summon the speed to stay with Tom until the last 300 yards.' And to Harry was given the advice, 'I don't think you have the speed to match Tom, nor the stamina to stay with Dick – but if they cut one another's throats, you will win.' And each runner knew that their coach was instructing them truly as individuals.
>
> There was another occasion when Lydiard adopted totally different tactics. Snell was having a little difficulty in regaining winning form and had been defeated by one half-miler a couple of times. Said Lydiard in his pre-race pep talk, 'If you let that joker get away from you tonight, you'll never beat him again.' And such was Snell's faith in his coach's prognostications that he simply buried the opposition over 100 yards in a superlative 1m 49.2s.

Whyman recounted his favourite story about Lydiard:

Although athletics and athletes will always remain his first
love, Lydiard was induced to invest in a half-interest in a
racehorse. And, as with most racehorses, it was taken to the
races as an object of supreme ability, inspiring unbounded
confidence. On the day, it had neither the speed of Snell nor
the stamina of Halberg.

'In fact,' said Lydiard, 'it was so fat I could have beaten it
myself.'

Such a condition – and presumably such a result – was an
immediate challenge to the trainer of world champions. As
with his runners, so with his half-racehorse. Arthur evolved a
training programme – and called it, of course, the Halberg
Schedule of Horse Training. The Halberg Schedule will
probably never revolutionise horse training – or even bring
Lydiard's horse home in record time. But then, thoroughbreds
can't be expected to have as much horse-sense as this coach's
pupils. THEY certainly know a good thing when they see him.

Lydiard's experience with horses and horse trainers rather
contradicts Geoff Whyman's confident conclusion but it was an
indication of the belief that many had in Arthur's capabilities.

Nobuya 'Nobby' Hashizume is a joyful Lydiard addict. He was
so impressed by the seminal book, *Running With Lydiard*, that he
moved to New Zealand for a year to study under Arthur. Upon
returning to his native Japan, he became a professional running
coach for Hitachi Ltd, working under the influence of legendary
coach, the late Kiyoshi Nakamura. Nobby was then out of the
running circuit for some time but his interest was rekindled after
he travelled to the Atlanta Olympic Games with his high school
hero, New Zealand middle-distance runner, Dick Quax, an
Olympian and former holder of the world 5000-metre record.
Nobby now lives in Minnesota. We thank him for his permission
to reproduce the following extracts from his 1998 article,
'Hanging with the Legends,' originally published in *Marathon
and Beyond*.

This story begins in late April of 1997 when Dick Brown of Eugene, Oregon, called to tell me that Arthur Lydiard and Bill Bowerman were going to get together at that year's Prefontaine Classic. There are perhaps half a dozen coaches who stand head and shoulders above the rest. Arthur Lydiard and Bill Bowerman are without a doubt two such coaches. I immediately booked a flight from my home in Minnesota to Oregon.

Nobby relates how Arthur and Bill Bowerman became close associates with a common interest and explains that Dick Brown, an established coach who tutored Mary Slaney to her two gold medals in the 1983 World Championships and who coached Vicki Huber and Shelly Steely, had become a disciple of Lydiard. Brown and Nobby meet the two coaches at Bowerman's home.

It is one thing to recruit accomplished athletes as some coaches do by importing Kenyan runners or by happening upon one outstanding athlete, but it is quite another to produce one good athlete after another over a long stretch of time. Bill Bowerman has definitely done the latter. And he actually hated recruiting, considering himself more of a teacher than a head hunter.

Bowerman is quoted as saying, 'You start making love to some high school kid too early, his head starts to get bigger and bigger.... If I join the tail-kissers, I'm just another donkey looking for another body to come out and run here. If I want to teach him and if I have something to offer him, we'll find out after he gets here.'

It is ironic to spend time with Bowerman, for the man who has taught others to excel from inside their bodies is stuck in a strange physical situation. His physical condition is a mess. He is 85 years old, his feet are swollen, he coughs once in a while, and he is rapidly losing his eyesight, the result of working in a too-small room with glue and rubber creating what would become the first Nike shoes. He suffered a heart attack some years ago, and he was also in a car accident several years ago. But when Bill Bowerman talks about running, he is animated and sturdy as a tank. He can also be somewhat intimidating, but if he senses his guest is sincere and interested, he responds in kind. It is the same quality I have found in Arthur Lydiard and the late Japanese marathon coach, Kiyoshi Nakamura.

Nobby says that Bowerman was firm on his policy of not wanting his athletes to double in the same competition. Later, when Nobby and Dick Brown attended the Oregon State High School championships they saw youngsters not just doubling but tripling because they were good athletes and the team needed the points. By the third event, they could hardly drag themselves to the starting line. Bowerman said: 'Give the other guys on the team a chance. It isn't all about winning.' Nobby is reminded of Nakamura's scientific training methods in the 1980s in which he combined mental, philosophical and almost Zen-like elements.

Coaches like Bowerman and Lydiard, whether intentionally or not, were already practising these elements. It is not the outcome (winning the championship or gaining the points) that is important, but the method of getting there for the sake of that method. With that philosophy, the results have a tendency to follow on their own.

[Arthur] doesn't seem to have aged. In fact, come to think of it, he doesn't seem to have aged from 1984 when I spent a year in New Zealand with him. Kathrine Switzer has perfectly described Arthur: 'Lydiard is an intimidating, imposing figure, that is, until you stand close to him. And then you realise that he is actually quite short, with a great gentleness and kindness behind the thunder, a total generosity. He is a man totally beloved.'

How good or not so good you are as an athlete is totally irrelevant to Arthur. He is often quoted as saying that it is as gratifying, if not even more so, to work with heart patients than to work with some talented athletes. 'Once they get up on the top of the dais,' he has said, 'they'll get big-headed and forget you. But others will appreciate you more.'

The quote sounds un-Arthur-like, given the loyalty and affection that still shows among so many of his former pupils.

Nobby continues: 'When Lydiard was in Japan in 1990, he was asked what kind of quality he looks for in an athlete he coaches. Without hesitation, his answer was simple: "Sincerity. By coaching and helping other people, you are giving up a part of your life. I can't afford to waste my time with fools." '

In his article, Nobby goes on to describe a dinner party, attended by Arthur and Dr Andrew Ness and his wife Christy, who coached figure skating champion Kristi Yamaguchi. (The Nesses applied Arthur's training principles to Yamaguchi's training, figuring that the two-minute short program and the four-minute long program were the equivalent of running a half-mile and a mile. By using Arthur's aerobic conditioning methods, Yamaguchi raised her VO$_2$max from 44 to 60.)

Arthur explains that he's a little dehydrated from his flight. 'The best thing you can do is drink beer!' he declares. Several of Dick Brown's runners rise to the occasion and declare this is great advice from a great coach. Marla Runyan, a legally blind athlete who has run a 2:04 800 meters in heptathlon competition (and was a front runner in the 2003 Boston marathon) takes Arthur's advice and then asks for some input. As a heptathlete, she feels she's too muscular. 'That's got nothing to do with it,' Arthur contends. He uses Peter Snell as an example. He was a very big, muscular man. He had some difficult times completing Arthur's marathon conditioning. But also because of his muscularity, Snell's kick was so powerful and explosive that once he unleashed it, nobody could stay with him. After being around Arthur Lydiard, you quickly catch his philosophy that nothing about you is a disadvantage. 'Interval training is a lot of eye-wash,' Arthur says. 'It's just the icing on the cake, not the governing factor. But what do most American runners and coaches do? They go on the track with a stopwatch in hand and do more intervals, more intervals, more intervals.... They destroy potential, instead of developing it.'

After Arthur has sated his thirst with 10 beers over six

hours and after dozens of photo flashes go off around the table, we decide to wind down. 'We'd better get you back to the hotel, Arthur,' I say to him. 'Why?' he asks. 'Are you getting tired?' Approaching 80, Arthur had flown from New Zealand the day before, driven from Portland that morning, spent the day with Bill Bowerman on a film shoot, and had just reached midnight after six hours of talking and beer-drinking. Arthur is still a human dynamo.

Several years ago, he was tested in Texas. The results indicated a supposedly aged man whose oxygen uptake was at least a litre above the norm and who sported the muscle-tone of a 40-year-old. He was once asked about all the hype concerning running not being good for you. 'I guess all the years of running are killing me,' he replied.

Later, Dr Ness wonders if, 20 years from now, anyone will remember Arthur Lydiard and Bill Bowerman. It is unlikely that the average person training for a marathon realises how much of the training theories they use to make such a challenging event so accessible have come from these two men, who achieved greatness through common sense, hard work, and passion for the sport.

Nobby ends his article with a depth of feeling that probably speaks for thousands:

For the moment, I think about the generosity that has made them such accessible giants to those of us who have had the honor of meeting and speaking with them. Although I wish all the greatest success to running and runners, in a world seemingly gone mad with sports, I hope, probably unrealistically, that this access to the giants of our sport is never withdrawn as it has been in so many other areas of the sporting life. For this golden moment, though, it isn't. The giants smile upon us mortals. And it is our responsibility to pass their words on to the generation to come.

30

a life hard run

ARTHUR HAD JOGGED, run and pounded through tens of thousands of kilometres over all kinds of terrain and in extremes of heat and cold for half a century, but it wasn't running that, literally, brought him to his knees. Or, at least, to an acute awareness of them. He remembers the occasion vividly and is equally conscious of the series of disasters which followed as he tried to maintain his running regimen.

'I had never had any injury or illness problems until I beggered up my knee helping a guy to lift 365-pound [165 kilogram] concrete pipes in a drain on our property at Manurewa, where Eira and I were living before we decided to build at Beachlands. The ground was uneven and I twisted my knee. I didn't think too much of it and went for a sixteen-mile run that night. The next morning, the knee had blown up like a balloon. It was full of water. Over the next few months, I went to about six doctors with the problem, but there was no athroscopy in those days and all they did was drain the water off. It still didn't work. I kept trying to run on the knee for about nine months, but it was getting no better.'

Eira went to Finland to see her relatives and Arthur followed later. The day after he arrived, she told him he was wanted at the hospital in Turku immediately. She had been talking to the doctor there who had looked after Arthur's athletes and, when he asked how Arthur was, she had told him Arthur was pretty hard to live with because he couldn't run well any more with this persistent knee trouble.

Arthur says, 'The doctor said, "Send him up to me." I went

to Turku and they put blue dye in my blood to track the flow, X-rayed my knee and concluded that I had chewed up all the meniscus in it. There was also an arthritic lump on the knee which I got rid of later on.

'I had to get back to New Zealand so they put my leg in plaster and I came home and saw a surgeon, who cut my knee in two places and took out the pieces of mangled meniscus. I returned to running but I was favouring that knee and, a few months later, when I was out in a park with a girl I was training, I twisted the other knee. She was running too fast for me.

'I decided I'd better get that knee fixed the same way as the other, so I went straight back to another surgeon, who operated almost immediately. But, apparently, he used equipment that had not been sterilised properly because my knee swelled up and, when I bent it, pus burst out of it like water from a water pistol. I could hardly get out of bed, so I phoned a neighbour who had a key to my house and he came in and carried me down the stairs.

'I rang Dr Lloyd Drake, who has looked after hundreds of athletes in his career, and another neighbour took me to Papatoetoe, carrying me from his car and up the stairs to Lloyd's surgery. He took one look at the knee and said it had to be attended to straight away. I was operated on first in Remuera and later had to be taken to Mercy Hospital, where they bored holes all round my knee to try to get rid of the mess inside it.

'I found after that that I could still run to a degree but not properly and my knees began to bow out sideways as if I'd been riding a horse all my life. In the end, it got so bad I could not walk properly so I went back to Lloyd Drake and eventually to Mercy Hospital for more surgery, involving the total replacement of both knees. But I finished up in Middlemore Hospital because, during the operation, I suffered a small stroke which affected my left side.'

However, Arthur's legs were more or less straight again but he has remained weak on his left side because of the stroke. He can see the humour in it: 'I can't swim like I used to; I keep going round in circles. I should do more running in water because that is good therapy and a lot of athletes use it now to recover from injuries or to prevent them.'

Arthur's main problem is maintaining his balance. Straight-line walking is fine, but in a crowd he is unhappy and has difficulty manoeuvring because his new knees don't swivel as they should. When running became impossible, he took to cycling, but that proved difficult because of his unsteady balance. 'The only way I can get off a bike is to fall off. At the moment, I have the bike indoors on a roller. I still use a rowing machine regularly, but my weak left side means I can't do my twenty chin-ups any more.'

His mild stroke and the medication he is obliged to take have added another frustration. He suffers from a constantly dry mouth, which makes speech difficult. His mind remains razor-sharp, although he admits to some difficulty in remembering the past, but the famous machine-gun delivery has gone. Nevertheless, ask him any question about his philosophy on life or pose him any problem about training, and the answer comes swiftly, bluntly and confidently. He remains the ultimate guru.

It is possible to see an odd juxtaposition in Arthur Lydiard's outlook on life. In small things, he displays a concern about cost. On the broader scale, his generosity is unquestioning. This is probably a legacy of his life as a child and a young husband and father, when counting the small change was vital. As a world-wanted coach, he reaped some reasonably handsome rewards, yet still gave his time and knowledge unstintingly for no reward at all whenever he chose, which was often.

As he says, 'I have never been a money man. I've seen too many rich people not enjoying their lives, although I suppose that if, as they say, money makes you unhappy, at least it's better to be unhappy in comfort. You don't need a lot of money, but you do have to have enough, and when I was raising four kids I had to work hard to achieve a level of comfort.

'I have managed to send all my children overseas for trips and, after Jean and I parted, I used to send her money whenever I could. I bought her a car and I sent Bruce and his wife to Honolulu for a ten-day holiday on the condition that they took Jean with them. She said later it was the best holiday she had ever had.'

Arthur has married for the third time, to Joelyne. He met her when he went to Wanganui for a re-run of the Peter Snell mile record. As part of the trip he was booked to speak in Opunake, where Snell was born. On the way there, he called in to New Plymouth to see Joe Broughton, then president of the New Zealand Joggers Association. He introduced Arthur to Joelyne and asked if he could bring her up to Auckland some time to get Arthur's help with her training.

Arthur recalls: 'They arrived for a weekend and Joelyne then asked if she could come and stay with me to do more training. I was about to head off to Europe for a couple of months so I said she would have to wait. The day I got back, she phoned me and asked, "Now can I come up?"

'I said, "No, you can't. I've just got back from Europe and I'm bloody tired." I told her to run a cross-country race in Taupo and then come to Auckland. She did that and she's been with me ever since. We married in 1997.

'So, I've married three times, I've been around the world, I've had some great successes, but I've never become rich. It's interesting to think that Bill Bowerman, who always described himself as my apostle, became a millionaire as a result of picking up on my jogging principles. His book on jogging sold a million copies. It's the difference between hitting the enormous American market and the tiny New Zealand market. He also took my advice on gaining entry to the running shoe market, first with Tiger and then with the company now known as Nike.

'I have sent or taken Joelyne to run marathons in France, Australia and the United States but, apart from the Paris race, where she finished in the first twenty women in a field of 23,000 runners, she hasn't achieved anything much. In Paris, she had run for two and a half hours the day before the marathon because she got lost, so her placing in the race was excellent. She can be a very good runner when she wants to, but she isn't interested in doing the speed work and the harder aspects of training. I think she finds that anaerobic work hurts and she's one of those who can't take it.

'It's a pity and I know there are people who point to her lack of success as proof that my system doesn't work – the "the guy can't even train his own wife" sort of comment. It doesn't bother me.'

Nor should it. It's the same tall poppy reaction that sees the armchair critics writing off a runner, a coach, a footballer or cricketer the first time they fail to achieve the result the critic expects. Maybe a sportsperson's success gives couch potatoes a vicarious feeling of self-satisfaction. If so, any 'failure' suddenly becomes more important, more significant, than preceding victories.

In Arthur's case, this criticism is laughable, since his record of remarkable successes spans nearly half a century and most of the world, and he continues to turn average youngsters into stars of track and cross-country simply because they ask for his help.

Arthur has had his share of mockery and derision. It might have made a lesser person bitter and discouraged them from continuing, but Arthur is made of sterner stuff. His unwavering faith in his ability to coach and counsel anyone to be a better athlete at any sport has been underscored by the knowledge that he acquired in the most rigorous way possible – by using his own small and ordinary body as the sounding board for years of experimentation. He has seen his methods proven and believes they remain unequalled after many decades. He is the most natural and unquestionable motivator most people will ever encounter in their lives.

Thanks to him, men and women all over the world have gone on to achieve performances of which they might otherwise only have dreamed. Arthur Lydiard will not be a hard act to follow. He will be impossible.

appendix

Key performances of some of Arthur's New Zealand runners:

Bill Baillie
Fifteen national titles – two at half-mile; two at 1 mile; one at 3 miles; seven at 6 miles; two at cross-country; and one at 10-miles.
Ran for New Zealand at the 1954 Olympics and 1954, 1958, 1962 and 1966 Commonwealth Games.
World records: 20,000-metres (59:28.6), Auckland, 1964; one hour (12 miles 960 yards 7 inches), Auckland, 1964.
Best times: 220 yards, 24.4; 440 yards, 51.2; 880 yards, 1:52.3; 1 mile, 3:59.2; 2 miles (indoor) 8:31.9; 2 miles (outdoor) 8:34.8; 3 miles, 13:14.6; 5000 metres, 13:40; 6 miles, 28:07; 10,000 metres, 29:01; marathon, 2:20:13; 40 miles, 3:45.

John Davies
Five national titles – all at 1 mile.
Ran for New Zealand at the 1964 Olympics (bronze medal in 1500 metres), 1962 Commonwealth Games (silver medal in mile).
Best times: 220 yards, 23.6; 440 yards, 49.9; 880 yards, 1:50.1; 1000 metres, 2:19.3; 1500 metres, 3:39.6; 1 mile, 3:56.8; 3000 metres, 7:51; 5000 metres, 13:54.4; marathon, 2:31:32.

Murray Halberg
Eleven national titles – five at 1 mile; five at 3 miles; one at cross-country.
Ran for New Zealand at the 1956, 1960 (5000 metre gold medal) and 1964 Olympics, 1954, 1958 (3 mile gold medal) and 1962 Commonwealth Games (3 mile gold medal).
World records: 4 miles (unofficial), 18:22.6; 2 miles (indoor)

8:34.4; 4 x 1-mile relay, 16:23.88; 2 miles, 8:30; 3 miles, 13:10. Best times: 440 yards, 52.0; 800 metres, 1:51.7; 1500 metres, 3:38.8; 1 mile, 3:57.5; 3000 metres, 7:57.6; 2 miles, 8:30; 3 miles, 13:10; 5000 metres, 13:35.2; 6 miles, 27:29.9; 10,000 metres, 28:33; marathon, 2:28:43.

Barry Magee

Seven national titles – five at 6 miles; two at marathon.

Ran for New Zealand at the 1960 and 1964 Olympics (bronze medal in 1960 marathon), and 1958 and 1962 Commonwealth Games.

World record: 4 x 1-mile relay, 16:23.8.

Best times: 220 yards, 25.0; 440 yards, 54.8; 880 yards, 1:57.4; 1500 metres, 3:51.1; 1 mile, 4:07.2; 3000 metres, 8:06; 2 miles, 8:40.2; 5000 metres, 13:39.2; 10,000 metres, 28:50.8; 10 miles, 48:49; 1 hour, 12 miles 318 yards; 30,000 metres, 1:34:47.4; marathon, 2:17:19.

Peter Snell

Six national titles – four at 880 yards, one at 1 mile, one at cross-country.

Ran for New Zealand at Olympics in 1960 (gold medal at 800 metres) and 1964 (gold medals in 800 metres and 1500 metres) and Commonwealth Games in 1962 (gold medals at 880 yards and 1 mile).

World records: 1 mile 3:54.4 (1962), 3:54.1 (1964); 800 metres 1:44.8; 880 yards, 1:45.1; 1000 yards (indoors), 2:06.0; 880 yards (indoors), 1:49.9; 1000 metres, 2:16.6; 4 x 1-mile relay, 16:23.8.

Voted New Zealand Sportsman of the Year in 1960 and 1964 and New Zealand Sportsman of the Century in 2000.

index of names